# Zen Conversations

## The Scope of Zen Teaching and Practice in North America

Richard Bryan McDaniel

*For Saphira,*
*Child of multiple heritages*

Wonder
Awe
Gratitude
Reverence

ZEN CONVERSATIONS
The Scope of Zen Teaching and Practice in North America
Richard Bryan McDaniel

Text © Richard Bryan McDaniel, 2021
Cover graphic: NataLima, Shutterstock
Author photo: Joan McDaniel
All rights reserved

Book design: John Negru

Published by
**The Sumeru Press Inc.**
PO Box 75, Manotick Main Post Office,
Manotick, ON, Canada K4M 1A2

LIBRARY AND ARCHIVES CANADA CATALOGUING IN PUBLICATION

Title: Zen conversations : the scope of Zen teaching and practice in North America / Richard Bryan McDaniel.
Names: McDaniel, Richard Bryan, author.
Description: Includes index.
Identifiers: Canadiana (print) 20210213035 | Canadiana (ebook) 20210213329 | ISBN 9781896559742 (softcover) | ISBN 9781896559759 (EPUB)
Subjects: LCSH: Zen Buddhists–Canada–Interviews. | LCSH: Zen Buddhists–United States–Interviews. | LCSH: Zen priests–Canada–Interviews. | LCSH: Zen priests–United States–Interviews. | LCSH: Zen Buddhism–Canada. | LCSH: Zen Buddhism–United States. | LCGFT: Interviews.
Classification: LCC BQ9298 .M35 2021 | DDC 294.3/927092271–dc23

 For more information about The Sumeru Press visit us at *www.sumeru-books.com*

# Table of Contents

Introduction . . . . . . . . . . . . . . . 7
1 – Discovering Zen . . . . . . . . . . 23
2 – The Function of Zen. . . . . . . . 47
3 – Zen Practice. . . . . . . . . . . . . 71
4 – Adapting Zen to the West . . . . 99
5 – Compassionate Action . . . . . 123
6 – Ecodharma . . . . . . . . . . . 149
Epilogue in Island View . . . . . . . 171
The Interviews (Index). . . . . . . . 177
Glossary. . . . . . . . . . . . . . . . 179

# INTRODUCTION

Once – crossing into Maine from New Brunswick, Canada – I was asked the purpose of my visit and replied that I was going to attend a workshop in Portland. The border official asked what kind of workshop. "A Zen workshop," I told him.

"You know, I keep trying to get my Zen on," he said, handing back my passport, "but I just can't do it."

I knew what he meant, even though we were talking about two very different things.

This kind of lop-sided conversation isn't unusual for Zen practitioners.

Robert Waldinger is the resident teacher at the Henry David Thoreau Zen Community in Newton, Massachusetts. He also works at the Harvard Medical School, which he describes as one of the most conservative institutions on the planet. "If I go away on retreat, I tell people partly because as a physician when you're off the grid you need to be sure you've got coverage, and people have to know you're really off the grid, that you're not this sort of fake 'I'm away, but I'll answer all my e-mails.' So people have to know that I'm not going to look at my phone for days. So when I get back, people will ask, 'How was your retreat? Was it really relaxing?' And I say, 'No, it was intense. Good. But not relaxing.' I have to explain it's not about relaxation. It's not about self-improvement. It's about a radical understanding of the self in the world and what it means to be alive. That's the elevator speech."

...

The word "Zen" has entered the English language in a peculiar way. It not only refers to a specific Buddhist tradition; it has also become a descriptor implying tranquility, peace of mind, and – perhaps – spiritual accomplishment. The online *Cambridge Dictionary* defines it as the quality of being relaxed and not worrying about things one can't change. Relaxation and lack of worry may be side-effects of Zen practice, they may even be what draw people to the practice, but they are not – in themselves – what the practice is about.

"Zen" is a Japanese term derived from the Chinese word *channa* – 禪那 – which, in turn, is a transliteration of the Sanskrit, *dhyana*, meaning "meditation." As a form of Buddhism, it is distinguished from other schools by the emphasis placed on attaining direct personal insight not through study and the acquisition of information but through the practice of seated meditation. Because it's a practice rather than a theory, it has been possible for non-Buddhist forms of authorized Zen teaching to arise in the west. Although the majority of Zen Centers still identify as Buddhist, they don't need to. Whether they do or not, all forms of Zen recognize that they are rooted in the enlightenment experience as a result of which the Indian prince, Siddhartha Gautama, came to be acknowledged as the Buddha – or the "Awakened One." The conventional story relates that Siddhartha – after numerous preparatory lifetimes and extensive study – determined that the search for meaning could not be attained from someone or something else. With that understanding, he took a seat beneath a fig tree outside Bodh Gaya, India, and turned inward. He sat with eyes lowered but open, and, when the Morning Star appeared on the horizon, he achieved complete and unsurpassed awakening or enlightenment. At the moment of his enlightenment, he is said to have exclaimed: "O wonder of wonders! All beings just as they are are whole and complete! All beings are endowed with Buddha Nature!" All beings, in other words, have an inherent capacity to realize that their basic nature – their true nature – is no different from that of all existence.

This was not a unique perception. It was one already recognized in the spiritual traditions of the time. In Sanskrit it was called *advaya*, which can be translated as "nonduality." While people generally have a sense of themselves as entities within the world confronting other entities, in advaya there is no sense of a self separate from all else. What distinguished the Buddha's awakening experience was not so much its uniqueness as its depth. Awakening is a subjective experience and, therefore, essentially non-transmittable. Nothing the Buddha said could give another person the experience he had had, any more than any amount of description can convey how figs taste. Enlightenment has to be encountered directly and personally. Nor were Buddha's teachings the content of his awakening, although they were derived from it. They included guidance about how followers could seek to attain awakening, but much of the teaching presented a description of the world and humanity's place in it that had become apparent to him as a result of his awakening. As it happens, we don't know with certainty what those original teachings were. The sutras – the sermons attributed to the Buddha – weren't written down until 400 years after his lifetime. Until then they were transmitted orally, a process during which they were inevitably modified, clarified, organized, and expanded. Historical analysis has established that new teachings were composed and attributed to the Buddha long after his death. What is now regarded as the body of the Buddha's thought and teaching, then, is not the product of a single enlightened mind but the collective reflection of generations of minds over a period of centuries. The corpus is massive. The earliest version of the collected teachings of the Buddha published in English was fifty-seven individually bound volumes long. Buddhist thought examined the nature of interdependent being, the process of causality, human psychology and behaviour. In some ways, Gautama's legacy is more like that of the early Greek philosophers – who were contemporaneous with him – than it is with the religious traditions which arose in the Middle East 500 years later.

Early Buddhists practiced meditation as one of the steps in the Noble Eightfold Path which describes the appropriate way to overcome suffering and unhappiness, but much of their time was spent studying, memorizing and promoting what came be called the Buddha's Dharma,[1] or teachings. Schools and universities were established in India which drew students from as far away as Korea, China, and Tibet. Buddhist missionaries promulgated the teachings throughout Asia.

By the time Buddhism made its way into China, around the 3rd century BCE, it was no longer a single system of thought. Competing theories and interpretations of the sutras had led to a proliferation of schools, including the establishment of two broad traditions, the conservative Theravada (Teaching of the Elders) now found in Sri Lanka, Myanmar and Thailand, and the more liberal but also at times more fanciful Mahayana which spread into China, Tibet, Vietnam, Korea, and Japan. In China, a unique form of Buddhism evolved from the encounter between Indian Mahayana and native Daoism. This school was called Chan.

The adherents of Daoism sought to cultivate calmness of mind in order to harmonize their lives with the natural order of the universe – termed the *Dao* or "Way." When they learned of Buddhism, they were less intrigued by its various and complex teachings than they were with the idea of personal enlightenment and a methodology to achieve the insight of nonduality which Gautama had acquired.

---

1. "Dharma" – or dhamma – is a term which originally meant law, custom, nature, quality, correct order. It also referred to the structures operative in nature and the universe. The Dharma as attributed to the Buddha, therefore, is the set of teachings which reveal the structure of Being, the way things are. In this sense it can mean both Teachings and Truth.

Robert Kennedy is a transmitted (that is, authorized) Zen teacher, who can trace his personal teaching lineage back to the 7th century Chinese Chan Patriarch, Huineng. He is the resident instructor at the Morning Star Zendo in Jersey City. He is also a Jesuit priest.

"Zen is a practical way of doing Buddhism," he explains to me. "It was put together by the Chinese around the 6th Century. As Buddhism came from India, it was rather scholastic and academic. And the Chinese wanted a way of 'How do you do this? How do you practically do it?' That was the beginning of Zen. The great work of Zen was done by the Chinese between the 600s and the 1200s. That would be roughly the Golden Age of Zen. 'How do you practically do this?' So that was the question. And that was how Zen was formulated."

If it's a practical way of "doing Buddhism," I wonder what purpose it serves in the Roman Catholic tradition to which Kennedy remains loyal.

"Well, first of all, the practice of seated meditation – or *zazen* – is not necessarily confined to Buddhism or to any faith. There's a wonderful teaching in Buddhism that Buddhism must leave Buddhism itself in order to enter the field of blessing. Buddhism recognizes that the truth of Buddhism is not simply Buddhist. It is human, and it is for all people. We are grateful to Buddhism for ordering Zen, bringing it about, answering some of the questions about how do you do this? But it's not confined to Buddhism. Now some Buddhists might disagree with this; they might say, 'No. Zen can only be done in Buddhism.' But this is not what the great Yamada Roshi[2] of Kamakura taught me. And I think this is the truth of it. Anyone can sit quietly and breathe and pay attention and stop thinking. And to his own great profit."

•••

By the 9th century, there were five major Chan traditions – or "Houses" – descendent from specific teachers who succeeded Huineng. Three fell into abeyance by the year 1000. The two that remained – the Linji [Japanese: Rinzai] and the Caodong [J: Soto] – would spread throughout Japan, Korea, Vietnam, and eventually North America and Europe.

Buddhism was one of several elements of Chinese society adapted by the Japanese during a period of cultural growth which began in the 6th century. The forms early Japanese visitors to China encountered were those popular in the port cities of the coast; contact with the Chan communities hidden away in remote mountain sanctuaries was slower to come about. But by the beginning of the Kamakura Era (1185-1333), the Linji and Caodong schools of Chan had been established on the islands and began to evolve into Japanese Rinzai and Soto Zen.

---

2. Roshi literally means "Old Teacher." In North American Zen, it has become an honorific title designating a fully qualified Zen teacher.

Soto Zen became a popular devotional religion in rural areas, and the number of Soto temples in the country easily outnumbered those of the Rinzai tradition. Nevertheless, Rinzai became more influential. The national leadership were Rinzai patrons, and, by the 14th Century, it had become the semi-official religion of the samurai class. Rinzai temples were also charged with providing schooling for the sons of the upper classes. The large number of lay people from influential families trained in the temples resulted in Rinzai Zen having a pervasive impact throughout Japanese culture.

By the 19th century, as knowledge of Buddhism in general spread outside of Asia, Rinzai and Soto practices were easily distinguishable. Rinzai emphasized the importance of achieving awakening or *kensho* – seeing into [ken] one's true nature [sho]. The practical means to this end is meditation and working with koans – a series of short anecdotes or "riddles" that help the participant achieve an initial insight then deepen it and integrate into their life. One of the best-known *koans* – popularized by the Japanese Rinzai reformer, Hakuin Ekaku – asks what is the sound of a single hand. The most frequently assigned initial koan is based on a brief story told about the Chinese Tang Dynasty Zen master, Zhaozhou Congshen, who was asked whether – as was commonly taught – even a dog had Buddha Nature. His monosyllabic reply was "*wu!*"[3] – which means "no" or "nothing."

Awakening in the Rinzai tradition, then, is a state to be acquired or attained. And the assumption is that once attained, it has the capacity to alter both the way in which an individual perceives reality and the way in which one interacts with the world. The fundamental purpose of Rinzai training, for both monks and lay people, is attainment of this insight, which is deemed to differ from the Buddha's awakening experience only in intensity. Initial kensho experiences may be shallow but are capable of being developed and growing more profound. They can also be very powerful and emotional. The enlightenment story of Koun Yamada – with whom Robert Kennedy had studied in Japan – is an example:

> I was riding home on the train with my wife. I was reading a book on Zen by Son-o, who… was a master of Soto Zen living in Sendai during the Genroku period [1688-1703]. As the train was nearing Ofuna station I ran across this line: "I came to realize clearly that Mind is no other than mountains and rivers and the great wide earth, the sun and the moon and the stars."

---

3. *Mu* in Japanese.

I had read this before, but this time it impressed itself upon me so vividly that I was startled. I said to myself: "After seven or eight years of zazen I have finally perceived the essence of this statement," and couldn't suppress the tears that began to well up. Somewhat ashamed to find myself crying among the crowd, I averted my face and dabbed at my eyes with my handkerchief.

Meanwhile the train had arrived at Kamakura station and my wife and I got off. On the way home I said to her: "In my present exhilarated frame of mind I could rise to the greatest heights." Laughingly she replied: "Then where would I be?" All the while I kept repeating that quotation to myself.[4]

Traditionally the validity of a kensho needs to be confirmed by a teacher who has personally experienced this shift in perception, and Yamada sought and received confirmation from his own teacher, Yasutani Hakuun.

Although viewed as a spiritual perception, Rinzai Zen understands that the attainment of awakening has application to secular as well as religious activity. Yamada, at the time of his awakening, was a lay hospital administrator. Artists, craftspeople, and even military figures saw value in undergoing formal Rinzai training in order to acquire awakening. For career monastics, the practice of koan reflection deepened their initial insight. Students could be guided through a koan curriculum of as many as 1700 cases[5] before receiving "transmission," or authorization to take their own students.

Japanese Soto practice is based in large part on a literal acceptance of the Buddha's claim at the time of his awakening that all persons "just as they are... are endowed with Buddha Nature." Therefore, awakening is not something to be sought. Rather one only has to recognize that one is already awakened. That recognition can come about without the need for intense experiences like kensho. It is viewed as an accumulative process. One analogy compares it to the way in which, while one walks through a field of grain in the morning, one's robes will naturally and gradually – even imperceptibly – become soaked by dew. Kensho isn't denied, but it is not seen as requisite, and, by the end of the 19th century, it was a policy of the Soto establishment that kensho wasn't a necessary qualification for a person to be acknowledged as a master of Zen practice.

---

4. Quoted in Philip Kapleau et al., *The Three Pillars of Zen* (New York: Anchor, 1989).

5. The origin of the term "koan" refers to "a public record" – "case" – in the sense of records kept by law courts to establish precedent in jurisprudence.

Soto monastics can spend even greater amounts of time in seated meditation – zazen – than their Rinzai counterparts, but the specific practice is usually different. Soto monks can and do work with koans, but their primary form of meditation is *shikan taza*, literally "just sitting so." One sits without formally focusing on anything and without seeking to attain anything from the practice; instead, all one needs to do is to forget the individual "self" (one's personality) in order for the larger Self (Buddha Nature) to become apparent. In a short work called *Fukanzazengi* or *Universal Recommendations for the Practice of Zazen*, the founder of Japanese Soto, Dogen Kigen, wrote: "firmly and resolutely," one thinks "about the unthinkable. How do you think about the unthinkable? Non-thinking. These are the essentials of zazen."[6]

A third school of Japanese Zen was established by Yamada Koun's teacher, Yasutani Hakuun, in the 20th century. Yasutani had been the student of Daiun Sogaku Harada, a Soto priest who – dissatisfied with the level of understanding he'd acquired through Soto practice – undertook koan study with a Rinzai teacher and came to awakening. Yasutani, in turn, went through the koan curriculum with Harada and achieved kensho. In 1943, after he had been authorized to teach, Yasutani broke with the official Soto tradition and established an independent school he called Sanbo Kyodan.[7] While the Harada/Yasutani lineage is not of much significance in Japan, it has been a major influence in the spread of Zen beyond Asia. Currently there are Sanbo Zen communities throughout North America, Europe, Israel, the Philippines, and Australia.

Common to all three schools is the understanding that wisdom (*prajna*) is capable of growing more profound and that it needs to be integrated into one's life for the benefit of others. This is *karuna* or compassion. The stages of Zen practice are portrayed in a series of illustrations called the Ten Bulls. They begin with a man setting out to seek the Bull of wisdom, finding its tracks, eventually mastering it, then "transcending" it and "returning to the source." The final image is of the seeker coming back into the market place with "gift bestowing hands."

•••

It could be argued that Zen in the west has largely been a literary phenomenon. Certainly more people in Europe and the Americas have read books on Zen than have ever done any formal practice with an authorized teacher. In the period between the two world wars, when Zen was first established here,

---

6. Francis Dojun Cook [trans.], *How to Raise an Ox* (Boston: Wisdom Publications, 2002), p. 66.

7. "The Fellowship of the Three Treasures." In 2014, the school was renamed Sanbo Zen. Yamada Koun was the head of the Sanbo Zen lineage from 1973 until his death in 1989. The Three Treasures are Buddha, Dharma, and Sangha (community).

Western understanding was almost exclusively based on the writings of a single Japanese scholar, Daisetsu Teitaro Suzuki.

Suzuki was a lay student of the Rinzai Master, Soyen Shaku, the first Zen teacher to visit America. Shaku had been invited to take part in the World Parliament of Religions staged in conjunction with the Chicago World's Fair in 1893. By the end of the 19<sup>th</sup> century, as post-Darwinian thinking cast doubt on traditional Christian teachings, there were people who sought for a more rationally based spiritual tradition. Some felt it could be found in the various forms of Eastern thought recently being studied by Western academics. There was a lot of charlatanism in groups like the Theosophists and Rosicrucians, but there was also a growing scholarly interest in Buddhism, a system of thought which did not assume a supreme being external to and responsible for creation. When a publisher invited Shaku to help prepare editions of Eastern texts for Western readers, the Zen master demurred, suggesting that the young Suzuki – who spoke English – would be a more suitable choice. It turned out to be a fortuitous recommendation.

Over his career, Suzuki published more than 100 books in Japanese and another thirty in English. Although he was not a formal teacher, he is accepted as being almost single-handedly responsible for introducing Zen to the West. And for Suzuki, Zen was Rinzai Zen. It would be decades before people outside of Asia realized that there was more than one variety of Zen practice. Suzuki's work captured the attention of Western thinkers like C.G. Jung, Thomas Merton, and Martin Heidegger.

In 1905, Shaku returned to the United States to give a series of lectures on Zen, bringing another student with him, Nyogen Senzaki, to serve as his attendant. Shaku's hosts in San Francisco misunderstood the nature of the relationship between the two men and considered Senzaki essentially a houseboy. They put him on staff, but their housekeeper dismissed him because of his poor knowledge of English. Instead of coming to Senzaki's defense, Shaku decided it would be better for the younger man to remain in America on his own. Shaku suggested Senzaki find work in the city and take the opportunity to learn as much as he could about the country and its people. "Do not utter even a syllable, don't even pronounce the 'B' of Buddhism for seventeen years," Shaku reportedly told Senzaki. "You must come to understand these Americans before you will be able to teach them. Work in anonymity for at least seventeen years. Then you will be ready." Senzaki never formally received transmission, but he did as his teacher advised him. He found employment for a while as a household servant. When conditions in San Francisco forced him to leave the city during the 1920 Anti-Japanese Crusade and Congressional Hearings on Immigration, he worked on a farm near Oakland. After the hysteria in the city abated, he returned and found employment in a hotel where he held a number of positions: porter, elevator operator, telephone switchboard operator, and bookkeeper. He eventually became the manager and even, for a while, was a part-owner of a hotel. But he wasn't a natural businessman, and the hotel failed. In his spare time, he meditated in the Japanese Gardens in Golden Gate Park and spent long hours at the public library reading American and European philosophy. After the seventeen years passed, he arranged to give his first public lecture on Zen in 1922.

On the other side of the country, a second generation successor of Shaku – Sokei-an Sasaki – established himself in New York City. He had earned transmission from Shaku's direct heir, Tetsuo Sokatsu, and became the first fully authorized Zen teacher to choose to live in the United States. In 1931, he established a small community that was incorporated as the Buddhist Society of New York. It drew the attention of a wealthy society woman, Ruth Fuller, who along with her daughter became active in the community. The daughter, Eleanor, was married to a young Englishman, Alan Watts, who would become an influential literary promoter of Zen.

During the Second World War, both Senzaki and Sasaki were interred by the federal government. Ruth used her influence to arrange Sasaki's release in 1943, and the two married in the following year. Sasaki's health was poor, however, and he died a few months later. After his death, the Buddhist Society was renamed the First Zen Institute of America, and – under Ruth's direction – it committed itself to preserving Sasaki's legacy. Ruth, herself, went to Japan to continue Zen training. She became both the first woman and the first Westerner to be ordained in the Daitokuji Temple system, and she established the first zendo in Japan specifically intended to receive Western students.

Although Zen was becoming a popular philosophical concept in Western culture, it remained largely theoretical until another literary event – the publication of *The Three Pillars of Zen* by Philip Kapleau in 1965.[8] Kapleau was one of a very small group of Western explorers who – initially inspired by D.T. Suzuki – travelled to Japan to undertake formal Zen training. He studied with both Daiun Harada and Hakuun Yasutani. *The Three Pillars of Zen* provides readers with Yasutani's detailed instructions on how to practice Zen

---

8. Kapleau's "authorship" of the book is a controversial issue. Sanbo Zen still doesn't recognize that Kapleau was an authorized teacher and maintains that *The Three Pillars of Zen* was the collective effort of three people, Kapleau and two others he identifies as his "collaborators" in the Editor's Preface – Koun Yamada and Akira Kubota – but whose names don't appear on the title page. The actual wording on the title page states that the book is "compiled and edited, with translations, introductions and notes, by Philip Kapleau." Yamada and Kubota both succeeded Yasutani as abbots of the Sanbo Zen school.

meditation. Perhaps even more importantly, it includes eight first-person narratives of modern individuals – four Japanese[9] and four Western – who attained kensho, demonstrating that Zen provided a practical means of achieving that insight into the nature of being – which is recognized as "enlightenment" in Buddhism – and that non-Asians were as capable of attaining it as their Chinese and Japanese contemporaries.

In 1965, Kapleau returned to America and – with Yasutani's authorization and the financial patronage of Chester and Dorris Carlson – established the Rochester Zen Center. Carlson was the inventor of electronic photocopying, and he and his wife had an interest in Eastern spiritualities. Kapleau's first Zen students were members of a study group organized by Dorris, which consisted mostly of women in their forties who were exploring various religious traditions. Kapleau taught them how to sit zazen and set up a regular schedule of sittings. The group, however, did not show up on Sunday mornings because they were also regular church attendees. Eventually they found the training methods Kapleau imported from Japan overly harsh and fell away from the practice. Then – to Kapleau's bewilderment – a much younger group of people, many who self-identified as hippies, began to show up at the door. They had read *The Three Pillars* and had made their way to Rochester seeking enlightenment.

•••

Soto Zen entered North America by a different route. Beginning in the 1920s, the international headquarters of the Soto sect – the Sotoshu – established missions in west coast cities like Los Angeles and San Francisco for Japanese immigrants and their descendants. Although these were closed during the Second World War, they were among the first organizations to be re-established after the war ended and became centers of community life, places where traditional Japanese values were retained and respected in an environment which still often remained hostile.

In 1959, a Soto priest named Shunryu Suzuki was sent to San Francisco to take charge of Sokoji Temple. He had been a temple priest in a small community in Japan and welcomed the opportunity to come to America. He was a modest man – often explaining that he was the "small Suzuki" rather than the "big" D.T. Suzuki – who never talked about awakening or kensho, and his activities at the American temple were largely ceremonial. There were regular Sunday services at which the temple priest – addressed as "Reverend" – was expected to preach a sermon. Although there was a shrine room, there was no zendo or meditation hall. Zen might be the "meditation school" of Buddhism, but, like most Japanese, the temple members considered zazen an activity for monks rather

---

9. Including Koun Yamada quoted above.

than lay people. The temple membership tended to be middle-aged or elderly and traditional. They welcomed Suzuki graciously but expected him to carry out his duties without fuss. It would became a matter of serious concern for them when unexpectedly their temple began to attract scores of non-Japanese hippies.

•••

A Zen boom occurred both in North America and Europe beginning around the mid-'60s and continuing for nearly 20 years. While Zen was in fact fading in Japan, authorized teachers – both Asian and Western – established centers throughout the United States, Canada, and elsewhere around the world. There were Chinese, Korean, and Vietnamese variants of the Rinzai school as well, although the inquirers who sought them out usually were unaware of the differences between the various lineages.

Those inquirers came from a variety of backgrounds. Several members of the Zen Center of Los Angeles would become significant figures in the transfer of Zen to the west. Bernie Glassman – founder of Zen Peacemakers and the teacher from whom Fr. Kennedy received Dharma Transmission – was an aeronautical engineer; Gerry Shishin Wick – founder and Spiritual Director of Great Mountain Zen Center in Colorado – was a physicist and oceanographer; Jan Chozen Bays – co-abbot of Great Vow Monastery in Oregon – was a pediatrician; and John Daido Loori – who established Zen Mountain Monastery in the Catskills – was a professional photographer and chemist (who invented the artificial flavor for lime Jell-o). But the majority of people showing up at the centers were members of the counter-culture movement.

While in Japan, youth were turning away from Zen – which they perceived as one of the archaic institutions responsible for their country's involvement in a humiliating war – in the West, young people turned to Zen as a way of seeking release from what they perceived as the stifling social conditions in which they lived. Those arriving at Sokoji in San Francisco or at Philip Kapleau's Rochester Zen Center in New York State were usually disaffected with the religious traditions in which they had been raised and, often inspired by psychedelic drug use, sought alternative spiritual paths. Interest in Zen became part of the zeitgeist of the era.

It is also the case that early North American Zen enthusiasts were not a very diverse lot. They tended to be college-educated and from well-to-do backgrounds – so they were able to afford to take the time to attend week-long retreats or do even longer monastic stays – and they were predominantly white. This is the generation from which most contemporary teachers have come, and, as a result, the people now leading centers continue to be primarily college-educated whites. One hopes that as Zen communities become more diverse, there will be greater diversity among teachers in the future.

At one time it was traditional for a Zen student, at a certain point in their training, to undertake a pilgrimage – an *angya* – to visit teachers other than their own in order to deepen their understanding of the Dharma. From March 2013 until the COVID-19 outbreak in March 2020, a small inheritance allowed me to visit Zen centers throughout North America. The tour took me from San Francisco, on the west coast, to Halifax, Nova Scotia, on the east; from Montreal, in the north, to New Mexico, in the south. I interviewed 124 teachers and long-time practitioners representing the spectrum of Zen/Chan/Soen/Thien[10] practice in North America.

It was a lengthy journey, and several of the teachers I met have since died including Albert Low, Bernie Glassman, and all three of the abbots – Steve Stücky, Mel Weitsman, and Blanche Hartman – I interviewed at the San Francisco Zen Center. I consider myself fortunate to have been able to record them while they were still alive.

In almost all locations, I was welcomed warmly and had the good fortune to encounter impressive, friendly, and approachable individuals who responded to my (at times impertinent) questions with frankness and good humor. As I have written elsewhere, almost all of them turned out to be the kind of people one would enjoy spending an afternoon with drinking beer (or tea) and discussing topics other than Zen. Those interviews became the basis of three books I published with the Sumeru Press in Canada, in which I deliberately chose not to argue on behalf of one school or another but simply to chronicle what I observed. The schools do differ though.

A Roman Catholic attending mass in Venice, Oaxaca, or Ottawa would find the experience essentially the same. For that matter, a Rotarian attending a luncheon meeting in Italy, Mexico, or Canada would expect the format to be similar save for, perhaps, a few cultural differences. A Zen practitioner, however, visiting two centers in his own community might well find them so different that they scarcely appear to have anything in common.

Books on Zen are almost always presented from the point of view of a particular school, but what intrigues me is the scope of the Zen lineages that have now been established in the west: the differences and similarities between the way in which contemporary teachers first came to the practice (Chapter 1), their views on the intention of that practice (Chapter 2), the way they present formal meditation (Chapter 3), how close they feel they have to remain to Asian – and even Buddhist – models (Chapter 4), the emphasis they place on social engagement (Chapter 5) and, in particular, environmentalism (Chapter 6).

---

10. Zen is known as Soen in Korean and as Thien in Vietnamese.

I began writing this book during the Covid-19 pandemic, and one of the recurring questions that arose during the time of composition was the degree to which this practice helped practitioners cope with the situation in which we find ourselves. Few events in contemporary history have demonstrated so clearly the basic Buddhist principles of cause-and-effect and interdependence.

More than 2500 years ago, the Buddha identified that existence was marked by three characteristics: all things are impermanent; all beings lack a permanent self; and that disappointment is inevitable in our lives. Zen maintains that this is a not a bleak assessment of life, but it is a realistic one, and if one can face it directly and honestly one can find satisfaction, fulfillment, and even joy. As Robert Waldinger told me, "It's not about relaxation. It's not about self-improvement. It's about a radical understanding of the self in the world and what it means to be alive. That's the elevator speech."

# 1
# Discovering Zen

A highly romanticized fascination with the "Mysterious East" arose in European and American literature and thought during the 19th century. It was confused with ideas about spiritual masters who communicated with students by telepathy, hidden enlightened societies and secret orders, fairies, and the occult. Figures such as the Hindu Paramahansa Yogananda attracted celebrity followers in America during the early 20th century, some of whom even practiced meditation. Madame Blavatsky's Theosophical Society opened chapters in many Western cities. The impact of all this activity on the broader society, however, was minimal.

What was extraordinary about the late '60s, the '70s, and early '80s was that Zen not only attained an intellectual respectability in the West that other Asian philosophies had failed to do, it also attracted a large number of skilled young people willing to take on what was often a long and arduous training. Many of these men and women later became instrumental in establishing the practice throughout the West.

No two individuals come to Zen in exactly the same way – the factors that drew a Jesuit priest are necessarily different from those that drew a New York folksinger – and yet there are commonalities in their stories.

### Hozan Senauke

Hozan Alan Senauke was the Vice Abbot of the Berkeley Zen Center when I met him in the autumn of 2019. A year later, the center's Abbot – Mel Weitsman – died, and Hozan became Head Priest of the Center.

When the non-Asian membership at Sokoji in San Francisco expanded, the ethnic Japanese congregation felt overwhelmed and disregarded. A break finally came about in 1969 when temple officials pressured Shunryu Suzuki into resigning his post. With the aid of his new students, he established what became the San Francisco Zen Center in a former women's residence on the corner of Page and Laguna Streets. As membership continued to grow, satellite centers were created. The first of these, in Berkeley, was inaugurated even before the move to Page Street.

While Mel Weitsman and Shunryu Suzuki were establishing a flourishing Zen community in California, Alan Senauke was occupying the administration building at Columbia University in New York.

"I was socially engaged from pretty early on." Hozan is a cautious speaker and will, sometimes, start a sentence two or three times before finding the way he wants to express himself. "I felt quite isolated during my first eight years of school where I went to private school. And then in ninth grade I transferred to the public school in my town, and that's when everything took off for me. That's when I became involved. I heard folk music and took that up, and it really was all one thing. Politics, music, elements of a lifestyle were all rising together. I was involved in civil rights work and in 'Ban the Bomb.' I think concern about race and civil rights is a continuous thread, and I was very involved in the anti-war movement. I went to Columbia, and, in the spring of 1968, we took over the university."

Students protesting the university's involvement in the Vietnam war occupied the administration building. The police intervened with force. 132 students, four faculty members as well as twelve police officers were injured, and over 700 protesters – including Senauke – were arrested.

"The occupation of Columbia was a huge experience. In certain ways a traumatic experience. We had to stay in New York for another few weeks to wait for the disposition of our trials or our cases from the arrest. Then we just wanted to get out of there." He and a group of friends decided to go to California.

"Everything was happening in California. But we arrived in the middle of People's Park.[11] We had an apartment for the summer in Berkeley, and it was rather disturbing to arrive in the middle of People's Park, because we moved into what seemed very much a police state. There were curfews. Cops in pairs and quartets were parading down the streets. There were violent demonstrations. It wasn't exactly an escape. But that was the time when we also began to sit zazen."

---

11. On May 15, 1969, People's Park, near the campus of UCLA Berkeley, was the site of a confrontation between students, the police, and the National Guard which resulted in one student bystander's death; 128 other students were wounded so severely they required hospital attention. Governor Ronald Reagan – who had referred to the Berkeley campus as a haven for Communist sympathizers and sexual deviants – declared a State of Emergency after the event and deployed 2700 National Guard troops to police the area.

The friends who had come with him had been part of what he describes as the poetry and literary scene at Columbia. "We were also involved in psychedelics."

Hozan and I are the same age, so share a lot of cultural history, including psychedelic use. Psychedelics were significant to many early Zen inquirers for several reasons. The experience often gave one a sense of interconnectedness with the whole of Being, what was termed "Cosmic Consciousness" by some. In doing so, it demonstrated that our usual dualistic view of the world wasn't the only way to understand things. A popular dorm room poster at the time quoted the 19th century American psychologist, William James:

> – our normal waking consciousness, rational consciousness as we call it, is but one special type of consciousness, whilst all about it, parted from it by the filmiest of screens, there lie potential forms of consciousness entirely different. We may go through life without suspecting their existence; but apply the requisite stimulus, and at a touch they are there in all their completeness, definite types of mentality which probably somewhere have their field of application and adaptation. No account of the universe in its totality can be final which leaves these other forms of consciousness quite disregarded.[12]

"We had an idea that psychedelics were in the field of mystical experience, and that there were probably other ways to access that field. And the most logical way, according to my literary and, certainly my explorations in religio-philosophical writing, was in the Zen tradition. *The Three Pillars of Zen* had come out that year or the year before, which was a very important book for a number of us. 'Cause it was the first book that really communicated that this was something you could do. It wasn't just a philosophical position. So we came out here, and one of our intentions was to figure out where could we do this."

The Berkeley Center turned out to be half a mile from their apartment.

"It was a big old house, and the zendo was in the attic, and it was quite lovely. All roughhewn, but there was something really special about that space. And I remember sitting under the eaves, just sort of looking at the place where the roof joined the floor, facing the wall, and feeling both comfortable and uncomfortable there. And then we would stay for chanting, and the chanting was all in Japanese, so we didn't know what the hell we were chanting. So actually one of the things was, I went out there not realizing that the approach to Zen

---

12. William James, *The Varieties of Religious Experience: A Study in Human Nature*, 1902.

was quite different than what I had read in *The Three Pillars of Zen*, and I had some problems with *The Three Pillars of Zen*, particularly around this kind of pretty overt valorization of *satori*.[13] Coming from a very status-conscious suburban high school background and then going to an Ivy League school and pushing for all these years, I didn't want to push for anything else. So that didn't appeal to me, and it was confusing. Because the Zen atmosphere I took up from reading Chinese and Japanese poets completely appealed to me, and meditation appealed to me, but the idea of striving for something, some kind of cosmic breakthrough, was not appealing. And I never quite got the fact that the kind of orthodox Soto approach that you'd find in Suzuki Roshi's school was somewhat different from what Yasutani Roshi was pushing."

At the end of the summer, he and his friends returned to New York. "So I went back for my last year of school. But we had bought *zafus* and *zabutons*,[14] and I actually enrolled in a Japanese language class and had some idea that maybe I would go to Japan. Because that's where the real Zen was. But that idea got interrupted by events of the day, the political upheaval that just could not be avoided or ignored."

Over the next few years, he remained politically active and yoyo-ed between the two coasts playing music. Then came what he calls "a difficult personal time." His marriage broke up, and he left the band he had been playing with.

"Then I was really lost. I was lonely. And it became clear to me that there was a limit or a ceiling to where my music was going to go and that I was close to it, and that there was something I was supposed to *do* in life, but I didn't know what it was. So I got involved in psychotherapy – which was very good – and in the course of one of the sessions I asked my therapist, basically, 'What am I doing on the planet? What is my life supposed to be?' And she said, 'That's really a great question, but it's not a psychotherapy question. It's a spiritual question, and you should maybe think about looking for a spiritual response.' And I said, 'Oh! Okay.' And I had been reading some Buddhist or Buddhist-based literature around that time. I read Shunryu Suzuki's *Zen Mind, Beginner's Mind* – which hadn't been published when I first started practicing – and that was really powerful because it both contained concrete instructions, and it had a kind of energy that was – to me – very much like what I was reading in the Japanese and Chinese poets, and it appealed to me very much just by the way in which ideas and the language was presented. Other books as well, and all these things were

---

13. Another term for awakening or enlightenment, derived from the verb "satoru" – to know or understand. Kensho usually refers to the initial glimpse. Satori implies a deep, more mature understanding.

14. "Zafus" – literally, Buddha-seats – are meditation cushions; "zabutons" are the mats on which the cushions are placed.

really influential. I've had this sense in my life in other areas where I will read something or experience something or hear about something, and this internal message comes up, 'I could do that.' And that's what I felt. And so I just did."

He decided to go back to the Berkeley Zen Center.

"But it turned out it wasn't where I had left it. It had moved. I didn't know where it was, but I found the number in the phone book, and I called them up, and somebody answered the phone, and I said I had had some experience in zazen instruction years ago, and I'm thinking about taking up the practice again. 'What do you suggest I do?' And the person on the other side of the phone said, 'You should find a blank wall and sit down and stare at it.' And I thought, 'Wow. That's really a peculiar response to somebody cold-calling on the phone. That's the place for me!' So I drove over. I had zazen instruction. I started to sit, and immediately I just knew I was home. And – you know – it was physically hard. It was painful. But there was nothing else to do. I felt like I had run out of script and was just going to do this. Which is what I did."

I ask if he remained politically engaged.

"That was another thing. When I came back, I found out about the Buddhist Peace Fellowship, and Berkeley was where it was headquartered. There were quite a number of people active in BPF at Berkeley Zen Center. I joined. I was sort of a lurker for a time. Then shortly after I was ordained and got married, I was offered a job there. So I was Executive Director of Buddhist Peace Fellowship for ten years straight, then left for a year, and then came back and was a key person for another four years. And that really shaped my life."

The Buddhist Peace Fellowship had been established by Robert Aitken, a teacher in Honolulu who first learned about Zen while being held captive in a Japanese prisoner-of-war camp during the Second World War. Several American Zen enthusiasts – including the poet and environmentalist, Gary Snyder – were engaged with it. "People who understood fundamentally that the nature of suffering that Buddhism is so good at describing and working with, that that nature was not individual. That it manifested individually, but that manifestation also had social dimensions. In other words, suffering was also related to systems of oppression, systems of suffering. And that I think is a common understanding for a small group of people; it was an *uncommon* understanding in the context of the general approach to Buddhism in the west, and in the East for that matter, at that time.

"The Buddhist Peace Fellowship became a national network, and it went through its growing pains, and I came in in 1991 as the first Gulf War was happening. And it just happened that that was a period of great expansion for us. People were really having a hard time knowing how to process this war that we were in. And we grew, and I grew the organization very substantially in the course of time that I was there. We had chapters; they were involved in anti-nuclear work, were involved in anti-intervention work, anti-war work, and then we became quite involved in Buddhist prison work."

## Bernie Glassman

Around the same time that Hozan was working with the Peace Fellowship, Bernie Tetsugen Glassman and his wife, Jishu, were establishing the Zen Peacemakers Movement in New York.

Bernie – as everyone called him – died in 2018, but I had an opportunity to spend a day with him at his home in Montague, Massachusetts, in 2013. He is one of the most significant figures in the transfer of Zen to the west.

He was born in 1939 in the Brighton Beach area of Brooklyn, a low income, immigrant neighborhood – "So I've always felt comfortable in poor areas" – the fifth child and only son of parents who had come to the United States from Eastern Europe.

"My mother died when I was eight. She had three sisters in the States. The rest of the family died in Poland."

"During the war? They were Holocaust victims?"

He nods his head. "Right at the beginning. And her sisters in the States were all in the Communist Party. My father wasn't really socially involved, but he had three sisters, and *they* were all in the Communist Party. I was brought up in that kind of environment. My cousin was the head of the Communist Youth Movement."

He was an inquisitive child and took to disassembling and reassembling small appliances, radios, and television sets. This innate curiosity led him to study engineering. "The school at that time was called – maybe it still is – Polytechnic Institute of Brooklyn. It merged with NYU. Had a very good mathematical department. I was focusing on aerodynamics, but when I graduated, I went into interplanetary work. There's no air," he says, chuckling, "so we were much more concerned with dynamics. I oversaw the development of manuals for trajectories to go to Mars, manned missions to Mars. It was that kind of work. But in 1958 when I was a junior, in an English class one of the books we had to read was *The Religions of Man* by Huston Smith. And there was one page on Zen, and it really caught me. So I read everything in English on Zen.

"After I graduated, I was sitting in a pizza place with a friend – he was in my graduating class, also an aeronautical engineer – and he said, 'What do you want to do with your life?' And I said, 'Well, there's three things I want to do. I want to live in a Zen monastery.' So this is 1960. 'I want to live on a kibbutz in Israel. And I want to live in the Bowery, in the streets of New York.' And now

I've done all three.

"So I hired into Douglas – it's now McDonnell Douglas – and in '62 I left. I quit, and I went to Israel to explore living there. I would have been drafted if I had just left McDonnell-Douglas, so I wound up getting a teaching assistantship at the Israel Technion in Haifa. I was there a year."

"What led you to the kibbutz?"

"My early readings. Around Bar Mitzvah time, somewhere between twelve and fourteen, I did this major exploration of – not religion so much – but I called it 'reasons for and against the existence of God.' So I read through lots of literature, and I got very interested in the kibbutz movement. This one kibbutz observed Shabbat as a day of silence, and they did a lot of meditation, and those ideas were totally in line with everything I was reading. But Israel was too chauvinistic for me. Like everybody had a chip on their shoulder, and 'This will never happen to us again.' And 'We're not going to be servants to anyone.' That was my experience at any rate. So I decided not to stay."

He had, however, met the woman who became his first wife – Helen Silverberg – on the ship over. Back in the United States, he sent out his resumé to appropriate corporations, and, once again, McDonnell-Douglas made the best offer, so he returned to them. He and Helen married and settled in Santa Monica. It was the early '60s, and there was a growing interest in Zen and related issues among young people. Bernie became involved with a group of similarly minded individuals who read *The Three Pillars of Zen* and tried to follow the zazen instructions it provided. They even paid a visit to the ethnic Japanese temple in LA, where Bernie first met the man who would later become his teacher, Taizan Maezumi.

When Bernie received authorization to teach from Maezumi in 1976, he returned East and established the Zen Community of New York three years later. His zendo operated traditionally for a while, but it wasn't long before he was experimenting with radically different forms, such as holding street retreats in which the participants lived with and shared the conditions of the city's homeless population.

## Genro Gauntt

For Grover Genro Gauntt, experimenting with Eastern Spiritualities was simply part of the cultural ambiance of the '60s and '70s.

"So in university, I was searching. So I was looking at all the occult religions from Tibetan Buddhism to whatever. You know, there was Alan Watts and D.T. Suzuki in Buddhism in the late '60s, so I read that. And finally was attracted to Zen – I don't know – end of college possibly? And it was Suzuki quoting Joshu.[15] Somebody asked him, 'What is Buddhism?' And Joshu said, 'The cypress tree in the garden.' And it just floored me. I was, like, 'Yeah. That's absolutely right. That's it.' You know? And I can't say I had a kensho at the time, but it was fairly big opening for me. And so from then on, I widened my studies and found Maezumi Roshi in 1971 or '72. Started to attend for 22/23 years."

"Why had you been searching?" I ask.

He reflects a moment before answering. "Because from the time I was a child, I knew that I wasn't just this person. I was something bigger and something far more unchangeable and eternal. I knew that. I knew a lot of things like that, more generally than specifically, so for me to find out what the path to realization was was deeply important, more important than anything else. So that's what drove me. It wasn't pain. It wasn't suffering. It was like I knew, and I wanted to experience and acknowledge myself, verify myself. I think many people – and this doesn't mean a huge number – but we're born with that kind of conviction. You know? It might be that I should be a solo pianist or I should be a psychiatrist or an author or something. And I think many of those paths are deep, but they weren't meant for me. Spirituality was the path and the way."

In the '70s there were only a handful of Zen communities active in the US, and it so happened that one of them was located in Los Angeles where Genro was living.

"There was an advertisement in the *LA Times* that a Zen teacher – a resident monk – was going to speak at the Philosophical Research Society in LA. I said, 'I gotta go hear this guy.' And so I did. And it was like all the bells just rang, and I showed up at the Los Angeles Zen Center the next weekend."

The head monk at the Center was Bernie Glassman. "He had already been there with Maezumi since like '67. He was Maezumi's first student."

Another student[16] from that era described the Zen Center of Los Angeles as a mixture of hippie commune and Zen monastery. I ask Genro if that had been his experience. He explains that it may have felt that way to residents, but he didn't move into residency until the '80s. "I did not consider myself an insider. I was a commuter, and although I had many good friends in the *sangha*[17] I left all the time. So for me it was a place of deep practice, 'cause I was there several times a week. I was having *dokusan*[18] all the time, and I went to *sesshin*[19] almost every month. At least part of them if they were long. And for me it was

---

15. Joshu Jushin is the Japanese rendering of Zhaozhou Congshen.

16. Jan Chozen Bays. Cf, *Cypress Trees in the Garden* (Sumeru, 2015), p. 276.

17. The community. One of the Three Treasures of Buddhism.

18. Soto term for private interviews with a teacher. Called *sanzen* in Rinzai.

19. A Zen retreat, usually seven days long.

just a place of deep practice."

In the mid-'80s both the Zen communities in Los Angeles and San Francisco were rocked by scandals. Teachers were discovered to be engaged in sexual relationships with students, and Taizan Maezumi publicly admitted he was an alcoholic and went into treatment.

"There was a huge breakdown because of stories you've probably heard. Until then it was a smoothly operating community in my experience. Because I was still working, I was practicing coming and going. I didn't hang out in the community. And when it finally broke down, half the people left. It was a huge, hard transition and healing period."

Bernie Glassman had already been in New York for several years by this point.

"You stayed?" I ask Genro.

"I stayed? Of course. Maezumi Roshi was my core teacher at a guru level, and I wasn't going to leave. I wasn't going to let my judgments – which there were a few – get in the way of my practice. So I was there. I was still on the board. I became chairman of the board – I don't know – the last seven/eight years. Something like that. I was there to support him, and that was my position. I was there to serve him and the rest of the community to the best of my ability. And my faith and devotion didn't waver."

After Maezumi died in 1995, Bernie invited Genro to come to New York, where he immediately become involved with the newly formed Zen Peacemakers and the street retreats.

"Bernie always had the vision from early on to build a multi-faith community of people working on behalf of society and doing social service in a vast variety of ways," Genro tells me. "So, Zen practice really isn't about learning a Japanese form and being able to do it well. It isn't about striving for enlightenment for yourself. It isn't about gaining anything or knowing anything. So the street retreat was a beautiful way to have people in a very short time throw off all of their identities as fast as they could, as much as they could, be in old clothes – you know – look unpresentable, have no money, no ID – maybe one piece – and dive into the streets in whatever city we are and have no idea of how it's going to work out. Just throw yourself to life. And it works really fast. You know, to be in a street retreat, to be in one of our Zen Peacemaker Bearing Witness retreats, is to do like years of practice in a couple of days because a lot comes off."

## Robert Kennedy

Father Robert Kennedy is Professor Emeritus of Theology at St. Peter's University in Jersey City. He is also one of Bernie's Dharma heirs and is the teacher at the Morning Star Zendo, where he is addressed as Kennedy Roshi. One day in the early '70s, Kennedy was listening to the radio while driving and happened upon a talk about Zen.

"The speaker was Alan Watts, and he said, 'Have you noticed that nature is never symmetrical. Or rarely symmetrical. It's more like sand thrown in the wind.' I don't know why that statement hit me with the strength that it did, but I remember that I had to stop the car and think about this extraordinary moment. I forget the purpose of the talk and everything else about it except for that one statement. Which is the way, I think, that we learn sometimes. It's like striking a match. Sometimes it lights, and sometimes it doesn't. But that made me stop and begin to sit. Now why I began to sit, why that question in my mind made me sit is another thing I cannot answer. I'd lived in Japan for many years and had no interest in Zen or Buddhism at all. My interest had been elsewhere."

In fact, his ordination as a Catholic priest had taken place in Japan. "I was there for almost eight years. I was studying Japanese and teaching in a Jesuit high school in Kobe and doing theology in Japan. And then I returned to the states for graduate studies, and I finished that in 1970. And it was shortly after that I had this experience."

"Without any formal instruction, how did you begin meditating?" I ask.

"I took a blanket off my bed. I folded it and put it down on the floor, and I started sitting. I can't really be more specific than that. Of course I started reading about Zen. I felt it was a way to go. There was something in my spirit that said I had to stop doing theology and turn to experience. Turn away from theory and learn from my own doing. Because Zen isn't a thinking thing. It's 'let's do it.' And I realized I had to *do* it finally.

"It was, as Catholics say, a great grace, a great gift. Although at the time I didn't know it, I was filled with a lot of confusion. Of course, this was after the Second Vatican Council when there was a great deal of confusion in the church and some experimentation, and I was part of that generation. So I sat for a few years by myself, and then I knew I had to have a teacher. I had a sabbatical in 1976. I went back to Japan, this time not as a teacher but as a pilgrim. And the Jesuits there helped me by introducing me to Yamada Roshi of Kamakura.

"I remember the first time he walked into the zendo before I met him personally. I was sitting in the back, up against the back wall. I remember vividly the way he walked in to light the incense and to begin the day of sitting. Again, I cannot explain it. The very sight of him walking into the zendo was life changing. Why? I cannot explain. He was younger than I am now, but he seemed old then. He was 68, and stocky, a heavy-set man. But gentle. He was a gentleman and gracious and welcoming which was tremendous in itself. He drew many foreigners to him. He was open to foreigners, open to Christians, open to Catholic priests and nuns, and we came to him in great numbers. There must have been a dozen priests and a dozen nuns who were actively sitting.

"I remember him saying, 'I'm not trying to make you a Buddhist. I want to empty you in imitation of your lord, Jesus Christ.' And that was a wonderful, liberating experience. He swept away, in a sense, all talk about Buddhism. And this was something Maezumi – his Dharma brother – also shared in California. I remember Maezumi shouting to a student once, 'Stop talking about Buddhism! Go into the zendo and sit!' And, in a more gentle way, that is what Yamada Roshi wanted us to do. He opened his home to us; he opened the zendo to us. And truly our faith did not matter. What mattered was our capacity to pay attention. As he said, 'Some foreigners come to Japan, and their will power is strong. Some come and their will power is not so strong.' It was interesting. He focused on will power, on our ability to concentrate. He never asked about what faith we had."

Kennedy spent the spring semester of 1976 in Japan, after which he returned to the United States. "Yamada Roshi recommended I go to Maezumi, his Dharma brother, in California, and that's what I did. And I finished my sabbatical year by sitting in Los Angeles.

"Maezumi Roshi was considerably younger than Yamada Roshi, maybe 25 years younger than Yamada Roshi, and a different person entirely. He was a great teacher, just a different personality. He used the stick[20] a lot. Yamada never did. But Maezumi believed in it. And it worked too. It really gave you energy. The purpose of the stick was to give you energy not to encourage thoughts. And he was not afraid to use it. And he was running – with Glassman Sensei[21] really – almost a hotel with many students who were living right there in ZCLA. So I became part of that world. I wasn't living there, though. The Jesuits have a high school in Los Angeles, and I lived there."

After his sabbatical year, Kennedy returned to New York where he was on faculty at St. Peter's College. "That's where the Jesuits assigned me. I was teaching theology and Japanese language to beginners in the business program. And at that time I was without a teacher. I went back summers to sit with Maezumi. But it was around 1980 when Glassman came to New York and set up shop as a Zen teacher there that I became his student. He became my teacher."

---

20. The *kyosaku* – or "Encouragement Stick" – is a long rod tapered at one end, used by monitors during zazen to encourage (or wake up) drowsy meditators.

21. *Sensei* is a title meaning teacher, in American Zen, usually implying less authority than a Roshi would have. It is commonly used in martial arts as well.

# David Loy

David Loy is also a Dharma heir of Yamada Koun Roshi, although he admits he hasn't followed the same type of path that most of Koun's successors have.

"Just about every other person who is a Dharma successor of Yamada Koun has ended up creating a community in their homeland. But in my case, I was an academic and moved around a lot, so that hasn't happened. In a way, I'm connected now with the Rocky Mountain Ecodharma Retreat Center, and that feels like a kind of home – a Dharma home – and I have some personal students I communicate with individually. But I have not created a community. And I think I'd be a terrible organizer, so unless somebody else was going to do all that work, I don't think it would work out very well."

"You're a freelance Zen teacher," I suggest.

"Pretty much. Although I don't know that I identify as a Zen teacher only."

He tells me he was raised Catholic. "But it never really took. I was a navy brat, so I grew up a bit of everywhere. I was born in the Panama Canal Zone actually, but I don't remember it. We were only there a year or so. Then I lived on the east coast, west coast. When my dad retired, the family returned to my parents' original home in Illinois, but I was there only a couple of years before I took off for college and basically I've kept moving ever since. That's one reason that I haven't had a sangha, I've just lived so many different places."

He first learned about Buddhism and Zen while in college where he studied philosophy. "Somebody like Heidegger is a good intro to Buddhism in a way. I've written about Heidegger in a couple of my early books, and I think there's a kind of natural progression to something like Buddhist practice. There's a famous – perhaps apocryphal – quotation that is attributed to Heidegger. Evidently somebody came across him reading a book by D.T. Suzuki, and he said, 'If I understand this fellow rightly, he's saying what I've been trying to say in all my writings.'"

David's interest was initially academic. It was a while yet before he took up practice.

"In 1969 I graduated from Carleton College and became a draft resister, eventually working with the draft resistance movement in the San Francisco Bay area. It was only as the war wound down that I realized I also needed to work on myself, that it wasn't sufficient to be concerned about social change. I had to look at my own anger and whatever was going on inside me."

"Did something specific prompt that?"

"Well, I suppose a sense of dissatisfaction about some of the things going on in the movement… the anger, the dualism. The way that military people, in particular, were objectified. But the Vietnam War was a real wake-up for our generation in another sense, too. We realized that our government lied to us. That the world wasn't what we thought it was. And I think that's a good prep for Zen too, if you think about it. You start seeing through the cracks and realize that the world is actually quite different. When you're studying philosophy, you do get some sense of constructivism, that the world as we normally experience it is not what it seems to be, that it's an individual and social construct. Once you have that general sense, it's not such a big shift to seeing the point of meditation. The other thing that I would add —and I'm curious how many of your other interviewees have mentioned this – is that psychedelics were an important part of my transformation too."

I admit that several of the people I'd spoken with acknowledged that psychedelics had been a factor in bringing them to practice.

"It's certainly no accident that after the Psychedelic '60s we had the explosion of interest in Buddhist and other meditation centers in the '70s," David continues. "For me it was mostly LSD, but LSD had a hard edge to it. You were never sure how pure it was, and it did take a toll on the body. I think it was Ram Dass[22] who said, 'It's a window, not a door.' That shift from psychedelics to meditation was obviously not something everybody made, but I think that was an important factor in the Buddhist-convert explosion in the '70s."

David first experience of formal Zen practice occurred in Hawaii.

"A friend and I decided we were going to travel around the world. As I remember, my vague intention was to spend some time in India and find a guru or a cave in the Himalayas. And so we got a ticket, first stop Hawaii, where I got stuck because I didn't have any money. So I ended up living there for five years, but it turned out to be not such a bad place to be stuck. I was crashing in a number of places out of my backpack, mostly in Molokai but also in Honolulu. I liked to hang out with a friend in Waikiki, smoking marijuana together and fantasizing about enlightenment, and one day he said, 'There's a Zen center near the university. Let's go check 'em out.' It was Robert Aitken's Koko An Zendo. We went there one evening. Afterwards, over tea, some of the residents told us that starting the next weekend they were having a sesshin with a visiting Zen master. My friend and I looked at each other and said, 'Cool! Can we come?' And the guy said 'yes.' So we ended up doing a seven day sesshin with Yamada Koun Roshi, despite having no idea what a sesshin was; I literally did not know what we were getting into. Needless to say, it was seven days of hell, not only physically, but also because I didn't have much perspective on

---

22. Baba Ram Dass, born Richard Alpert. Along with Timothy Leary, he studied the effects of psychedelic drug use at Harvard. Later, he became a Hindu Yogi and was instrumental in popularizing Western interest in Eastern spiritualities.

what was going on in my mind, so I really thought I was going crazy. It was only afterwards that there was some experience, and I became hooked on Zen practice. That was the beginning for me.

"Afterwards I was still going back and forth between Honolulu and Molokai, where I would camp out in Halawa Valley on the east end of the island. But I was doing quite a bit of meditation on my own, and when Yamada Roshi came back for other retreats, I signed up for them too. It was maybe after the third retreat that Bob Aitken invited me to Maui. I told him, 'I don't have any money,' but he said, 'Don't worry about it. It's only $50 a month, room and board, and I can lend you the money.' Which he did, and I'm happy to report that I later paid him back."

Although David did formal training with Aitken, he felt, because of his initial sesshin, that Yamada Koun, was his "root teacher." "So eventually I moved to Kamakura in Japan and practiced with him."

## Bobbie Rhodes

Soeng Hyang Soen Sa Nim is the Guiding Teacher of the Korean Kwan Um School of Zen founded in America by Korean teacher, Seung Sahn Sa Nim. Her birth name is Barbara Rhodes, and she invites me to call her Bobbie.

She laughs when I ask her how she first became involved in Zen.

"Well, being born and suffering. As I think any child who comes into this world, you see a lot of pain and you have confusing situations. You observe hypocrisy and suffering."

"Hypocrisy?"

"Well, my family went to church regularly, and I didn't think the people there walked the talk. I always questioned why people weren't more pure or more forthright in their actions, how they were saying a certain thing in church and not doing it in their daily life. I guess I started to notice this more when I was around twelve or so."

Her family was Episcopalian. "And I stayed with it, but it just got more and more difficult. I started to faint in church. It was pretty dramatic. Every time we would come to the Apostle's Creed, I would faint, and I was really trying not to. I tried to sit near a window and get more comfortable and not kneel. But no matter what I was doing, I would just start to get dizzy. When I later told my teacher, Zen Master Seung Sahn, about this, he said" – mimicking his accent – "'Oh! Buddha was trying to get you out of the church!' He said it as a joke, but it was actually something that was pretty visceral with me.

"So I just started to teach Sunday School. Not really teach Sunday School but go and watch and color with the four- and five-year-olds and watch them while everybody else was in church because I still felt kind of religious in the sense that I wanted to be part of things. Then one day this kid came up to me. He was four or five years old, I guess, and he asked, 'Where's Jesus?' And I said, 'God! I don't know.' That was my first koan, really. I swear, it hit me like a koan. He goes, 'Where's Jesus?' I said, 'I don't know.' And he said, 'Well, he was here last week.' And I said, 'He was?' Like that, talking to him as if he was an adult. He said, 'Yeah. You know, he was sitting over there with the black robe and reading us that book.' And what that was was somebody's father had worn a choir robe and was reading Bible stories to the kids. And I said, 'That wasn't Jesus. That was somebody's father.' And he goes, 'Oh!' And that was the end of my Christian experience in the sense of in a church." She was sixteen at the time.

"But then I had to take my brother to his first communion. Nobody was around except for me that was willing to take him to church because my parents were on vacation. So I walked him up to church, and I hadn't been in there for, like, two years. And of course, he was scared because he had to go up to the rail and take communion. So I went up with him. And then the Apostles' Creed started, and I had to leave the church because the same thing started to happen. And I was trying so hard, because my brother really wanted me to hang in there with him. But I had to walk out."

After high school, she entered a nursing program and was assigned to "a really acutely active hospital in Washington, DC. That was really my first temple. We worked non-stop, and, back then, you only had two weeks of vacation a year. But I loved it. I loved medicine, so I was just thrown into the scene. There was a *huge* amount of physical suffering and psychic suffering in the hospital. And while I was there, Martin Luther King got killed and Washington burned; parts of the city were in flames. It was a really amazing time in my life to be in nursing school. I took care of somebody who tried to burn himself in front of the Capital Building. I spent a whole eight-hour shift with him and watched him die. He had the most beautiful eyes. I couldn't talk to him. He was totally wrapped in bandages except his eyes and his mouth, and he was so sick. But just having things that intense happen, watching people come in with gunshot wounds, all those years of actively seeing so much suffering – and a lot of joy as well – that was my first Zen experience, I think. Being in that hospital for those three years.

"And when I got out, I still hadn't done psychedelics. I wasn't drinking or anything. I was just working. So for someone my age – I was seventeen when I went in and twenty-one when I left – when most people would be partying in college, I was working. But happy. I never went to a bar in my whole life until a couple of times on vacation when I got much older, in my forties. I remember sitting at a bar with someone and saying, 'This is the first time that I've sat at a bar!' You know? So it's not like I was a substance person. But after I graduated from nursing school, I worked in a free clinic for Mexican-American farm laborers in the San Joaquin Valley, and the doctor I worked for was into psychedelics. And he introduced me to marijuana and LSD, which was really good for me. I was out there for about two years in the desert. I never did drugs at a party or at a concert. I would just walk out and be with nature. And really it was a *huge* lift for me to do that. But after two years, I had had enough of it. I was tired; I wasn't learning new things from it. But I always bow to those things because they woke me up. I saw the potential that consciousness has.

"So I just started talking to people about stuff, and somebody turned me on to Krishnamurti[23] and D.T. Suzuki. I just loved that stuff. And I sort of leaned towards Zen because I thought it was so direct. You know? And I wanted to do koan practice. So I went to the San Francisco Zen Center, but they don't do koans."

Eventually she returned to New England.

"My parents were living in Rhode Island, just outside of Providence, and I hadn't spoken to them for two years, because I just needed a break. So on an acid trip, this voice came to me: 'You've got to go make amends with your parents and go meet your teacher.' Some intuitive thing knew my teacher was out on the east coast. And they were both in the same state, that teeny little state of Rhode Island."

She searched for an apartment in Providence, and one of the places she looked at was above Seung Sahn's temple. She didn't take the apartment, but, after overcoming some anxiety about doing so, she came back and knocked at the temple door.

## Melissa Blacker

Spontaneous examples of the type of "Cosmic Consciousness" which some achieved through psychedelics – and which sometimes led those who experienced them to spiritual practice – are not uncommon. Children can have them.

"I was raised in a secular household," Melissa Myozen Blacker tells me, "so I never had any religious training. In fact, my parents were very suspicious of religion."

---

23. As a child, Jiddu Krisnamurti was discovered by the Theosophical movement and declared to be the new World Teacher, following in the line of previous masters like Jesus and the Buddha. As a young man, he disaffiliated from the movement and denied any supernatural status. He remained a popular spiritual teacher nonetheless.

Melissa is one of the resident teachers at the Boundless Way Temple in Worcester, Massachusetts.

"But I had these spontaneous experiences when I was a little girl that I tried to talk to my parents about, and they didn't know what I was talking about. I see it now as a kensho experience, but I was just a little kid. I had no idea. There was no framework for it. I was at a summer camp, and we were camping on the beach at Martha's Vineyard – a beautiful island off the coast of Massachusetts. And on this island, this particular beach faced east. And I got up out of my tent and went, spontaneously, to sit on the beach in – what I now recognize as – Zen posture. I was sitting there, little folded legs and just very, very still – and I'd never sat still like that before – and watched the sun come up. And what happened was that everything changed… like there was this incredible sense of the aliveness of the world. I saw the individual motes of light come up and then the sun, and I was *utterly* transformed by it, and was so excited. And, being a kid, the first thought I had was, 'This must be what grown-ups know. This is the great secret of being a grown-up.' So I was very excited to see my mother the next day when I got on the ferry. And when she picked me up, I said, 'Mommy, Mommy, I saw the sun come up!' But, you know, this was code for, 'I get it now!' And she looked at me. She was a very loving mother, and she said, 'Oh, that's so nice, honey. Sunrises are beautiful.' And I totally knew she didn't know what I was talking about. So at that moment, I thought" – she lowers her voice to a whisper – "'I've got to keep this to myself. Nobody's going to understand this.' And, I would say, for the next ten years – I was just entering being a teenager – I studied and read and asked questions, and I got interested in Buddhism through reading, and Hinduism, yoga."

### Shinge Chayat

Shinge Chayat is abbot of the Dai Bosatsu Zendo Kongo-ji monastery in the Catskill Mountains. Her father died during the Second World War, and her mother remarried when Shinge was four years old.

"It was very dramatic. A huge change for me. Even though there was this underlying sense of sadness after my father's death, there was great love. When my mother remarried, my step-father wanted to take us away. So we moved from my grandmother's house. He was an extremely difficult man. Right away my grandmother and I felt kind of great fear. I remember being still in her house, and he would come over. And I was playing with a friend one day in the sun-porch, and we were chatting away, and he came out and screamed for us to be quiet. So I tried. And I guess we started yelling again. So he came out and taped my mouth shut. And that was the beginning of what I experienced with him as a kind of an ongoing, terrifying violence of one kind or another. Sometimes not physical but emotional.

"We went to New Mexico for a year, then we ended up in New Jersey, and I spent my childhood in a kind of strange mix of disbelief and incomprehension. And anger. And grief. And I didn't understand what had happened. Why did the whole world change so radically? And I started getting hives all the time. Nobody knew what was wrong, but it was emotional/psychological stress. And one day, I just sat down under a tree. I was just filled with so much turmoil, and I just let it go. I was sitting with my hands clasped together, and I felt so still, almost as though I had turned into a statue. And at the same time, the feeling of my small bubble of pain completely opened. The entire universe was… It's very hard to say exactly what happened, what was coming through me. And I felt that so strongly, and it was like a wonderful blessing."

"How old were you?" I ask.

"Maybe eight or ten. And then I started doing that. I would sit on a window-seat in my room and do the same thing. I would sit very still. And my hands would become almost as though they were the size of the of the Earth. Everything became very still, and my sadness would lift and everything would just take my small painful existence and open it up to the vastness. And I became this vastness. This became something that I would do from time to time, particularly when I was feeling – oh – just terribly oppressed or confused.

"I was a good student. I loved going to school. Anything to get out of the house. One day in eighth grade we were reading a textbook on various world cultures. I turned to the section we were to read, and it's about Zen Buddhism. I can still feel… Sitting in that dark room – there were so many of us baby-boomers, the first of the baby-wave – and they had cut the cafeteria in two with a kind of a pull-apart door, so that we'd have a room. Had no windows. So we're in this dark room with – you know – one single light in the ceiling, and looking at this page and thinking, 'This is what I've been doing.'"

## Henry Shukman

Henry Shukman is the resident teacher at the Mountain Cloud Zen Center in Santa Fe. He was 19 when he had an experience "that fell on me out of the blue that resolved everything for me, answered everything, and I didn't know what it was. And for ten years I suffered rather a lot, actually, trying to forget about it. Or else trying to address it and not knowing how to."

I ask if he can describe it.

"Well, it was a run-of-the mill experience of oneness, I guess. I was watching the sunlight on the ocean. I had actually just finished writing my first book, and I was very happy. And I was watching the sunlight on the ocean, far from home – I'd been working abroad – and all of a sudden the sunlight on the ocean... Well, I was trying to figure out if the sea was very, very dark or very, very bright. 'Cause it seemed to be so dark where the light was not shining on it and so dazzlingly bright where the light was on it, and the light was shifting about. So was it completely black? Or was it utterly white? I just couldn't work it out. And all of a sudden, it simply wasn't outside. It was impossible to say whether it was inside or outside – you know – there it was and here I was watching it. Yet there just was no separation whatsoever between it and me. And in that moment, I was flooded with this great sense of love. And the love seemed to be everywhere. And possibly because of my background as a half-Jewish guy in England, where there was still a certain amount of latent anti-Semitism, actually, even when I was growing up in the '70s, I guess one of my issues had been, 'Did I belong?' Or, 'Where did I belong?' And, at this moment, I realized that I belonged beyond belonging. 'Cause I was made of the same fabric as the whole of creation! There was absolutely no difference. And it... it was totally, overwhelmingly marvelous. I felt like I'd been taken over – claimed – by a greater love that included everything. But I had no idea what it was. I was stone-cold sober, by the way, and I didn't know what to do next."

## Joan Sutherland

I first met Joan Sutherland when, like Henry, she was living and teaching in Santa Fe. Shortly after that meeting, she ceased active teaching for health reasons but continues to write about Zen. Along with her teacher – John Tarrant, a Robert Aitken heir – she has been influential in adapting the koan tradition to America.

"When I was about thirteen, I was living in Southern California on the west side of Los Angeles, and I could take a bus in one of two directions. One was to the ocean where I would go surfing, and the other was either to the big bookstore right outside of UCLA or the museum downtown. Hence that was sort of my life, defined by the bus lines. And one day I was in the big bookstore outside of UCLA, and I found the *Daodejing*, and, with a kind of thirteen year-old's arrogance, I thought, 'Someone understands! Someone sees the world as I see it!' So when I got to college, which wasn't too long after that, they said, 'What do you want to major in?' And without even thinking about it, I realized I wanted to learn the languages so that I could read Daoism in the original, because I had an intuition that that would be important. So that's how I got involved in language studies. And I'd also been doing my own kind of spiritual stuff, meditating.

"When I was in high school, one of the only games in town was the Vedanta Society.[24] You could go there and learn to meditate and read their books and stuff like that. And that's how I got into it. And then when I was at university – at UCLA – I had a professor, Professor Ashikaga Ensho, who asked me if I wanted to do a seminar with him, and I said, 'Of course.' And I showed up, and I was the only person there. So it was a one-on-one situation, and we were translating *The Gateless Gateway*, one of the koan collections, together. And it was really a transformative experience, and I began to understand – as he was teaching me – that he wasn't correcting my vocabulary or my grammar, but he was really giving me the Mind behind the koans, and it clicked. I understood that there was this really vast, beautiful tradition and that there was a practice attached to it. And so then I began wandering through Zen and a little bit through Tibetan practice, but I was a..." – she laughs – "...I was a failed Zen student until I found the koans."

Her first exposure to Zen had been through one of Shunryu Suzuki's students, Jakusho Kwong, in the Soto tradition.

"In what way a failed student?" I ask.

"Mine was an unrequited love."

She graduated with a degree in East Asians languages only to discover there was little she could do with it. "My one job offer was from the CIA. Which I declined. And – oh – I kind of held it for a couple of decades, actually, not really knowing why I'd done that study. I went off and did other things."

Unrequited or not, she continued to practice with Kwong, and, when he suggested she become a Buddhist, she began the formal preparations to do so. "I thought if my teacher invited me, I needed to show up."

It was at the time of the AIDS crisis, "when it was still called Gay-Related Immune Deficiency and stuff like that." A fellow student also preparing to become a Buddhist was a gay therapist, who "was doing this amazing, brave work where he was going to the prisons and talking with people, because people who were HIV-positive in prisons were being beaten up and murdered by the other prisoners because they were afraid of them." He and Joan became friends. "Several years later he died, and I went to his funeral, and the roshi who was conducting the funeral was John Tarrant. And for the first time in a while, I thought, 'Huh! There's something there. There's something that I can really feel.'"

She began to study with Tarrant and rediscovered the koan tradition Professor Ashikaga had introduced her to, and, as she puts it, "I knew I was doomed."

---

24. Prior to the Zen boom, the Vedanta Society was one of the earliest examples of Asian spirituality to be promoted in the United States. It was affiliated with the Ramakrishna Hindu Mission. The first society was founded in New York City in 1894.

## Robert Waldinger

Bob Waldinger is a Dharma heir of Melissa Blacker. He came to Zen relatively late in life. He was in his 50s when he began formal practice. "I had been interested in meditation since I was in my 30s because someone I did my training in psychology with casually said one day that she and her partner had spent a weekend doing a silent retreat. And I said, 'You mean, you didn't *say* anything?' I couldn't imagine spending time with my girlfriend being quiet. So I think she recommended *Wherever You Go, There You Are*, the Jon Kabat-Zinn book,[25] and I read it and was really drawn to basic Buddhist philosophy. The idea of impermanence resonated so much because since I was a teenager at least, reading some of the poets like Yeats, I realized that I was worried about all this stuff that didn't matter, and that all these ideas about what we were supposed to achieve and what people were supposed to accomplish had this kind of absurdity about it because it was all going to pass away. And that really struck me deeply as an adolescent, but I didn't have any way to talk about it, and nobody else was seeming to think that way. So I did all these very achievement-oriented things, but all the while kept thinking, 'There's a part of this that's completely made up and absurd.' Traditional religion hadn't worked for me. I was raised Jewish, and – like – I would be in services with my family and wanted to stop the action and go up front and say, 'Okay, raise your hands. How many of you really believe this stuff?' Of course I could never do that. So there were these ways in which I was hungry for a spiritual practice and a way to make sense of the world."

He dabbled in various meditation traditions before meeting Melissa's teacher, James Ford. "My son's friend in middle school had a coming-of-age ceremony at the Unitarian Church where James was the minister. And I sat next to the friend's mom, and she knew I'd been interested in meditation; she pointed to James and said, 'You know, he's a Zen master.' So I emailed him and asked if I could come see him, and he said, 'Sure.' So one weekday morning I went to his office, and it was just a total mess, and he came in with his shirt-buttons wrong and – you know – was just James. And was very down to Earth. And I thought, 'Oh, I could probably learn from this guy.' One of the first things James said to me was, 'We do scruffy Zen.'" Bob accepted an invitation to try sitting with the group that James was running at his church. "And I went up to him afterwards, and I said, 'You know, I was really uncomfortable with all the bowing and the chanting.' And, of course, being James, he said, 'Good!' And that was sort of a dare to come back, so I came back, and…" He shrugs. "I drank the Kool-Aid."

---

25. Published in 1994. Kabat-Zinn is a significant figure in the Mindfulness movement.

"As long as you recognized it's Kool-Aid."

"Well, that was actually one of the most helpful things. The Zen I know doesn't present itself as anything but Kool-Aid that eventually you'll put down.

"The structure of Zen works for me, these frequent interviews with teachers are important because I tend to get discouraged. Doubt is a big part of my experience. So I would sit there and think, 'What the hell am I doing? I might just as well be phoning this meditation in.' And so it's really helpful to have another human being working to remind me what this is. So I found that structure helpful. And when Zen talks about 'already Buddha' – you know? – what the hell is that? And that seemed to me to be really important and much more... um... both surprising and real than what I understand from some of my friends in other traditions. Well, they eventually deconstruct all these levels. But most of us never get to that point. Most people don't get far enough along the path to deconstruct the various levels. What I like about Zen is it keeps knocking you back down and saying, 'We're going to deconstruct it moment to moment.'"

## Koun Franz

Koun Franz of 1000 Harbours Zen in Halifax, Nova Scotia, came to Zen after it had become well-established in North America, but he still went to Japan for formal training.

He grew up in Helena, Montana, which he describes as "disproportionately Catholic and disproportionately Mormon." His family was Catholic. One of his earliest encounters with Zen came when a friend of his father gave him a copy of *The Three Pillars of Zen*. "He has this karmic burden on him now that he did that," he says chuckling.

It also happened that a teacher at his High School was Buddhist and introduced him to like-minded people. It was a small group, but his involvement with it deepened his interest, and, after graduating from college, he decided to go to Japan. He found work at a private school but when he inquired about Zen temples, "What I got was this confusing message that there *were* Zen temples, but nothing that I could participate in at all. That was not what I expected. But most Japanese Zen temples don't have any zazen component at all." He shrugs. "So I came back to the US and went to graduate school."

It wasn't long before he realized he was "kind of hooked on Japan, even though it had been a failure according to all the metrics I had assigned to it. So throughout the time I was in grad school I was figuring out how to go back to Japan."

During his second visit, he found his teacher. "I was in a little tiny town, Takamori, inside the caldera of a volcano in Kyushu. And the first day I was there, I was determined. I said, 'Is there a Zen temple in this town?' They said, 'Yes. There is one. It's over there.' And I heard a temple bell coming from over there. So the next morning I got up, and I had a bicycle, and I waited. And when I heard the temple bells, I just started going in that direction. Found a temple; it had a bell. There was a little guy in back wearing overalls, but he had a bald head. My Japanese wasn't great, so the best I could do was ask 'Is this a Zen temple?' He said, 'Yes.' I said, 'Do you do zazen here?' He said, *Of course* we do zazen.' I said, 'Great! Can I come do zazen here?' He said, 'Okay. Sure. Come tomorrow.' So I went the next day, and he was there, and he was wearing really fancy robes and the incense was going, and he set me up. And I sat there in front of the altar, and he walked around with the kyosaku and hit me a couple of times. And when it was done, they kind of rolled in this fancy table, and there was a meal, and his wife served me breakfast. Then they saw me to the gate, and I said, 'This is great. Can I come tomorrow?' And that was not what they expected. They thought they were giving me a kind of tourist experience. They had really done their best at it. And he said, 'Ohhhh... okay.' So I went back the next day, and the next day it was a little less of a show, and the next day it was less of a show, and eventually it wasn't certain whether he was going to be there or not. But I just went every day for two years. And eventually I just kind of had a key to the place, and I would sit, and I would clean the grounds, and then I would go into their kitchen and have breakfast with the family"

"I'm guessing this was a community temple," I say.

"Yeah, it's community service, a community center. One of the things I've enjoyed since coming back to the US – one of the ways I can tell that someone is just full of it – is if they ask me who my teacher is and I tell them, and they nod, and they say, 'Oh, yeah. Yeah. I know who that is.' 'No, you don't. Because even the people in the next town over don't know who he is.'"

The priest's name was Kosoku Honda. "So he became my teacher; he became my ordination teacher. I was ordained at the end of those two years."

# 2

# THE FUNCTION OF ZEN

## Melissa Blacker

"What's the purpose of Zen?" Melissa Blacker muses. "Well..." She pauses and sighs. "I don't know if Zen does anything. I think it's important to realize that part of our tradition is about non-doing. And especially – you know – in the Soto School, we quote Dogen a lot, 'Doing not doing.' There's a big connection with Daoism and the blend of Indian Buddhism with Daoism. So, for me, what Zen does in the world is it finds a way to talk about an experience which is very hard to talk about, because whenever we put words to it, it divides it up. And it's this experience of a reality that's sort of beyond the reality that we ordinarily experience – what I like to call 'consensual reality' – it's beyond 'consensual reality.' It's the real, true perception – not an idea – of everything being one fabric, of everything just being this one thing that's multi-faceted and it's continually alive and going on. And in that aliveness, there's a sense of freedom and a sense of liberation from old ideas.

"We're all story-tellers. We all tell really great stories, and we're masters at being able to tell stories about reality. There's nothing wrong with stories – they help us to function in the world – but sometimes they can get in the way of direct perception. So I think Zen is a way of using a different kind of story to point to a life beyond stories. And one of the reasons I got involved in Zen in the first place is that I also love stories. I love every form of story: story-tellers, books, movies, TV, every way that stories can be told. But one of the things that's important to me is to know when story-making is happening and see it for what it is and then to see what's beyond the story. So in a way, the function of Zen is to see beyond the constructions of the mind that blind us to reality."

## Myokyo McLean

Zengetsu Myokyo McLean is the abbess of Rinzai Enpuku-ji in Montreal and the Buddhist chaplain at Concordia and McGill Universities. When still a young woman in the early '80s, Myokyo went with a boyfriend to Mount Baldy in California to take part in a sesshin directed by Joshu Sasaki. The boyfriend had to return to Canada on family business. Myokyo stayed. After the retreat, she wanted to remain at Mount Baldy for a longer period, but it wasn't possible, so she returned to Nelson, British Columbia, where she worked in fabric and paper design, earning just enough to maintain a studio and be able to fly down to do annual retreats with Sasaki.

Then, in 1984, he suggested she consider taking part in the extended winter training period. "But I couldn't do that because I'd just borrowed money for supplies for fall and Christmas sales. But the seed was planted for me to go for a training period, and, the next winter, I went." And there she remained until Sasaki encouraged her to open a center in Montreal.

"Zen is a practice," she tells me. "It's not a lifestyle. It's not a way of thinking. You don't need to believe anything when you start Zen practice. It's a practice. And everyone does the same practice. And through the practice of zazen peoples' minds become clearer, and – you might say – you dissolve the mind that separates us from everything else in this world."

•••

The point that both Melissa and Myokyo are making is basic to Zen's understanding of the human condition. Much of human unhappiness – *dukkha* – is rooted in our failure to see the way in which we are connected with the rest of Being. Our minds normally view the world dualistically even though biologically and sociologically it is obvious that we are thoroughly interconnected with one another and with the environment that supports us and without which we would be unable to survive. The concept of interdependence – or nonduality – is expressed in a variety of ways. One of the most bewildering for people unfamiliar with Zen practice is the concept of Emptiness, which is – in part – to be empty of all the assumptions which color one's perception, to be empty of the stream of ideas, opinions, and strategies which flow through the mind creating the sense of being a particular self separate from everything else. When these are interrupted there can be the flash of insight – kensho – which makes it clear that we never had been separate from the rest of being.

For many Zen teachers, this insight is fundamental to Zen. Yamada Koun put it bluntly: "Doubtless, kensho is the very core of Mahayana Zen. Without kensho, Zen lacks the religious power to save people in the truest sense of the word."²⁶

The teacher with whom I worked for many years, Albert Low, was equally frank:

> Nowadays in the West the pure waters of Zen are being muddied, and more and more it is said that Buddha and the patriarchs did not really mean one should search for one's true nature. Some say the essence of the Way is living an ethical life, others advocate just sitting in meditation and forcing oneself to take up the lotus posture even at risk of knees and ankles. Others prefer to read books and attend conferences. But the word Buddha means *awakened*. To be awakened is to be awakened in, and therefore to, true nature Zen teachers who teach anything less than this are cheating their students...
>
> Without awakening, kensho, satori, call it what you will Buddhism has very little to offer the West except more abstruse philosophy and an ethical system in no way superior to the Christians.²⁷

## Joan Sutherland

It is a point of view Joan Sutherland shares. When I ask her what the function of Zen is, she responds without hesitation. "Awakening. Without question."

"And that means?"

"Awakening is a process. It's not a sudden event, which is why I use 'awakening' rather than 'enlightenment' which is a word kind of obscured behind" – she chuckles – "a cloud of projection. So awakening is a process that happens over the course of our whole lives, and if I had to define it really simply, I would use one of the Chinese synonyms for enlightenment which is 'becoming intimate.' It's a matter of becoming intimate with the world. And so the practice is a lot about clearing away what gets in the way of our intimacy with the world. That's a kind of powerful deconstructive quality. And when the clearing away has been done, and we stand on the bare ground, we've made ourselves fetchable by something else."

---

26. Yamada, Koun, *The Gateless Gate* (Boston: Wisdom Publications, 2004), p. 211.
27. Albert Low, *The World: A Gateway* (Rutland, VT: Tuttle Publishing, 1995), pp. 268-69.

"We've made ourselves?"

"Fetchable. Able to be fetched by the whole of the universe. And so it becomes a kind of return from a feeling of exile to a feeling of belonging to something. And there are moments where that 'being fetched' is very powerful, and those we call opening moments. And then there's all the deconstructive work that leads up to that, and there's all the integration work that comes after such moments. And that whole process is the process of awakening.

"I have this crazy notion that the whole universe is involved in a kind of large project of awakening. And what Zen and the koans are about is allowing us to join in most freely and most hopefully in that large process of the awakening of the universe."

## David Loy

During my first conversation with David Loy, he told me that "according to Zen and/or Buddhism we are not fully awake. There is something we need to realize about ourselves and about the world, and this path is to help us wake up." Later, I ask him what that "something we're not aware of" is.

"There's a lot of ways to answer that, because there's a lot of different aspects to it – right? – but for me what stands out is nonduality or nonseparation: overcoming the delusion that there's a me *inside* that is somehow separate from you and the rest of the world *outside*, and that therefore my well-being is separate from yours and others' well-being. The delusion of self. Kensho – the 'opening' as some people prefer – is a letting go of that and realizing or experiencing the world at least momentarily in a nondual way. So we need to wake up to. And then we need to integrate the implications of that into how we live. It's not enough just to have a moment of insight, but how does that affect how we actually understand our lives and how we relate to others?"

"So kensho is an opening in the sense of an initial insight?"

"A taste of insight, a taste of nondual experience. It obviously has to go beyond some kind of intellectual understanding. Yamada Roshi had a nice analogy to explain why it is that every genuine kensho is qualitatively the same but quantitatively different from, say, a really deep *daigo tettei*.[28] He said to imagine your teacher asked you to polish a wall, and he gives you something to polish with, a rough sponge or something like that. You don't really understand what's the point, but he tells you to do it, so you do it. Kensho is the moment of realizing that it's not a wall; in fact, it's a pane of glass, because you can see there's something on the other side. Kensho is the moment when you realize that. The

---

28. "Unsurpassed and complete awakening."

danger is that, having had that moment, someone might think, 'Well, that's it. I've got it.' Instead, it's important to continue polishing, to make the glass completely clean, and then the great enlightenment is when the glass shatters, so there's no longer anything between yourself and what's on the other side."

## Rinsen Weik

Rinsen Weik is a university professor of jazz guitar, an aikido instructor, and the abbot of the Buddhist Temple of Toledo. He has a shaved head but a long ZZ Top-style beard. In what he calls his library, there is a stick of incense burning on the altar beside his desk as well as figures of Manjushri (the Bodhisattva of Prajna/Wisdom) and Kannon (the Bodhisattva of Karuna/Compassion).

"No seated Buddha figure," I note.

"No. I take care of that part," he says, laughing. He's fun to talk with. He laughs frequently and has an irreverent sense of humor. "Words are great. I love them. I'm surrounded by them," gesturing at the shelves, "but they won't ever scratch the itch. So what has to happen is people have to first be able to see into the true nature of themselves – which means letting go of the linguistic processing of that and actually just experience it – and then we have to be able to communicate that to each other. It's learning a language, like jazz; it's learning how to speak and express this ineffable, unspeakable, what-the-fuck-it-is thing. It's about achieving the fullest and deepest potential of the human being."

"I couldn't achieve that any other way?"

"I'm sure you can. I know there's probably lots of way to arrive there, but in my life I have never found a system which is all that Zen is. I've never found a system that is as effective and specializes in that. Zen has a long lineage, and it has a historically adaptable system to fit whatever society and culture it's in and really have this awakening and heart of compassion be real. And I think people in our society are plagued by isolation, and they're plagued by the 'surfaceness' of things. And so increasingly people know that, and they're sick of it. And so Zen offers not just a surface, but the rabbit hole goes all the way down. So that's an incredibly deep thing. This isn't just a seminar or a consultant or a cool book that you forget about; there's actually a lifetime's – multiple lifetimes' – worth of depth to be had. And that itself is very attractive, and it also has community, an actual connection with other folks in your life that really matter. And it's not just you get yours and you get your nondual thinking on and you're good now. It's not like that. So this tradition has baked into it actual guidance from teachers who actually know what they're talking about – hopefully, right? – and it's got actual depth to it and not just the surface of everything, and it's got real community. Now, there's lots of places to get all kinds of good in the world, and I would never say that Zen is the only way to do this, but it certainly is *a* way, and those are certainly some unique characteristics."

## Koun Franz

Not all Zen teachers, however, emphasize awakening. One of the things that attracted Hozan Senauke to Mel Weitsman as a teacher was precisely that Mel did not promote "this kind of pretty overt valorization of satori."

Koun Franz – like Hozan and Mel – is a priest in the Soto tradition and has reservations about the value of seeking "enlightenment," although his introduction to practice was through *The Three Pillars of Zen*. The influence of that book had been, in large part, due to the fact that it posited not only that the experience of awakening was real, it was achievable.

"And," Koun admits, "that was very exciting. But at this point in my life, I really don't have any interest in enlightenment. That was such a driving force for so long, but to me, now, it doesn't hold up. The people I've met, by and large, who claim to have had some sort of enlightenment experience are no more mature – by any measure – than anyone else that I know. What I'm really interested in is maturity and I think Zen offers a vehicle by which people can grow up in a profound way.

"I tell this story a lot: When I was in my senior year in high school, I was about to graduate, I went to a Hallmark store in my town, and they had the graduation gifts – you know they always had the shelf for the season – and one was this little framed thing, and it said something to the effect of, 'Being an adult means taking responsibility for your actions.' And for me – I was 17 or something – that was a tiny 'falling away of body and mind.'[29] I looked at it, and it was absolutely true. And I knew it, and I didn't want to hear it. I wished I hadn't seen the sign. But I knew that was right. And I think what the Zen path does is it offers – through the model of the Bodhisattva[30] – a way to take responsibility for your actions that goes beyond what we usually think that is into a much, much broader vision of adulthood. That's inspiring to me."

"I wonder, then, what it is that the people who seek you out in Halifax are looking for. What brings them to your door?"

He considers my question before answering. "I think people come because they're suffering. And they want something. They want some kind of clarity. They want something that's different. In many cases, they want something

---

29. *Shinjin datsurakuh*, a central element in the presentation of Soto Zen practice.

30. An enlightened (Bodhi) being (sattva) who seeks wisdom for – and dedicates their life to – the benefit of others.

that's not Christianity or not something they grew up with. So they're still hoping there's some kind of spiritual answer to something."

"And why do they come to you rather than going to the Vipassana[31] people, or a local yoga studio, or maybe taking a mindfulness seminar online?"

"Well, I think there's the occasional person who actually does their homework, and they listen to my talks and things like that, so they kind of know what they're showing up for by the time they show up. But I think most people have no idea and then don't come back. So it's not that people are choosing to visit Koun's community because they know that Koun is offering the thing they need. It's that they have no idea what they're looking for, and they show up. And what happens with me is they find a guy who's saying, 'We offer nothing. There is nothing here for you, and you will be disappointed for the rest of your life. Would you like to sit with that?' Right? And some people resonate with that and some people don't."

"You said that you came to Zen because of Kapleau's book." He nods. "The whole focus of which is on the attainment of kensho."

"Which I have *no* interest in at all."

"And yet people have kensho experiences which are acknowledged by others. So, what are these?"

"What's kensho?"

"Yeah."

"It's an experience. It's like..." He pauses and laughs gently. "The first thing I wanted to say is that it's like a burp of the mind. I mean, it's a good experience. No one would say it's not. I think it's positive when people have those experiences. It's not a negative. It's not like, 'Go put it back.' But it is as temporary as anything. It doesn't mean anything. It means you had a good experience. Right? It's like a drug experience. If someone takes mushrooms, and it encourages them, inspires them to look more deeply into their mind, sort of to think in a more universal way about something, great. If they take mushrooms and the first thing they do is want to go back and take more mushrooms, they blew it, as far as I'm concerned. They missed the opportunity. For me, Zen practice is about a kind of honesty. and it's about a kind of maturity. And that doesn't require some kind of mind-blowing episode. Period. At any time.

"Zen offers a particular vision of responsibility that's very much in line with the current kind of humanistic direction of the world. It doesn't rely on anything. You can take away all of the different jenga pieces and it's fine; it doesn't rely upon any particular mythology. Now I'm speaking about this through my own lenses obviously; my teachers would speak about this differently because

---

31. Meditation techniques associated with Theravada Buddhism.

they *would* incorporate more of the mythology, and they *would* incorporate a more specific world view than what I'm presenting. But I think Zen has space for this. There's a way of examining your role in the universe that does not impose upon it a description of what the universe is. That, to me, feels really useful. It doesn't require you to believe something new. It just requires you to look at something that's present. Temperamentally there are people who will want that, and other people who will find that either boring or absurd or repellent. That's fine."

## Domyo Burk

Domyo Burk is also a Soto priest. She is the guiding teacher at the Bright Way Zen Center in Portland, Oregon.

"I'm dear friends with several people who've had certified kenshos, and I'm like, 'Well, clearly that didn't solve all of their problems.' They sometimes still struggle with a personal sense of inadequacy and insecurity and all that stuff. It's a little surprising, like, 'Huh!'"

"So, if not awakening, what is it that you hope for the people who come to you?" I ask.

"The word that springs to mind is 'liberation,' but it's difficult to put one's finger on 'what does that look like?' But maybe a sense of that transformation where – and it doesn't happen all at once – but over time you see people get comfortable in their own skin and free from some of the grief and neurosis that cause them so much suffering. Once some of that central doubt and suffering has been resolved, or at least there's enough faith in the practice that whatever residual doubt and suffering there is the person is confident 'We'll deal with it in time,' then there's kind of a turning outward, when people become more aware and attentive of others. More patient with others. More interested in serving others. So there's many different dimensions. *And* I'm kind of implying that I'm talking about a complete transformation, but every little point of transformation along the way is also beautiful. It's so inspiring when I see someone overcome their sense of social anxiety and recognize that they belong in the sangha or something like that – see these little openings people have – and whenever I see that, I feel like my job is totally worth it."

## Mitra Bishop

In Zen's spotted history there have been sufficient examples of teachers whose personal behavior was questionable in spite of their "awakening" to validate the point Koun and Domyo are making. But most teachers who focus on kensho recognize that an initial experience, in and of itself, isn't adequate.

Mitra Bishop is one of Philip Kapleau's heirs. Her zendo, Mountain Gate, is located on a secondary road branching off the old High Road between Taos and Santa Fe. The main structure is an adobe building surrounded by an arid landscape that looks, to my Canadian eyes, like desert although I'm told it's actually an agricultural area.

On the zendo door there is a calligraphy by Shodo Harada Roshi[32] that states: "Great effort without fail will produce great light." The great light referred to is the light of kensho, but Mitra points out that, "It's not enough to have had a kensho, or even two or three. There is what Torei Enji, Hakuin's premier disciple and Dharma heir, called the Long Maturation. Kensho allows us to see a bit more clearly, but then we have to work with what we become aware of in our own behavior and bring it into line with that clear seeing. Kensho isn't anywhere near complete until we have integrated it into our daily life so that everything we do or say or think accords with what we've realized. Kensho has to manifest in our daily life to be of any value whatsoever."

"How would you describe kensho?"

"Kensho is an opening..." she starts, then pauses. "No... Let me back up a minute. Kensho is a temporary – and it can be more permanent depending how deep it is – clearing of the misunderstanding, the delusion, the misperception of reality so that we can see more clearly. And, of course, kensho varies significantly. It's been said that kensho these days in the west are pretty shallow because we have so many things to play with, to take us away from that search."

Serious Zen training, in her opinion, isn't satisfied with an initial awakening no matter how profound. There needs to be "a continuing motivation to go deeper, either by being prodded or from our own innate sense that there's something that we need to continue this. And people who have had a certain degree of transformation in their lives are often, but not always, motivated to go deeper in this way."

## Rebecca Li

Rebecca Li teaches within the North American Chan tradition. She is a second-generation Dharma heir of Chan Master Sheng Yen, whose Dharma Drum Foundation now has affiliate centers in fourteen countries. Although she was raised in Hong Kong, she was introduced to Buddhism by her American-born husband. "Most people just assume that I made him Buddhist. People are always surprised that it was the other way around; it was this white

---

32. A Rinzai priest and admired calligrapher. He is the abbot of Sogenji monastery in Japan, and maintains a temple in Washington State called Tahoma Sogenji.

boy from Kansas. My family is not religious. My parents are quite confused how they ended up with me and my brother. My brother is an evangelical Christian. He lives on the west coast, and I actually go to church with him twice a year."

"And if one of the members of that congregation were to ask you about Chan, about what it does, what would you say to them?"

"I would say, 'It is to help us understand how our mind works so that we can understand clearly why we do what we do.'"

"Okay. How does it do that?"

"So, one important aspect of this – engaging in some sort of meditative practice – is to have you settle your mind so that it is possible to begin to see the subtle actions of the mind. A lot of the time we don't actually know the thoughts and the feelings that are behind our action. Meditation can actually make you a better Christian or whatever faith you are. Because if you're devoted to becoming a more ethical and wholesome person, one thing that's keeping you from doing that is your habits, these habitual tendencies or influences. In Chan we call them habits of vexation. Habits of craving or aversion. But they are very entrenched and show in many subtle ways, and so they just take over without your awareness. So in Chan practice, what we're doing is knowing that they are there, and we're not all the time aware of them, and that's why they take over. By cultivating 'more clear awareness of it' what I mean is you become very familiar with how they show up, how they work. Because any kind of habit is our reaction to what's going on, but it's thought after thought after thought. You perceive it as that, and that perception's based on your preconceived notion, or your certain belief, and all those odd thoughts, subtle thoughts. And then we engage in meditative practice so that the mind is still and clear so that we can see these very subtle thoughts coming up in very rapid succession. Then we can say, 'Oh. Okay. It's this chain.' But they're not on auto-pilot. It *feels* like they're on auto-pilot because of the habitual tendency. But actually every thought that we follow we can stop. We don't have to add to that. We don't have to pick this next moment and take that step. So instead of taking the next step, you can think, 'Okay. I'm standing here.' But we are compelled to keep taking that step when we don't know what's going on. It feels like we're being pushed to act in ways that are not wholesome, and we feel helpless. We feel we can't stop it. And I think a lot of frustration of people who want to be a better person, and follow the Bible, and study any kind of faith, that they use their faith to help them but feel like they're failing. That's their frustration in life. I think that's where the practice can really help them. They can continue to use their faith to give them strength; especially if that's what's helpful for them. And also Chan provides this ability to see the habits of their mind, and they can see actually they are capable of choosing; they can choose to not walk down that path. They can just not take that step. Then they say, 'Ah! Okay.' So that is what I would say."

## Taigen Henderson

Taigen Henderson is the teacher at the Toronto Zen Centre. Established in 1967, it was the first satellite center of the Rochester Zen Center, and it is also the first official Zen practice center in Canada. Taigen originally came there as a student in 1970. He tells me that what drew people to Zen practice at that time – when it was still seen as somewhat exotic – is different from what appears to draw people now that Zen has become more fully integrated into Western culture.

"When I first started practice, the Vietnam War was in full swing. There was a lot of turmoil in society, mainly amongst young people. There was a lot of questioning. And I think a lot of that questioning was basically, 'What are we doing this for?' You know? 'What is going on with the world?' And society had done kind of a flip because the old order was really being questioned. Today people don't have that kind of questioning, so they come for personal reasons. If you ask people, 'What's bringing you to practice?' they'll talk about feeling better or they're discouraged about things in the world, but they won't say, 'I want to be enlightened.' I don't know anyone in our time who didn't say, 'I want to be enlightened. That's what I'm coming for.' But I'm not sure if that's because they don't believe in it or it's not on their radar quite so much somehow."

"Does their understanding change as they become involved in the practice?"

"Yes. Definitely. You know, people come for all kinds of reasons, but they're really drawn for karmic reasons, and they may or may not be aware of that karma, that affinity. And then we talk about it; we talk about where you are and why you're doing this and the transformation possibilities. So if they're hearing *teisho* or if they're coming to *dokusan*,[33] if they come to sesshin, then people start to kind of turn a little bit, slightly nervously" – he turns his body a little, almost reluctantly, to the side – "and then say, 'Well, I think I'd like to try to – you know – realize my mind.' And then you realize they're starting to get ready to work in a different kind of way. But I think a lot of people now have trouble believing in the reality of awakening."

---

33. Teishos are talks given by the teacher during sesshin, or retreat. Dokusan is the private meeting between student and teacher, also called *sanzen*.

# Robert Waldinger

The members of Robert Waldinger's Henry David Thoreau Zen Community in Newton fondly refer to it as "Hank."

"Sometimes when people come to Hank initially, we do little orientations and ask what they're looking for, and if they say they're looking for relaxation, we say, 'Well, that's a perfectly good thing to look for. That's not what you'll find here. But there are lots of other places you can find it. In fact, we can even point you to some of those places.' So we do that, and usually most people come visit us once and don't come back."

"What about the ones who do come back?" I ask. "What are they looking for?"

"I think they're looking for something that feels authentic. You know, nobody's telling them what to believe. We're saying, 'Try this on. See if it resonates.'"

"Why would they even care? They're looking for something authentic? Authentic for what? For what purpose? To what end?"

"Oh! Because many people feel that there's something wrong, there's something missing. And then it's the old bait-and-switch. They're coming because, 'I want to get over this grief; I'm coming because my relationship failed; I'm coming because dot, dot, dot.' And the promise – we don't promise it – but the promise that they seem to see is, 'This is gonna help me manage this.' And then – you know – the bait-and-switch is, 'Now we're going to ask you to face *toward* it.' But usually the people who stay are the people who find, 'Yes, facing toward is difficult and yet at the same time nourishing in some way.' I think the people who stay – in my experience – are the people who find that it calls to them in ways they don't fully understand. You know, sort of this 'opaque to the mind and radiant to the heart.' Certainly in the beginning I didn't always know why I was doing Zen. It just kept calling me back, and I kept going. I'd never been as unambivalent about something – in spite of the doubt – I'd never been as unambivalent about something as I have been about Zen. It just kept calling me. I can't rationally tell you why. I mean, I could make up stuff, but it was really just a kind of heart thing. And I didn't know I was looking for it. So I think maybe the bottom line is, I'm not sure people know what they're looking for, and I'm not sure they can put it into words."

# Mike Fieleke

Mike Fieleke is the resident teacher at the Morning Star Zen Sangha also located in Newton. Both he and Robert Waldinger are teachers in the Boundless Way collective, and he has authorization in three lineages: Soto, the Harada-Yasutani school, and Korean Soen. His experience of what new students look for when they first come to Zen is similar to Robert's.

"I would say often what they're looking for – initially – is stress reduction. 'I'm so stressed out I just want to find a way to calm down and be at peace.' That's probably the most common thing that brings people through the door. There are other people who have studied the practice or who had practiced in other groups who don't come in with this agenda and who come in to deepen their insight into the nature of themselves or reality and to continue to deepen their own practice that they've cultivated over some amount of time."

"What brings them to you, though?" I ask. "After all, where you are there in your part of Massachusetts, you're in the heart of the secular mindfulness industry."

"Hmm. Yeah. I guess the best way for me to put it is the lack of agenda. The idea that we aren't there primarily as a self-improvement project, and the goal is not to be different from what we are, but to *see* what we are. And there is a faith that that in and of itself is liberating.

"I took the mindfulness-based stressed reduction course many years ago and took an intensive course in learning how to teach it, and I think there's good in it, in those practices. You can really bring people into the moment through a kind of connectedness to their body and their breath and an awareness of what's unfolding. And I think the notion that it makes you feel better in some way, that it will relieve your stress – stress-reduction in the title – is sometimes true and great marketing, and it gets a lot of people in the door. In Zen, while there is a grain of truth that stress can fall away, still I worry that there's a little bit of a disservice in that goal. I think that for me what has been most liberating about Zen and what I think it offers is that, of course, we can make changes in our lives and in our thoughts and behaviours and all that, but that we don't necessarily have to. We can simply see, and things unfold – everything unfolds – everything goes its own way and we have the capacity to have faith in this unfolding and that whatever is alive in the given moment is the Dharma, is exactly what we're seeking. So I guess it's that quality of being met in the instant that I love so much about Zen. And I think there's aspects of our tradition that allow for us to challenge the hidden practices that people come into mindfulness with in a very direct way. I found it much more difficult in the mindfulness teaching to do that. Eventually I gave that up. I decided people could get caught on the idea that 'Life will get better some day if I keep doing this.' And that isn't to say that Zen, in my view, doesn't make life better. It does. I think there's a lightness and a quality that we can experience. Appreciation. But not always."

"What do you mean by hidden practices?"

"The idea that if I keep sitting in this way that I won't suffer any more. That I won't feel stressed any more. That this is gonna make me feel better. That that's my goal, to get rid of stuff. And when I'm able to get rid of this stuff, then I will be happy, then I will finally feel complete. And that stuff is usually stuff that makes me feel stress or anxiety or sadness, grief."

"Many of the early Zen teachers in North America put a lot of emphasis on the attainment of kensho," I point out. "They even suggested that the kensho experience was essential, that, in some sense, real practice didn't begin until you'd had kensho. It was preliminary to everything else. Some even argued that the only suitable response to Mu[34] is kensho. Anything short of kensho fails to respond to it adequately. Is that the case within Boundless Way?"

"We do have a certain level of expectation around, particularly, the source of Mu. I would say we are looking for a kensho experience in that. But I guess I would say that we allow for different intensities of that experience. We aren't looking for 'great kensho,' per se. It might, for some, be like just a subtle release, maybe a tear in the eye, maybe some laughter, but not necessarily *great awakening*," he says, deepening his voice. "And to go back to what people are looking for when they come in, I think you're right, fewer people come into practice thinking, 'I'm going to get enlightenment.' More people are coming in, like I said, saying, 'I just want to feel less stressed.' And so the way that we meet people maybe has shifted based on peoples' hopes. I wonder if part of our de-emphasizing around this awakening – although it is the heart of the matter – doesn't align a bit with the Soto tradition. And I think that's really woven into the fabric of who we are, to acknowledge that it's already true. There's nothing to attain. We just need to realize that. But I think another aspect of it might be that we are meeting people where they are when they come through the door. And if we suddenly say to them, 'I know you want less stress, *but what you really need is...*'"

We both laugh.

## Henry Shukman

"The practice was set up originally for one purpose only, which is to help people with their suffering," Henry Shukman tells me. "It's a pragmatic practice. It has a practical intention."

"So that's the function? To help people deal with suffering?"

"To help us to suffer less. And to become more compassionate and other-oriented. But I want to say something else about this actually, which is that some people come *knowing* why they're coming, and they may leave. And

---

34. The first koan in the *Mumonkan*, often assigned to students as their initial koan. Cf. p. 13 above.

some people may come *not knowing* why they're coming, and they may stay. In a sense, we don't exactly know what process it is that we're engaging in. None of us really know what we're letting ourselves in for when we enter Zen training, and we couldn't possibly know. And I think that actually becomes even *more* true when we train. So whatever conception we have of what we want, what we're looking for, in a sense is not the whole picture. Even before you've started. Actually, I was talking about this in sesshin recently. I think it's Dylan Thomas who wrote, 'The force that through the green fuse drives the flower.' The flower doesn't know what's going on. The green fuse doesn't know what's going on. But the bloom is coming out. It's just the same with us. We don't know why we come to practice. I mean, we don't know what brings us here. We can have these great reasons: I'm unhappy and want to be happier. Or I'm anxious; I want to calm that. Or I've got high blood pressure. You know? Or the world is full of suffering; I don't know what to do about it. Solid reasons – we think – but actually who knows? Maybe they're just a tip of an iceberg. Or they're just something that's been grabbed to be used as a handhold to get us into the journey of training by some other force that wants to make something happen. And we don't know what it is.

"What is it to sit zazen?" he asks a little further on. "What is it for us? Maybe there is some strange sense of rightness that you can't put a finger on. I don't know why, but it feels right. Or it feels, somehow, *real*, feels just one little step closer to some kind of reality that I don't even know what to call and haven't clearly tasted, but I can taste a little bit now. But I don't know what it is. I think it's like that. It's outside what we know – it really is – and it may be best that way. On the other hand, of course, it can be helpful to have some kind of a notional map of Zen training, to receive that early on, which you would do if you read *The Three Pillars of Zen,* and you would do if you glanced at the Ox-Herding pictures.[35] You get some sense, 'Oh, there is a kind of a process here.' But if you try to understand, for example, the Ox-Herding pictures with the mind of the first Ox-Herding Picture, you couldn't come close to whatever the later ones might mean. Because in a way as you get further down, it's different, meaning is less involved. Understanding is less and less involved. It's like trying to understand the flower coming out of the green fuse. What can you understand about it?

"I've heard that back in the '60s, '70s, '80s, when people showed up at a meditation center and were asked why they came, very commonly they said, 'I want enlightenment.' *These* days when people show up at a meditation center – typically – you ask them why, and it's about anxiety; it's about depression; it's

---

35. Also known as the Ten Bulls. A set of ten traditional pictures illustrating the stages of Zen practice.

about fear of the future, uncertainty. It's about managing difficult feelings. It's a different level of practice. Now, I'm teaching koans! They're about awakening. Every single koan – as you know – is an expression of awakening and an invitation to broaden our capacity to allow awakened existence to show itself, or however we might express it."

As with Mitra, he doesn't view awakening as a single event. "I don't quite buy the whole mythology of kensho as a one-off fix. There's a koan that ends, 'You've got to break through seven times and see through eight times.' I forget which one it is. I like that. Because, you know, there's so much to integrate. And there's always further to go. It's not just about waking up. The waking up must permeate deeply through us, so that it actually affects, ultimately, every moment of our life and how we do everything. That's not gonna happen in one flash. The one flash may be a sufficient flash, but then there's going to have to be *years* of training to make it actually permeate."

There are multiple forms of meditation available to people in North America now, and what, only a short time ago, would have been seen as a peculiar practice has become mainstream.

"In 2012 they reckoned that 30 million Americans had meditated. In 2012. There was some survey. By now it's probably 50 million. But the vast majority would have been doing mindfulness practice, which is very expressly about self-regulation, and about maybe improved performance in whatever area it might be. It may be about improved connectivity or relationship-building. Self-regulation and relationships and performance are maybe the three main things. Self-regulation meaning the ability to pacify and stabilize the nervous system and to be less reactive essentially. Not living in stress all the time and all the benefits that can come from that. I'm sure that 99% of those *huge* numbers that meditation practice is now seeing, to whatever extent it really is – some of those may be one-timers, you know; some may be small steady practice – but I'm sure the vast majority of that is on that level. The level of what in the Sanbo Zen tradition would be called the 'first fruit of practice.' The 'second fruit' is being awakened, enlightenment. I am quite explicit about teaching a path that I believe does lead to awakening. It's not like I keep that out of the picture or something, and focus only on the first fruit. I'm front and center – you know? – because most weeks I talk about a koan. And you can't talk about a koan without addressing that.

"Still, if we really pursue it, and we're guided in doing so by our teachers, practice can really turn around any somewhat miserable ordinary life. I mean, if we have really serious psychosis, schizophrenia, we may not be the best fit for it – I don't know that we definitely *aren't* – but if we have average depression, average anxiety, even sometimes strong anxiety, and typical disgruntlement, and that life of quiet despair – what used to be called neurosis – Zen can show us that our life is the most marvelous jewel, most marvelous gift, marvelous opportunity, beyond all reckoning. And Zen as you and I have known it (and by the way, there are many other styles of Zen) still offers a path to the most incredible fulfillment of a human being, that can become something that is practiced daily, and that radiates out from us and is hopefully of benefit within a small community, then beyond that rippling out wider and wider. Who knows how far it may ripple out?

"And I actually believe, Rick, we're on the brink of a titanic shift. And by 'titanic' I mean on the scale of the titans, like Prometheus who stole light. I think it is coming to light that more and more people are realizing the sense of self is a trick. It's an illusion. It's an evolutionarily supported misunderstanding. And that we're reaching a point where, somehow, awareness of this is growing. And there are various human activities that are helping to make it apparent. They're not all as wholesome as meditation. They may be drugs; they may be psychedelics; they may be going to raves; they may be doing extreme sports. But there's definitely a growing awareness that our sense of self is not trustworthy in its own terms. *That* is growing. As it's growing, some people are going to be drawn to quick paths of escape from self like psilocybin, but others are gonna put their trust in ancient ways that are saying the same thing and that have tried and tested methods that are maybe not infallible, maybe not foolproof, but by and large it's not improbable that they will help. Not only that, but the level of reality that they emerge from can be sensed by people, even before they have a direct experience themselves. They may not sense what it is exactly, but they have some sense that this place, this center – whichever one they may have visited – is upholding something that's true, and it's not a fairy tale. You don't have to believe a thing. You know, it's not a path that requires belief. It does require trust, it's true. Or it requires at least determination, or it requires resilient, patient resolve to keep going. So I think all those things remain pertinent and relevant as long as there are human beings. I don't know what we're going to do – of course I don't – but it could be that we're gonna get a Western globalized society where meditation practice of some form is widely recognized as beneficial and maybe even important to everyday maintenance."

### Rinzan Pechovnik

Rinzan Pechovnik is a Rinzai priest – or *osho* – in Portland, Oregon, and the guiding teacher at No-Rank Zendo. He is also a psychotherapist and tells me that he wears traditional Zen *samugi* when meeting with patients. Samugi are work clothes that Zen priests often wear when not in their formal robes.

"Most patients think it's pretty cool that their psychotherapist is also a Zen Buddhist priest. They often comment on the fact that I wear my 'robes,' and I tell them that my robes are much fancier than the samugi. 'These,' I explain, 'are more like my pajamas.'"

Rinzan believes that the desire for "awakening" is as strong as it has ever been but that people have grown shy about admitting it. "This is part of our culture. I think people are afraid of coming off as being arrogant or highfalutin. That's why you don't hear it as much; people give a soft serve in terms of what they want. They'll come in and say that they just think it's good for them, but most of my students are doing koan work, and you can feel the desire to go beyond. They want to wake up. That's the word I prefer, 'to wake up' rather than 'become enlightened.' This helps people realize that it's already out there. There's nothing to attain."

"So when people who say they're coming to Zen to relieve stress or anxiety..." I start.

"It's mostly because they're shy. Because they feel they would be putting on airs if they said they wanted to wake up. Although, there's one student that I have that probably, if you said, 'Do want to be enlightened?' – he'd go, 'Prrp! What's enlightenment?' Which gives me a nice sense of his frame of mind. It's like, 'Okay. You're good. Nothing to attain. Now... Work harder!'"

## Tetsugan Zummach

I met Tetsugan Zummach in Portland, Maine, when she and her husband, Dosho Port, were offering an introductory workshop on Zen. I ask her if she had any sense of what drew people to the workshops.

"We always begin by asking people to say something about why they're here, and what they hope to get out of the workshop. More and more people are struggling with anxiety, depression, stress; they often say they want to learn how to deal with stress, how to regulate their emotions, how to be more calm and present. The secular mindfulness movement has really taken off, so they've heard about mindfulness and they want to learn how to be more mindful. Or, they're looking for a sense of meaning and purpose in their lives."

"So what does Zen do?"

"What does it do? Well, on one hand, Zen doesn't *do* anything. Spiritual practice in and of itself is not going to solve all your problems. What it does provide is a path and a container for exploring and really living in a deep and authentic way. Another way of saying that is that Zen doesn't do anything; *you* do Zen. It's really about what you bring to it and what you put into it. 'Big shout, big echo; little shout, little echo'; it's that sort of thing. If you're interested in stress reduction, or you just want to connect with like-minded people in community, that's fine. You can come and engage to that extent. But, if you really want to *transform* your life, you've got to throw yourself into it wholeheartedly."

"What's awakening?"

She pauses a long while before replying. "Well, one way of thinking about it is, through practice, coming to the realization that you are not who you think you are. We're generally conditioned to believe that we're our personalities, our hairstyles, our hobbies, or our careers. And through Zen practice, there's the opportunity to see through all of that, to realize that what we truly are is change. Impermanence. That's the great matter of birth-and-death."

"And why would I want to realize that?"

"That's a good question," she says, laughing. "Well, the idea you have about yourself often causes you to suffer. And that's why a lot of people come to Zen practice; that's why I came to Zen. I wanted to understand, to look deeply into what it is that causes me and others to suffer. In my early 20s, following a turbulent childhood and adolescence, I reached a point where things began to settle down and my life became more stable. I met and married a good partner, I had a decent job, we took fun vacations, and I enjoyed life at times. But in quiet moments, I still felt like something was missing. So, the question arose, 'What else is there?' and I was haunted by the idea of settling, of living life only partially fulfilled. Through the course of practice, I began to realize that my happiness – or really, any state of mind – isn't dependent upon external circumstances; it's not dependent on having or not having. Sure, if you're living in abject poverty, and you don't know if you're going to have enough food from one day to the next, that tends to lead to a lot of misery. But there have been people in the world like Mother Theresa and Gandhi, for example, who lived with very little and yet were content and peaceful, who lived lives of *purpose*. Waking up to the truth of this life, then, has the potential to cut through a lot of our self-imposed suffering and to help others do the same.

"What I discovered was that my happiness wasn't dependent on anything outside of me, but it's not dependent upon anything *inside*, either. And with that insight, there began to be this sense of freedom within the container of life and practice and also from the tyranny of self-clinging. Rather than accepting the belief that Western culture attempts to feed us about freedom being found in endless choices and doing whatever we want, whenever we want, ultimate freedom, from a Zen perspective, is about developing the capacity to harmonize with whatever circumstances we find ourselves in – to be the 'snake in the bamboo tube,' we say. When we can be right where we are, open and present to whatever is arising, inside and outside drop away along with struggling and suffering."

## Zen Mountain Monastery

In 1980, John Daido Loori founded Zen Mountain Monastery outside of Woodstock, New York. Monasticism is not a common calling in either the West or the East, but there have always been a few people who choose to withdraw from society and dedicate themselves to lives of spiritual discipline. At the time of my visit in 2013 there were thirty-one residents, ranging in age between 20 and 86, about half of whom had taken monastic vows. The woman who organized my visit is one of these.[36]

"I was living in New York when September 11th happened." She was 26 years old at the time. "I had just started a new job. I was working in the corporate world, and I remember being just so completely freaked out and realizing for the first time – like, non-intellectually – that I was going to die. It could happen today. And what was I doing with my life? Was I happy? I didn't even know what 'happy' would mean. So I didn't recognize any spiritual questions, I was just really kind of freaked out. And so I started a process. I changed my career and my partner and I moved a bunch of times, read a bunch of books and went to churches and was just looking and looking and looking. I didn't really know that much about Buddhism, but I went to a Sunday morning program at the temple in Brooklyn."

Like ZMM, the Zen Center in Brooklyn is part of the Mountains and Rivers Order established by Daido. The day she attended the temple, Shugen Arnold – the current head of the order and abbot of ZMM – gave a talk. "And I was just like, 'Oh, my God! There's a religion that's based around answering my questions. That's so fantastic!' I resonated immediately with zazen. Something about sitting down and being quiet. And several months after that, I met Daido for the first time. He had come down to the temple, and I talked to him briefly on Sunday in my typical way, 'I just started practicing,'" – in a sing-song voice – "'What should I do now?' And he was like, 'Have you done a Zen training weekend?' And I said, 'No.' And he's like, 'You should do that.' And I came up here in May of 2005 for my Zen training weekend, and I walked into the dining hall, and it was just like, 'Oh, shit! This is it! But how am I going to do this?' And I steadied the urge to kind of talk myself out of it, and then I became a resident here a year later."

She admits that it isn't always an easy calling.

"There are times when I look around, and here we are in these grey polyester robes eating fruit salad with chop sticks, and I just think, 'What are we

---

36. Although everyone I spoke to at ZMM was willing to be quoted, several asked me not to refer to them by name.

doing? This is insane!' And yet! Here we all are! So, yeah, living in community is super challenging, and sometimes I really hate it. But that's just a feeling that I have because I still have some expectation that it shouldn't be this way. But it is this way. I mean, it's great too. I have a couple of friends among the residents, though not as many as a person would think. Most people here are not my friend; they're more like my family. The crazy family that you choose to live with. But that's what makes it a practice gold-mine. I mean, if you're up against it all the time, especially if you want to wake up, that's a huge benefit."

"What do you mean by that?" I ask. "Waking up? What does that mean to you?"

"If you want to be unconditionally free regardless of the circumstances you find yourself in. That's what it means to me. I'm super not into the whole enlightenment experience thing. I think it's important to have insight as you continue in your practice. But I'm so not interested in kensho or enlightenment. To me, if a person can disidentify with a thought, that's enlightenment. Can you pick up a napkin that's dropped on the floor? Can you help this person that you actually don't like? To me, that's enlightenment. When I use certain terms it's different from how other people may use them. So what I mean by the 'benefit of living in community' is, I really want to be free in my final moment of life, as I'm dying. And this is really good training for that, because the day is filled with 'I don't want to do that.' Or like Bartleby the Scrivener, 'I'd rather not.' You know? All day long. And so I feel like I'm training for my death in a way. And I mean that sort of joyfully." She laughs. "It's not the Death March to Bataan, even though I kind of make it sound like that."

### Phap Vu

Monastic communities are of varying degrees of strictness. At Zen Mountain Monastery, the residents are permitted to form committed sexual relationships (although if children result, they have to leave the monastery). The monastics at Blue Cliff Monastery in New York State, on the other hand, are not only celibate, males also commit to abide by 277 traditional rules of behaviour. There are 34 additional regulations for women, for a total of 311.

Blue Cliff is in Thich Nhat Hanh's Order of Interbeing, a form of Vietnamese Zen that has practice centers around the world. My visit was arranged by Brother Phap Vu. We have spoken several times since that initial visit, and he is no longer in residence at Blue Cliff although he remains a monk in the Order of Interbeing. He currently travels about the country giving retreats and providing support to other monastics through an online program called Dharma Pathways.

I ask him about the purpose of monastic life.

"To be Buddha. To awaken. To work all the obstacles that I find within myself, that inhibit my freedom, inhibit my interconnectedness with people, places, things. All things. That's what's being cultivated when we talk about 'practice.' The reason I use the term 'practice' is because our teacher" – Thich Nhat Hanh – "*really* stresses that. Really stresses the idea of 'your life is a practice.'"

"A practice of what?"

"Of the Precepts.[37] Of the understanding that comes from the Precepts. Of discovery, understanding, compassion. All the virtues of Buddhism that you find throughout the sutras. For example, sometimes I get frustrated. Sometimes I become impatient. Sometimes I feel anger. Now before I was a monastic, or before I was practicing – even though I was a lay person – if I was angry, I lashed out in anger. And usually it goes along the line of reasoning, 'Oh, *you* made me angry. Look what you did.' Right? When we talk about practice, it requires us to look inside, not outside. Looking at all those dynamics within me to get beyond this silly notion of you/me, 'you did this to me,' and whatever the storyline is that our mind creates."

"Well," I argue, "there are external factors which contribute to unhappiness. Your own teacher went through the horrors of the war, the refugee crisis that followed."

"Right. So how do you relate to that? How do you respond to that? It's not that we're isolated emotionally, intellectually. We're not. We're all very connected. But the question is, 'How do you respond?' How do I respond in the interior when I come across an event – and I could name a number – where it causes impatience or anger in me. What's my relationship to that? Do I accept that or do I try to push that away? Do I go with it and make it grow? Become more angry; become more impatient? Or do I work with that to find some equanimity or some compassion? That's the fundamental element here. Yes, there are exterior factors in life, but how do we respond? What's our relationship? Is it coming from a place of wisdom and compassion? Or is it just a reactivity?

"We all want to connect. We all long for connections. Even if we don't admit it. There will be people who when I give a talk on this, and they'll say, 'Oh, no. I don't need to right now. I'm good on my own.' Right? But, no, I don't believe them. We long for connection. And the question is, 'What stops that connection?' When we look at our lives, we can think our connection is, 'Well, okay, connection with my family – okay – and my neighbors and my small

---

37. Ethical teachings Buddhists commit to abide by. "Taking the Precepts" is part of the process of formally committing oneself to Buddhist practice.

community here.' But the connection is huge! It's huge. It embraces everything. The rock I'm looking at outside my window and the snow.

"Having this connection with all things, the language behind that is so inadequate compared to that actual experience and understanding and my perspective based on that understanding. Understanding that comes from an experience. So, going from the illusion of the individual to this interconnectedness of all things. This is a thing not of the mind – this is where people get it wrong so much – it's not a thing of the mind; it's a thing of the heart. And the thing of the heart is so important. You know, we live so much in our heads. We don't live enough in our hearts. And in order to understand and touch this connection, to get beyond our isolation, our heart needs to grow. In the west, we divide ourselves up into the mind and the heart. Whereas in Buddhism, traditionally, those two are the same thing. Yeah, we could do it on the intellectual level, and, of course, we need to. But can you touch things on the heart level? This is enlightenment."

## Chimyo Atkinson

Great Tree Zen Temple in North Carolina is specifically a women's residential center. The teacher is Teijo Munnich, a former Roman Catholic nun and Dharma heir of Dainin Katagiri. In 2018 there were several guests at the temple but only two permanent residents, Teijo and Chimyo Atkinson. Chimyo tells me that her official position is Head of Practice. When I ask what that means, she says, "I'm basically the... well... everything. *Ino* [manager], *chiden* [caretaker], *tenzo* [cook], *tanto* [assistant to the teacher], everything, because there's only two of us living here.

"Our mission at Great Tree Zen Women's Temple states that it's a way of allowing the feminine to manifest itself in a way some may not have been allowed to in the past – ancient and recent – simply because, as in anything in society, it's kind of dominated by men. And so the feminine aspect of what Zen could look like hasn't – maybe – been nurtured as much as it needed to be or celebrated as much as it needed to be. So here's a place where, because it is centered on women and women's practice, you see what comes up, what it looks like, and how is it different – if at all – from the way men's practice manifests itself? That doesn't mean that it's going to be different, but we're trying to give it a chance to develop and be what it can be."

"What are the women who come here looking for?" I ask.

"I think they're looking for compassion and empathy. I think they're looking for a place where they feel comfortable and safe in doing their spiritual practice, whatever that is. They have a sort of a sense of community with us and in a non-intellectual way. We do our study groups and so on, and we can get heady in those study groups, but I think – mostly because of Teijo – I think they feel a warmth and a nurturing here that is maybe unusual at some American Zen centers.

"Because we're a Zen center, people have this incomplete idea of what Zen is, and I think they come sometimes looking for that. The sort of peace/bliss kind of thing, or very heady, intellectual, kind of thing. I think the people that stick around are people who are looking for community and looking for a place to be that is open, where they don't feel judged, and can just have a conversation about anything, really, with people who care. Our conversations are about practice, but about practice in a way that's more directly about our lives, rather than – you know – talking about philosophy. We do emphasize the sitting; our main practice is shikan taza, but our practice is also being with each other and being of comfort to each other when we need to.

"The whole point of doing this practice is to develop compassion, to develop the sense of interconnectedness and empathy for each other. That's where the clarity comes from, so that you can act from that compassion, so that you can act from that understanding of connectedness."

## Albert Low

Early in the course of conducting these interviews, I visited Albert Low in Montreal. I had been doing koan study with Albert since 2003, and he had written the foreword to my first book. We meet in the ground floor parlor of the Center. Over the fireplace, there is a reproduction of *The Solitary Angler* by the 13th century Chinese painter, Ma Yuan.

"What is the function of Zen?" I ask.

Albert's reply comes as rapidly as had Joan Sutherland's. "Oh, there's no function of Zen."

"So why do people come here?"

"Because they think there is a function of Zen."

"And they discover?"

"There is no function of Zen. If they work long enough."

# 3

# Zen Practice

## Zen Mountain Monastery

There are various levels of engagement in Zen practice, ranging from individuals who occasionally visit a center to the far fewer people who commit themselves to long-term training at a place like Zen Mountain Monastery.

"We have a dozen monastics or so, so most people here are not monastics," Geoffrey Shugen Arnold, the abbot of ZMM, tells me. "There are people who come to the monastery or the temple in Brooklyn every Sunday to sit and do a service and hear a talk, and so, in a way, it's kinda like church for them. They may sit at home; they may not. There are people who may just want to be part of a community, and Buddhism resonates with them on some level. There are people who want to have an active meditation practice. There are people who want to formally study with a teacher, so they step in a little bit more. They may want to receive the Bodhisattva Precepts, so they step in a little bit more. There's a whole range of engagement, which I think is important."

What these individuals have in common is that they all spend at least some time in meditation. How significant that practice will be for them depends on the consistency and diligence with which they pursue it. Dosho Port of the Vine of Obstacles uses the analogy of attempting to start a fire. "It's like the idea of you think you're going to start a fire by rubbing two sticks together. But you rub for two seconds and then you stop. There's no heat. There's no spark. So consistency is important."

At ZMM they emphasize that meditation – *zazen* – should take place within a wider practice context. Daido Loori identified what he called Eight Gates, which are enumerated in a pamphlet I am given during my visit: 1) zazen, 2) the student-teacher relationship, 3) liturgy, 4) art practice, 5) body practice,

6) Buddhist studies, 7) work practice, 8) right action. "Grounded within a rigorous monastic matrix," the pamphlet states, "the Eight Gates training emphasizes practice, realization, and actualization of our true nature."

One of the residents explains the Gates this way: "The matrix here, the eight gates, are eight different fingers pointing to the moon. They're opportunities for people of different dispositions to find entry. So you have artists who immediately recognize the possibility of finding the Dharma in the creative act. And then you have others who resonate with the academic study. But all of us do all the practices to different degrees."

Zazen is identified as the first gate and is fundamental to all Zen practice, although the way in which it is presented and the instructions one is given can vary from one center to another.

The training coordinator at ZMM takes me through the instruction provided to new students here. It begins – as it does in most centers – with posture. Although there is no longer as much importance put on using traditional forms like the lotus posture[38] as there once had been, there is still an insistence on the importance of maintaining an erect spine.

"So I'll show you the positions, of how to place your body in a way that is strong and stable and is in accord with where you are right now. You can sit on a bench, a chair, a cushion. You don't have to worry about getting twisted up in any special posture. You will need to agree to being still for about 25/35 minutes. Then how to align your body so you can allow yourself to settle down. It's a skillful means that we offer here – which it may not be at other places – that we ask that you really don't move. There are other traditions where you can move, and it's much more open. But this is kind of an opportunity so that we can really see all the distractions that arise in our minds and see if they're worthwhile, have a chance to see if we don't need to keep following everything around.

"So we start with getting the body set, and then the beginning practice you'll work with is counting your breath. One to ten, then starting over. Silently, in your mind. And seeing thoughts. The count is so that you can stay focused. And how to let go, how to work with things that may arise as you're sitting. Like physical pain. Mental pain. How to work with that afterwards, when you get up. How to not suppress, but not indulge, not just keep spinning on the wheel, to just kind of empty yourself out, and then you just sort of settle down and see another aspect of our mind that we may never attend to or experience within ourself – or not for very long – which is stillness.

"You know, most people come in and say, 'I want to be present. I'm not present in my life.' I hear that a lot. 'I just want to be present. I'm not present.'

---

38. The familiar meditation posture in which the legs are crossed and the feet rest on the opposite thighs.

I say, 'Well, where are you?' You know?" she says, chuckling. "Where else can you be? But there's that division of body and mind; that's what they don't understand. That you can actually be in harmony. That you can actually do what you're doing while you're doing it completely. We just haven't had much training. And so this is what helps with this. Training our mind, to put it where we want it; develop some concentration."

## Elaine MacInnes

Elaine MacInnes is the first Canadian – and one of the very first westerners – to be authorized to teach Zen. She became a Roman Catholic nun after her fiancé was killed during the Second World War, and her order sent her to Japan. There she met the Jesuit, Hugo Enomiya-Lassalle, who was studying Zen with Koun Yamada. Sister Elaine became curious and decided that if Father Lassalle was practicing, "It had to be okay."

She acquired some fame after her order transferred her to the Philippines during the Marcos regime. She agreed to a request from the incarcerated dissident, Boy Morales, to teach him Zen. When he was released from prison in 1986 and was asked how he survived the treatment to which he'd been subjected, he credited Sister Elaine and Zen practice. Soon afterwards, Sister Elaine was invited to Britain to work with a prison program there.

I ask her how she introduced zazen to the inmates. "Well, we start with counting the breath. And I just try to get them breath centered as soon as I can. And then I go into, 'Be the breath. When you're watching something or counting something,' I said, 'You're two.' You know? 'But,' I said, 'Zen is an experience, and it is an experience of oneness. So I can't give you something that's two to come to One.' And so I would, as soon as possible, say, 'Be the breath.' And there's something about – if they're ready – there's something about that change that they can handle. Of course, prisoners go off fantasizing right away. I can tell by their posture. They go like this," demonstrating how their posture becomes slack. "And so you just go and touch them, kind of thing. And that usually takes them out of it, and they can go back to their counting."

## Hozan Senauke

"We put an emphasis on posture and breath," Hozan Senauke tells me. "And we give you one or two ways you can actually follow your breath – counting your breaths or just following it. Sometimes I give people the instruction to place the expression 'just this' on the breath. Breathing in on 'just' and out on 'this.' And returning to the breath and realigning your posture throughout a period of meditation. And just turning to that again and again."

"And what does that do?"

"I don't know." We both laugh. "I actually don't. But I do think that it allows you into a space that not many of us knowingly occupy. Unknowingly, we occupy it all the time. But here is a way of actually doing something intentionally. So that's where I would start with someone new. There's something else that I do, actually, that has not been the instruction here, but it's something that's evolved for me, which is when I sit down I plant a seed of bodhicitta.[39] Which means, very simply, I'll use the expression to myself – I made this up – when I sit down, I say to myself, 'May I be awake that others may awaken.' And I'll say it to myself three times. It's like dropping it into the pool of my body and mind as I start to sit. And that's it. I don't do anything with it. But that, to me, is a very simple way of establishing your sitting."

## Rebecca Li

Rebecca Li tells me that she spends a "fair amount of time" helping people unlearn "some of the misconceptions they might have developed around what meditation is about. A lot of people have this incorrect understanding about what it is about. The most common one is they believe meditation involves eliminating anything from the mind. They're supposed to cultivate a blank mind."

"Like going into a coma," I suggest, and she laughs.

"Yeah. They weren't aware that that's what they were trying to do. I think it has to do with the language being used, the words being used a lot of time in explaining how to meditate. So without adequate guidance – because a lot of people do it on apps and stuff – so they just use their existing idea about things to make sense of it. So that's another thing I talk about is actually we are bound to go about meditation the wrong way in the beginning because we take our usual habits, our usual mode of operation – which is all about causing suffering – into the meditation. So we use meditation to cause more suffering in the beginning. So that's where we start, and then we learn about how we are causing ourselves suffering by looking at how we approach our meditation."

## Myokyo McLean

Like Rebecca Li, Myokyo warns people to be wary of the assumptions they bring with them. "Anything you've read may or may not be something that's

---

[39]. The intention to achieve awakening for the benefit of others.

going to happen to you. But mostly what's going to happen to you is that you're going to be very uncomfortable sitting in a cross-legged posture, and you're going to really start thinking a lot about your notions of how life should be and what you should be like and how you are. And so you'll begin to question all that in the context of quiet sitting in this upright posture that actually has the potential for making you very present and very 'in the moment.' So an experience you're not having usually; we're usually way, way far away in our minds."

I ask her about the instruction she gives beginning meditators.

"I tell you how to sit. How to get in a cross-legged posture, so you'll be very discouraged and it will be really difficult physically for the first few times. Then the practice is always the same. So following the breath, but eventually that kind of tightly following the breath disappears. So just very basic zazen, and that's actually what I've done up to this point. Joshu Sasaki Roshi actually discourages us from latching onto any kind of focusing tool, including the breath. So maybe it is shikan taza after a while. You know, just sort of sit.

"I talk about seed thoughts: notions, ideas, feelings, physical sensations, or emotions. As we become conscious of one of these, we decide, first of all, whether we like it or not, or maybe it's neutral. If we don't like it, we stuff it back, way down somewhere back and get rid of it. If we like it or it's just neutral, we just add another thought and that carries on into a story. I reassure everyone that there's no problem with that. Our minds are creative. The creative process is what our minds are for. The problem is we think that that story is our life. And so in zazen you begin to learn that that's not correct; that our story is not our life. The effort is to observe what comes up and then to simply let it go away before you even begin to discriminate or make a judgement about that thought, to be so clearly present that you can actually observe what comes up in the mind and then let it go by.

"So people can visualize that or understand the words, but then when they go to do it, it's absolutely, absolutely difficult. And then, immediately, they're not present. Right? And so they know that, and I know that, and I say, 'Then you need to keep going back to the present.' You need to physically keep placing yourself here. Most of them probably won't have the... the.... What do you call it?... The verve, the desire... the *tenacity* to continue. But, you know, we need to be sparked by something to be tenacious. So I say, 'Probably most of you won't have it.' That's okay, too."

## David Rynick

David Rynick is Melissa Blacker's husband and one of the resident teachers at the Boundless Way Temple in Worcester. He was one of those who originally came to Zen "chasing enlightenment," although he notes that now people who visit the temple for the first time "don't often use that language. People often use the language, 'I want to be peaceful. I don't want to be anxious anymore. I want to have a clear mind.' So it's interesting that 'enlightenment' isn't often in the vocabulary of the people."

"And when people do come to the door," I ask, "what do you do? If you were writing a job description for a Zen teacher, what would it look like?"

"The first thing that comes to mind is I disturb people," he says, laughing. "I want to undercut their assumptions of life. But I would also say my job is to see the Buddha in each person. I think, that's probably the most important thing I do. And in that meeting of hearts when I'm with you and you are with me, if I see and appreciate that, then that shifts what's possible for you."

"So I knock at the door. I'm not looking for enlightenment, but I want to be a little more peaceful, a little less anxious. What are you gonna do for me?"

"I'm going to appreciate that you walked in the door. What an incredible thing! That you really want something, don't you? So I will inquire, 'What are you here for? What do you really want?'"

"You're not necessarily going to immediately introduce me to zazen?"

"It's not for everybody."

"I remember when we first met, you told me that when you started sitting you could last about two minutes."

"Right."

"I've told that story frequently since then."

He laughs heartily. "That's great! Right. I do encourage people to sit. Once we clarify what do you want – even 'I want to be free from anxiety' – I say, 'Wow. Yeah. So, let me tell you the way we practice here. We're actually not trying to control our mind.' And the truth is that sometimes human beings feel anxious. So what we are doing is increasing our capacity to be with what is here. And actually one of the new teachings that Melissa and I have is four steps of breath practice. The first step is being present with the breath. The second step is wandering away. This is an essential ingredient in breath practice. Most people are pretty good at it. But it must happen. The third step is something miraculous, that at some point you become aware that you have wandered away, and that is a moment of awakening. 'Oh! Thinking about dinner. Oh!...' And the fourth is then that we can choose to return to this moment, to this breath. And every time we return, we're strengthening our capacity to be here. So the more times you wander away," he says, chuckling, "the better your practice is, the more you increase this capacity."

"That's nicely put. But if I'm a new person, someone who has never sat before, and you present this to me, I think what I'd do next is ask you, 'What has that got to do with me feeling less anxious?'"

"Hmm. So I would say..." He pauses a moment before continuing. "Anxiety is unavoidable, but part of the problem we human beings have is that not only do we feel anxious but that we suffer because we don't *want* to feel anxious. And I would also say that there are mind states that we resist. I don't want to feel anxious. I don't want to feel angry. I don't want to feel sad. And what we resist persists. Whatever we try to push away gets more energy and gets bigger. So as we learn that human beings feel anxious, sad, happy, clear, cloudy, all of those, as we open up to what is here, then it comes and goes on its own accord."

"It?"

"Life comes and goes. Then anxiety is not a problem to be fixed but how I feel sometimes."

### Rinzan Pechovnik

"What do you mean by 'practice'?" I ask Rinzan Pechovnik.

He reflects a moment. "Okay, let's see where this goes... Zen is not an idea. It's not a concept. There's nowhere to get to. There's nothing to attain. And so all we're doing is living a life of practice. And what is practice? The analogy that I give people is, I'm a guitar-player – not a great guitar-player, but I play guitar – and I'm not going to get better at playing the guitar by wishing or thinking about it or imagining that I'm Eric Clapton or thinking about how Eric Clapton got to be Eric Clapton. What it requires is I put a guitar in my hands, and I start doing things with it. So this is an activity. So although I encourage people to read books and gather ideas, really the question is: Are you going to throw your body, in a fundamental way, into an engagement – I don't even want to say a way of being – but an engagement with the world, with existence, in such a way that you commune with all of this, everything, differently than our normally shielded, blinded perspective?

"The practice of Zen is basically 'open up.' At the most basic level, it is 'open up.' How do we open up? Well, there's a couple of techniques or skills. If I'm using the analogy of the guitar, what I'm doing is I'm putting my hands on the fret-board, and I'm pressing down strings, then with the other hand I'm plucking notes, and something arises. Music arises because of what I do with my body. When I say, 'open up' from a Zen perspective what I mean is get very still so there are no distractions, root yourself into the earth, breathe in a relaxed manner and open up the senses. This is just zazen – get rooted, use the breath as a kind of tool or a metronome to be present. Open up the senses, and then open even more by developing a sense of wonder asking, 'What is this?' Don't expect an answer. Just settle into open wonder. It's a matter of toning the body to this question that really doesn't have answers; it's an unending question. So similarly, if you're going to continue the analogy with the guitar, as I pluck, I'm wondering, 'What is this sound?' You know? What's coming out? These sounds, the tune that happens with the guitar? That's it at its most basic level. And we have ritual and technique and forms that help to pull that out, just as on a guitar you might have a song you're working on, you might have scales or something.

"The other aspect of my role as teacher is to point to the wonder that is shining brightly all around us. 'Do you see it? Look! Look!' That's another job. So take the veils off your eyes and be deeply engaged in just this. And the third part is to say, 'Not yet.' Rinzai was very clear about that. 'Not yet. Not yet.' There's no place to end. This is a life of practice. Now there's nothing wrong with having a goal in mind. I want to become a better guitar player. I want to be able to play this song. That stuff arises because we're human beings, but for me – and I think this is true more and more – when I practice it's just practice. It's just this life of practice forever.

"Anyway that's the description of it. Then people say, 'What do I do?' And I say, 'Let me show you some fundamentals of zazen.' Zazen is not a technique, and there's nothing to be gained from it. But that's hard to grasp onto. And so I'm going to give people some things to do while they're sitting, not moving for the next half hour or hour. I will describe posture to them. This is what we do with your body. We're doing something. It's an activity. You're doing something with your body; you're not moving. So first I'll help them with body posture. Then I'll work with them on breath. And my big emphasis with breath is *chi*.[40] This part of zazen is not often spoken of in the West. It's feeling the energy of breath, and I'll demonstrate that. It's not just thinking about breath but *being* breath. So this is chi-breathing. And then I'll say, open up your ears. Listen. Open up your pores. Feel. Open your eyes. See. That's a thing to do. That's an activity. And then just wonder, which is step number four. Tune the body to this questioning attitude. 'What is this?' Or 'Who am I?' Or 'What am I?' So they'll think, 'I'm going to try this and see what'll happen when I sit down and don't move for the next half hour.' Often then, maybe in a few weeks, they'll come and say, 'I must be doing it wrong. Nothing is happening.' And we can go down that road as well. 'Be more curious about nothing happening.'"

"You bring up the wondering element at the beginning?"

"I give everyone those four steps. All four are happening anyway, 'cause you're sitting there, you're already thinking, 'All right, I'm sitting. What's happening? What's gonna happen? What's going on?' Right there."

---

40. Fundamentally "energy" or "source of energy."

"Why the fuck am I doing this?"

"It's a good question. That's great doubt. So I frame that in terms of, you start by sitting, and these are the steps, and if you decide to go to step two, which is starting to breathe, and you get distracted, return to the body, and do a body scan, feel rooted in the body. Then move to breath. Then move to opening the senses. And then if you feel that you're stable, wonder, and then you can flow in and out of these four stages."

Most of the teachers with whom I talked emphasized the importance of a daily home practice as well as time spent at centers.

"This is what I recommend," Rinzan tells me. "Start with five minutes at home. This is my standard advice, start with five minutes, and don't do any more, don't do any less, to start to condition the body. I'm a radical behaviorist in many ways. Condition the body, just sitting on the cushion doing this practice. And making this part of your daily life. You have to make it the most important part of the day, so do it before brushing your teeth. I assume you brush your teeth every day, so prioritize this over brushing your teeth, just five minutes on the cushion. Don't go longer. Because if you go beyond five minutes and just finish when you feel like it, you'll finish when you're bored. So finish when the timer tells you to without any assessment or judgement. Then I'll wait a while, and they'll ask, 'Should I be doing more than five minutes.' I say, 'Yes!' 'How much should I be doing?' 'Well, how much do you think?' They'll say, 'I think I should be doing fifteen minutes.' I'll say, 'Yes. I think you should be doing fifteen minutes.'"

"David Rynick confessed that when he started he could only make it for two minutes. He'd set his timer for two minutes, and by the time it rang, he'd be just about jumping out of his skin."

"Yep. For me it was three. I set my timer for three. And I looked after about a minute and a half, thinking, 'Is my timer broken?'"

"So, I'm up to about twelve minutes a day, and then I ask you, 'Should I be doing this when I'm not on the cushion?'"

"Uh-huh. Yes. And then I would say, 'A wonderful time to do it is when you're doing your dishes. Or preparing a meal is another time to bring in mindfulness and a sense of wonder and make this all a practice.' And again I would give them tools to help them heighten their awareness that this is practice. This is music-making – holding onto that metaphor – you're making music. And so pause before doing the dishes. You can even ring a bell. And then bring your whole body into it. You're rooted to the ground with your feet. You're aware of your breath, and your senses are open as you're washing the dishes. And, if you can, you pull in not, 'Why am I washing the dishes?' But, 'What is this?' You know, this existence is, 'Wow! What?'"

"And what does all this do?"

"We are habit creatures, and we are creatures that are biologically designed to conserve energy, so we don't like to do anything that is out of the ordinary. In fact, in old age, we can just become automatons with very limited range. And what sitting still actually does is it puts a halt to all of our habit energy – it takes more energy to sit still than to just keep going – so we're interrupting the natural habits we're engaged in. And when I say we're conserving energy, it actually takes less energy to continue the way we're going than to put the brakes on. So we put the brakes on, and we don't move. And that gives us an opportunity to see something outside our normal range. And as we don't move and our thoughts just start to quieten, through using the breath, sitting still, we can become curious. We can become more and more intimate with this present moment experience, which is shining forth right now. There's nowhere to get. It's here. But what the practice allows us to do is to come into contact with it."

## Rinsen Weik

"We start with concentration on the breath and the awareness of the One Point and the *hara*,"[41] Rinsen Weik tells me. "So you're going to breathe in 'one,' breathe out 'two,' until you get to ten, start over concentrating on the One Point, and if you get carried away by scenarios, see it, acknowledge it, let go of it, and come back to the breath, starting the counting back at one. That's your basic start."

A large percentage of Rinsen's students move onto koan study. I ask if the initiative to do so comes from the student or from the teacher.

"I think it's case by case. In general I'm very specific about the process when you go from counting both the in and the out of the breath, then just counting each cycle of the breath on the exhale, and eventually you drop the numbers and just work with following the breath. And those are very specific, and I tell them not to fuck around with that. Like, if the teacher says this is your practice, you practice this. Right? You don't graze and do a bunch of stuff. And then once there's a level of *samadhi*[42] that's really kinda baked in there, typically what I'll get 'em to do is start following Mu instead of following the breath. So they're not questioning Mu. I'm not poking or prodding or anything like that, but we just insert Mu as kind of like a mantra, really."

"What do you tell them about Mu?"

"Very little. I'll recite the case. 'A monk went to Master Joshu and said,

---

41. The abdomen understood as a person's center in both martial arts and meditation.
42. Concentration.

"What the hell?" And Joshu said, "Mu.'" Then I say, 'Okay, what I'd like you to do now is a practice we call "following Mu."'"

"Okay," I say, "by this point, I'm holding up my hand to stop you because I'm one of those irritating people who really needs everything spelled out before I can proceed."

"That's kinda nice."

"And I say, 'What does "mu" mean?'"

"Don't worry about that right now, Rick. That's just a bunch of weeds you don't want to get into. What I want you to do now is just follow the thing. Okay? Then, bring me what you find. So now it's like I'm asking you to put on a snorkel and a mask and go dive. And then when you feel it, bring back what you have, what you know will dance. And see, there's a shift which is actually empirically verifiable to me when a student clicks into the samadhi of just being Mu. There's a thing that happens when they're just chanting Mu, and there's another thing when they *become* it. How exactly do I know? I don't know, but I do. And when that moment happens – and that can happen really quick or that can take a couple of years; I don't know why; karmic conditions, whatever – but when the person slips into that place where they're actually becoming Mu, then I'll spontaneously spring a checking question[43] on 'em. And if they misfire, I'll say, 'Oh, forget about it. I was kiddin'.' And then just go back to following, and they just keep baking like that. The other complimentary practice is called 'washing through.' And that's something that only happens in sesshin. If the person in question is someone I just meet at the occasional Sunday Sutra service with their kids and that's it, we're not really going to go here because it's not fair to them. Okay? But if someone's got the life circumstances and gumption to be able to do sesshin and they have a real shot at doing the deep work, well then I'll go here because I've got a chance at it. Okay? My opinion. So they're a sesshin person, and we'll start to have 'em follow Mu, and I'll have them 'washing through,' which is where you mentally imagine that you take Mu and you wash any solid object through with it. So for example" – he holds up a cup and passes his hand alongside it, as if through it – "and it goes, 'whooo.' So it's like a visualization practice. It's like there was a movie, *The Matrix II,* and there were these two bad guys who could turn into ghosts and come back to solidity. It's something like that. So I train the students in this visualization and to be able to see any object and to just wash it through with Mu very gently. So they're kinda getting nudged in this way of shifting perception. And then what ends up happening – and it works great, honestly – at a certain

---

43. There is a series of traditional "checking questions" – such as "How tall is Mu?" – used to test a student's understanding.

moment in dokusan, I'll ask them a checking question, and they'll just respond spontaneously. They don't think about it in advance, which is the way it oughta be. And then we start dancing the Mu checking questions together."

"Okay. There's a common Soto criticism of this type of work because the student is being told he's supposed to attain something – he's supposed to 'grasp' Mu or whatever – and in Dogen-style Zen the emphasis is that there is nothing to attain."

"I'd say that once one has a really positive and successful experience with koan study, they arrive at 'there's nothing to get.' And they get there really deeply in their bones and in their DNA, and that it's not an abstract thought. It's something they can actually live out of deeply, really deeply. So in my mind, koan study and shikan taza don't fight each other. In fact, we do this thing where the base practice is shikan taza, but the koan is kinda dropped in there sometimes. But for me, the koan is something you do in the dokusan room. Now I can see where if someone is monastically situated – as in traditional Soto training – and you're living in community for a long arc of time, with the ritual and the just-sitting shikan taza, that that can bake the bread pretty deep. I get it. But I think that if you're *not* in that monastic setting, and you just sit there for twenty minutes a day with nothing to attain, I think the results are kind of maybe tepid. So I think for people who are not living in monastic life for ten years, then this kind of expedient means of koan goosing produces a deep insight into that reality of 'I don't know' and 'there's nothing to get,' and at that point it's not a phrase or a bumper sticker; you've actually seen it."

"So if you were discussing this with your Soto colleagues, how would you describe the point of koan work?"

"The point of the koan work is to realize the Bodhisattva vows in your bones. To really see it. So, for me, it's about actualizing the Dharma – the Buddhadharma – and living from it. It's very expedient for a certain kind of person. Now there are some people who are wired in such a way that it's not a useful means, and so they don't need to do it. But for a lot of people – in fact, most people – it works great. We did sesshin last weekend; most people who are not really new are either in koan study or they're working towards it. And the thing that just raises the hair on my beard" – he grabs his beard and pulls it up and to the side – "is when people who have no access to this from any other thing other than their own zazen, their own Dharma eye, they have the same response to these things. And there's an intelligence behind it that I can see, because I can look at the whole thing and look at it from a pedagogical point of view that I couldn't see as a student. When you're a student going through it, you don't know what's going on. You're just on the stand, and the guy's calling tunes, and you're doing your best. But as the band leader, I can see the intelligence behind how this thing is set up, and it works. And what I mean by 'works' is, it actually does get people to a kensho that's meaningful and that shows up in their daily life."

## Ruben Habito

Ruben Habito is a former Jesuit priest, now the teacher in residence at the Maria-Kannon Zen Center in Dallas. He was born in the Philippines in 1947. His father was a university professor, and, as a young man, Ruben was aware of his family's privileged status. "I did not suffer the hunger or the deprivation or the discrimination or illness or the things that many of the people in my country had to – and still have to – undergo. There is so much injustice in the world, so much unfairness and so much suffering. And how can this be allowed if God is all-powerful and all-loving and so on? And so the basic question of whether God did exist or not became very acute for me."

"Did you ever resolve those questions?" I ask.

"Uh... I'd say the jury's still out on that one," he tells me with a smile.

The questioning eventually led him to enter the Jesuit novitiate, where he had a chance encounter with an American missionary returning from Japan. The young priest was Robert Kennedy, who – by his own admission – had had no interest in Zen during his original posting to Japan. "He gave a talk about how Japan was a very challenging place for Christians because they were less than 1% of the population – half of them Catholic – and that it was a country that was gradually becoming secularized and losing its spiritual heritage."

The talk inspired Ruben to ask to be assigned to Japan.

His first responsibility in the country was to learn the language "I was in the language school in Kamakura and our spiritual director happened to be Father Thomas Hand who had already started practicing Zen with Yamada Roshi for some years before I arrived. And he advised me, 'To deepen your spiritual life, and also to really deepen your knowledge of Japanese culture, why don't you come with me and join me in sitting in Zen with this group?' There were several Jesuits who were practicing Zen and integrating it with Jesuit spirituality."

Under Yamada Koun's tutelage, Ruben began koan study.

"A koan is a way of letting the discursive mind come to face a blank wall, and somehow pull it to a stop so that your intuitive mind might open up and allow you to experience reality directly without the mediation of the logical or discursive mind. When I was first introduced to Yamada Roshi, I was given the koan called 'Mu.' And so just letting that koan be the focus of my sitting led to an opening of something that gave me a very, very deep and profound experience of ecstatic joy. It was an experience of being one with everything and of realizing every moment as sacred. One cannot describe it in words, but it was so overwhelming that I jumped up in joy and started running up the stairs and knocked on the door of Father Hand, saying, 'I got it! I got it!' He looked at me with some surprise, and suggested I go and visit with the master to have it checked. And so I did. So after a couple of such meetings of being examined with the usual checking questions, I was confirmed in what is called a Zen kensho experience, an experience of seeing one's true nature. And so from there, from that point on, I was presented with a curriculum of 500 or so koans one has to go through, and it takes a good number of years to go through them one by one with the direction of the master in one-on-one consultation or a face-to-face encounter until one completes the curriculum. And then one can go back and do them over again and see them in a deeper way and so on.

"Koans are a very, very effective and methodical set of tools that open one's mind and heart to that realm whereby one realizes everything in the universe as intimately interconnected. They are gateways of the mind and heart, enabling one to see things as they really are, the wisdom that enables you to see one's interconnectedness with everything, with every living being, with everything there is. At the same time it opens up your heart in compassion, because you realize you are one with all and are enabled to share in the pain of all beings as well as the joy of all beings."

## Joan Sutherland

Joan Sutherland and John Tarrant, with whom she studied, have experimented with ways to adapt koan teaching to the west. They determined that a demystification process was needed in order to reduce the barriers between Western students and Asian koans. One aspect of this was simply to avoid foreign words whenever possible. Some terms remained because there was no appropriate English equivalent – *Dharma* and *Dao* for example – but when dealing with the koan "Mu," they used the English equivalent "No" instead.

"And it makes a huge difference," Joan tells me. "Let's use 'No' instead of 'Mu' so we have the same experience a Japanese-speaking person would have with 'Mu.' See what happens. 'No' became incredibly powerful in quite unexpected ways. So we said, 'Okay, that's good. We'll hold onto that.' And then, instead of looking for the student to 'answer' the koan, I would say 'respond to.' So we've moved from 'answer' to 'respond to.' And allowing people to understand that their response to the koan is everything that happens while they're keeping company with that koan. Not just the moment when they're in 'work in the room.'[44] And so asking them, 'What's it been like keeping company with this koan? What have you noticed in your life? What's happening in your dreams?' So that was a huge difference. Rather than having this encounter where you come in, 'What's your koan?' 'It's X.' 'What's your answer?' 'It's Y.' 'No.' It becomes, 'What's it like?' Which is a very Chinese way of asking the question. And listening for that and helping someone – if they need help – find a response that has the flavor of the traditional response as well."

"How do you first introduce students to koans?"

"It would be after establishing a good foundation of concentration practice. I tell them, 'Do your concentration practice until you're feeling relatively still and stable and the platform is sturdy.'"

Then she invites them to sit with a koan. "Bring it in and ask it a few times. Whatever it is. So, what is the sound of one hand? Ask it a few times. And then it's as if you're dropping a stone into a still pool, and you're going to watch the ripples. So you drop the koan into your meditation. Let it go, and just watch what happens. Stay focused on your breath. Watch what happens. If it gets too 'thinky,' if you feel you've lost the concentration, go back to your concentration practice, then bring the koan back up again. So it's a kind of repetition like that. Hold it lightly. That's on the cushion. Then as you're walking around during your day, take your koan with you. Ask 'what is the sound of one hand here on the corner of Cerrillos and Saint Michaels Streets?' What is the sound of one hand in this situation? Do 'No.' 'No! No! No!' What is it like to do 'No!' to every thought that arises, to every emotion that arises in every situation? What happens with that? Take it into your dreams. Fall asleep doing 'No!' Have it be a whole life practice."

## Henry Shukman

Most teachers see a qualitative difference between the first case assigned to a student – sometimes called a "break-through koan" – and subsequent koans.

"I'm only going to embark on koan training with somebody if they have been utterly shocked by something that's happened to them," Henry Shukman tells me. "Whose world view has been utterly overturned."

"You don't initiate that by assigning people a first koan? You don't use Mu as a way of achieving that?"

It turns out that I am misunderstanding him.

"Well, we don't consider Mu the start of koan training. We call that Mu practice."

---

44. Their English term for dokusan or sanzen.

"And you start with?"

"Sure – with Mu. But when 'koan training' begins is when we get onto things like 'Stop the sound of the distant bell'[45] and other early koans. But let me say, there are different depths of kensho. I don't think anybody should start koan study unless they've at least been shocked by Oneness, that all the multiplicity of phenomena are somehow one single phenomenon. Somehow all these disparate things are just One. That's a bare minimum for a kensho experience that can get you into the koans, meaning the koans after Mu practice. Because, they really have to see either Emptiness of Self or Emptiness of World. And at some point, by means of having one of those kinds of breakthroughs, we're enabled to get through Mu, and then we start on the koans. And doing those koans, we hope more things will happen, more pieces will fall off. It's like a house falling apart."

## John Tarrant

Many of the people I have interviewed – Melissa Blacker, Robert Waldinger, Rinsen Weik – are Dharma descendants of James Ford. James, along with Joan Sutherland, is the Dharma descendant of John Tarrant, the first of Robert Aitken's heirs. Which places John very early in the process of the transference of Zen to the West. He has been particularly influential in adapting the koan system to American and European practitioners. The way in which the system evolved in Asia resulted in what often became a very competitive practice in early American centers.

"Bob Aitken did this funny ceremony he got from his teacher, Yamada Roshi: when you passed your first koan – which in those days was always Mu – there were all these elaborate checking questions that you'd have to answer according to the Hakuin system, and then he'd have a ceremony and he'd announce you'd passed. You'd get a rakusu and you'd offer incense and bow to the zendo and walk around and everybody would *gassho*.[46] It was really a pretty simple ceremony but extremely irritating when the person who had had kensho was annoying to the community. Some people loved it and felt very encouraged and, of course, often the person who had had this experience was some stoner-girl who had just entered the zendo but had a wide-open mind. The really

---

45. "Stop the distant temple bell" is from a collection referred to as the "Miscellaneous Koans" which students are introduced to before taking up formal koan collections like the *Mumonkan* or the *Hekiganroku*. Other examples of miscellaneous koans are "All things return to the one; to where does the one return?" and "The stone woman gives birth in the middle of the night."

46. Bringing the palms together and bowing.

earnest citizens would be stuck forever, and so Bob really didn't want to do that ceremony. He just quietly stopped doing it and then at one stage Yamada asked him whether he was doing it still. And Bob said, 'No, no, I stopped doing that.' And Yamada said, 'You must start doing it again.' So Bob would wait and wait until the last possible moment, and eventually he just quietly dropped it and it ceased to be."

"Albert Low tells the story about when he was studying with Philip Kapleau and they would have that ceremony," I say, "and there would be these people who had been plugging away at Mu for years, and they'd see the stoner-girl with her rakusu and groan, 'Oh, God, not *her!*' So Albert did away with it as well."

"Well it was a good thing in a way. The good thing was, 'Why not her? Oh, what I've been judging as merit is probably unrelated to anything.' You know? And so I like that aspect of it actually. That was one of the nice things about the democracy of that system. It could be the sort of person that serious students would look down on but who actually had a wonderfully wide-open mind and was much more creative and a bit more spiritual than the rest of us, because we were so earnest and puritan about it all. That's the joke."

### Robert Waldinger

"I wouldn't say that koans bring about insights," Robert Waldinger tells me. "I mean, I've had some insights when I do koans, but not that much. It's more like they confirm them. For me, it's helpful to see that 400 years ago these guys were struggling with the same things. And it's that experience of humanness that koans kind of illustrate that I find really helpful. Like, 'Oh, yes!'" He feigns sighing as if in relief. "And sometimes the answer to the koan will reinforce something that's been arising on the cushion or just in my life. And so for me like… I don't know… I don't have the right way to express it. But it's more like it confirms and reinforces rather than it does something. And the other thing, it just gives you something to talk about with your teacher, which is kind of fun. We often talk about 'playing' with koans. Playing is really the joy of it for me."

### Koun Franz

For Koun Franz, the Soto form teaches individuals to embody the practice in a way he doesn't necessarily see it embodied in other traditions. "The people I've known who are perhaps most deeply steeped in the Soto tradition tend to take embodiment very literally. They stand up straight; they sit up straight; they take care with how they hold their hands, how they walk, etc. It's an internalization of form that I haven't seen, at least not in that way, among koan-oriented friends. It's an understanding of the practice as being very physical in nature."

Koun does not work with koans. He introduces his students, instead, to shikan taza, but admits that it's a more difficult form of meditation to convey. The term means "nothing but" (*shikan*) "just" (*ta*) "sitting" (*za*). To some extent, it has to be learned by feel, by doing it – much as one learns to ride a bike or to swim – rather than through verbal instruction.

"I keep it technical: posture, hands, eyes, then breath. I'm careful not to say what it might feel like, only that when the mind starts to become interested in something or when you find you're pursuing a particular thought stream, to come back to those basic elements: posture, hands, eyes, breath. Sometimes, at the very beginning, I'll ask people first to sit the way they would if they were bored or had no respect for someone who was talking with them, then to show how they would sit if they really cared or felt a deep respect for the person in front of them. Just that clarifies a lot about the energy of it."

He returns to the idea that Zen is – as he puts it – "a practice of form."

"So I have to say this acknowledging there are different Zens. Right? I'm not telling the whole story, but in terms of what I was handed, it's really important not to frame it in terms of your mind and your mental experience. Zen is that you're doing something. Zen is that you're giving expression to something. And you're exploring compassion, exploring wisdom, exploring whatever that is, through some kind of action. And the way that Zen has done that traditionally is by getting really interested in the way that you hold yourself in the world. And so the way that you walk, and the way that you sit, and the way that you stand, and those matter because by paying attention to those things, you're paying attention to who you are in this moment. And that's what Zen looks like to me. Zen, to me, is standing in line at the bank and remembering to stand up straight. Even though no one cares. That feels like it has a lot of juice. But when the conversation shifts to 'This is what it looks like inside my mind,' or, 'I feel like this when I sit,' or whatever, those are natural processes, but that's not really at the heart, for me, of what this practice is. Those are things we're kind of getting past so that we can focus on not being paralyzed and actually doing something."

## Domyo Burk

"I have a pamphlet that I wrote for my podcast," Domyo Burk tells me. "I made myself a challenge. Could I write instructions for zazen that would fit in fairly large text on a tri-fold brochure? What is the most important thing to teach people? And I think I teach it differently than the way in which I was taught, which was 'here's your instructions for physical posture, and then you can count your breaths from one to ten, and when your mind wanders you just bring it back to your breath.' But – honestly – I am with the Japanese Soto school. I don't think that's shikan taza. I don't think breath following is our Soto form of meditation. However, people have pointed out to me it's still useful to mention that tool to people because for some people, what they're really looking for is a break from really disturbing mental loops that they get on, and shikan taza may be too vague a practice at first. They actually need something to break out of those mental loops.

"So I mention that to people. Basically I say, 'There's many forms of meditation. You're welcome to do what you like when you come here as long as you're quiet.' And I say, 'Shikan taza means "just sitting".' When we're doing it perfectly, we're just sitting there. But if you've meditated at all, you know that's not necessarily as straight-forward as it sounds. What does that mean? If your mind is wandering, are you just sitting there? I think of this as a letting-go practice instead of a directed-effort practice. In most forms of meditation you choose a meditative object – whether it's your breath or maybe in other traditions it's a syllable or it's a visualization – and when your mind wanders you bring it back to your meditative object, and the idea is that after a while your mind settles down. And if that works for you, that's wonderful. It's a very straightforward form of meditation. For some of us – myself included – it's like that very effort to redirect the mind agitates the mind even further. I like to think that shikan taza is a very clever way to circumvent the mind and its attempt to always be central in our experience. Our emphasis really is on the physical act of sitting. That is, we're giving up all volitional activity except for sitting still and upright and trying to pay attention to simply being alive. So those three things. Any other volitional activity we're going to let go of, including trying to make our meditation experience any particular way, including trying to settle the mind or let go of thoughts or return to the present or anything like that. But the ironic thing is that if we find that we've been caught up in thinking, what we're actually doing is we're getting caught up in volitional activity. We're actually engaged in volitional activity. We're planning or fantasizing or doing *something*. Essentially we have got caught up and all we have to do is let go of that volitional activity and return to this incredibly simple just… just physically sitting there.

"I also like Uchiyama Roshi's metaphor of 'opening the hand of thought.'[47] What we've done when we get caught up in thinking is we've grasped some particular thought. All we have to do is open our hand. The thought, whatever

---

47. Kosho Uchiyama was abbot of the Soto Antai-ji until his death in 1998.

it is, will change. It will come and go. And I tell students, 'If you were to learn this form of meditation in Japan, they would tell you physically how to sit, and then they would say, "Let thoughts come and go," and that'd be all the instruction you would get.' Let thoughts come and go. No big deal. I find this shifts the emphasis off of my mind; when I notice I've been caught up in thinking and I'm planning my grocery list and whatever, so what? When I notice that, I just notice that. I just sit, and it's not a big deal. It's like the 'so-what-mind.' Do what you like. And my mind will actually settle more when I do this.

"But then there's a very tricky dynamic there which I don't tend to get into much in the really brief intro, which I have to keep coming back to with students, which is, 'This isn't a slack, lazy activity. You're paying attention to simply being alive as if this were the last time you were ever going to sit.' That's the level of awareness and attention and dedication – ideally – that we bring. And it's difficult."

## Dosho Port

Since Albert Low's death, Dosho Port is the teacher with whom I've continued playing with koans. He is a Dharma heir of both Dainin Katagiri and James Ford, and his training with Katagiri was in the Soto tradition where the focus is on monastic life and shikan taza – which Dosho prefers to refer to by the English rendering "just-sitting" – rather than on koan study. It was Katagiri's wish, however, that Dosho spend some time practicing in Japan, and, while there, he was introduced to koan work.

"I think the purpose of koan introspection and just-sitting combined with dignified behavior, the way it's taught in Soto monasticism, are the same," he tells me. "But if the goal is to realize the same mind as Buddha and live accordingly – or 'to practice awakening' as Dogen put it – koan work is more effective for most householders[48] than just-sitting, and, despite the continuing prevalence and power of the monastic narrative within Western Zen, about 99% of Zen students are householders.

"What Harada Daiun Roshi and Yasutani Roshi did in the 20th century was simplify the Rinzai koan curriculum so that it was portable, so that practicing awakening as a householder was within reach of anyone who approached the work with persistence and skilled guidance. I don't know that making it available to householders was their intention. It could be that they were just trimming the hedge that had grown up since Hakuin's time, but that simplification, or refocusing, made it possible for English-speaking Westerners to do

---

48. "Householders" is a traditional Buddhist term for lay persons.

post-kensho koan training without being Chinese classics scholars.

"At about the same time, Shunryu Suzuki Roshi, Katagiri Roshi, Chino Roshi, and others were here trying to figure out how to teach people how to practice in householder life in the West, and so they simplified dignified-behavior training from the Soto monastic system in a way that was similar to what Harada Roshi and Yasutani Roshi had done with the koan curriculum. But, in my experience, without the monastic container, the impact of dignified-behavior training is rarely as effective as the koan curriculum. It just isn't as obviously portable.

"Saying this doesn't make me very popular in some Soto circles, but that's my experience as a student and as a teacher, first as a teacher in the Soto system for twenty years and now as a teacher of the Harada-Yasutani koan curriculum for about ten. Without koan training, people can certainly have deep belief in the efficacy of the Buddhadharma, but it's rare to actually taste the truth of Zen in their life without some kind of koan work. It's possible, of course, and I've met about a dozen students, some of whom also started with Katagiri Roshi, who I'm convinced had clear kensho experiences while practicing just-sitting. But even if someone living as a householder has a first kensho, there isn't a system within Soto Zen in the West, at least outside of the few Soto monasteries here, that can help people move through and beyond the first opening. And post-kensho integration is really the more important part of training. Within the koan curriculum there are hundreds of barrier koans to pass through as exercises in the 'how to' of vividly practicing awakening – actually integrating the kensho experience within the nitty gritty details of the life the person is living."

## Bobby Rhodes

When I ask Bobby Rhodes what methodology is employed in Kwan Um practice, she chuckles and replies, "Well, pay attention to the moment Over and over and over again."

"Is that more centrally important than seated meditation?"

"Well, it's fluid. My teacher, Zen Master Seung Sahn, taught that lying down, sitting up, walking, eating, anything you're doing, brushing your teeth, to pay attention to that moment. So the sitting is not any more important than brushing the teeth as long as you're staying in the moment."

"Does the sitting have an impact on your ability to stay in the moment elsewhere?"

"I think it does. I think it helps train the mind. It's very difficult to do that in activity because you're already preconditioned to be thinking about something else. For example, using brushing the teeth as an example, you're already thinking about what you're going to do next. Whereas sitting – you know – you're supposed to be just being there. So I think the practice of sitting is very helpful. Yes."

"You said that when you were living at the temple, the practice supported your work as a nurse."

"It was like hand-in-hand. We sat every morning and every night, and it helped me with the *paramitas*,[49] with generosity and patience and gratitude and everything. It just opened me up. I always wanted to be a nurse, and I wanted to be a nurse even more as I practiced. It would help me be such a good nurse. And the koan practice helped too, because I wouldn't know how to help certain people or what they needed, and I would use it as a koan. So there I'd be walking to their room, I'd focus on who I was going to see and how they were and try to be there – in the moment – with them. And I really started to watch intuition kicking in much more than it had when I was younger. So I felt like the whole practice was helping my intuition and my patience and my gratitude."

"How do you present meditation to beginners?"

"Meditation is to understand your true self, to return to the moment, to see what's going on just now. So we teach a certain technique. Usually what we do, we have people sit for ten minutes before the talk, and we tell them to breathe in on 'clear mind' and to breathe out 'don't know.' That's our beginner technique. Breathe in 'clear mind,' breathe out 'don't know.' Just quietly inside. And try that for ten minutes. So after you've done that, we ask if you have any questions."

"Okay, so my question is, 'What do you mean by "don't know"? What is it that I don't know?'"

"You don't have to know what it is, just say 'don't know.'"

"So let's say I stick around and keep coming back to the scheduled sits. Then one day, I come and tell you, 'I've been doing this every day for a couple of months now, but I still don't know what I mean when I say "don't know."'"

"Correct."

"And that's your answer? I don't know what I mean when I say 'don't know' and you say?"

"Correct."

## Dang Nghiem

At Blue Cliff, Sister Dang Nghiem tells me people call her Sister D. She was born in Saigon and named Huong, which means "fragrance." Her mother had left the countryside as a teenager to work as a maid in Saigon. Eventually

---

49. The Six Perfections: generosity, ethical behavior, tolerance, diligence, concentration, and insight.

circumstances led her, as it did many young women at that time, to consort with US soldiers. Sister D is not certain whether her own father was American or Vietnamese, but it was clear from his light skin, facial features, and blond hair that her younger brother was of mixed heritage. This caused him grief both in Vietnam and the United States; in Vietnam he was taunted for his American ancestry, and in North America he was bullied and called a communist because of his Asian ancestry.

For a while, the two children lived with their grandmother, a devout Buddhist, in the countryside. But when a patron maintained Huong's mother in a private house, she brought her children to the city to be with her. It wasn't a healthy environment. Huong was conscious of and disturbed by the sexual demands made of her mother. Huong herself had been sexually abused by an uncle when she was only nine and was sexually assaulted by a drunken policeman a year later.

When Huong was twelve, her mother disappeared and was presumed to have been murdered. The children returned to the care of their grandmother. Fearful of the way her grandson was treated after the American withdrawal, the grandmother arranged for the children to emigrate to the United States under the auspices of the Amerasian Immigration Act. Sister D was 16 years old at the time.

She did well in school, excelled in her language studies, and was eventually accepted into medical school. During her medical training, she did internships in India and Kenya but felt increasingly ill at ease with the impersonality of her chosen profession.

"I finished medical school; I went to residency. Even though I was raised as a Buddhist, I never really practiced it. My grandmother was a very deep practitioner, but I just went along with her. In the US, as a teenager, I never went to the temple because I lived with foster parents who were Christian. In college and in medical school, I had no time for a spiritual life. Then while I was doing residency, one of the doctors said to me, 'You know, doctor, there is a Zen Master who's Vietnamese, and he's giving retreats all over the US. Maybe you'd like to attend one of his retreats.'"

The teacher was Thich Nhat Hanh. Sister D went to his retreat in Santa Barbara, and at it, she tells me, "I realized what we call the Four Noble Truths – the Buddha's essential teaching[50] – about this deep suffering in myself and in my

---

50. The Four Noble Truths are traditionally considered a summary of the Buddha's basic teachings: 1) All of existence is characterized by suffering (dukkha); 2) Suffering is caused by craving; 3) Suffering can be ameliorated by overcoming craving; 4) Craving can be overcome by following the Noble Eightfold path, which consists of right view, right intention, right speech, right action, right livelihood,

family. I mean, I always knew I suffered, but to have suffering as a noble teaching was something enlightening to me. What also moved me was that all these years, growing up, I thought of myself as a victim, but, in the retreat, I realized that I was the one perpetuating the suffering. I had become a perpetrator. I was no longer a victim but a perpetrator. Then I also learned that there's a way out. I saw that I could participate *actively* in the making of the suffering but also in the transformation of the suffering. This realization moved me so deeply. It also changed my views about religion, about Buddhism, because I had thought of religion as something like a superstition; however, in that retreat, I saw it was really a deep practice."

Back in her residency program, she saw "even more clearly how my suffering continued because of the daily pressure and stress as well as because of my ingrained habit energies. I had so little time to care for myself. Therefore, when difficulties of the past arose, I couldn't really take care of them. This awareness made me even more depressed than before. Then it happened that my partner died in an accident."

He had gone swimming in the ocean and didn't return. His body was never recovered. "His death woke me up. He lived a spiritual life, and, when he passed away, I didn't regret it for him, because he had lived a deeply joyful and meaningful life. His death woke me up because even though I had all the conditions of happiness, I was unhappy and even desperate at times. If not by the stress and pressure of the present moment, I would be suffering from nightmares about the past. I realized that if I were to die suddenly like him, I would not have peace in my heart. I could not have said that I had lived my life peacefully. I could not have said that I had truly lived my life so that I could just die then like my partner. This realization made me want to change the direction of my life. I wanted to live in such a way that if I were to die anytime in the midst of the day, it would be okay."

She left medicine and went to Nhat Hanh's Plum Village in France, where she eventually took vows as a nun.

"Our teacher tells us that the practice of meditation is like a bird with two wings; one wing is stopping, and the other one is deep looking.' So we always start a meditation with stopping. And that means stopping, bringing the mind back to the breath and then to the body. The Buddha taught this in the Sixteen Exercises of Mindful Breathing. So we always start with breathing: 'I'm aware that I'm breathing in; I'm aware that I'm breathing out.' And then a few exercises. 'Breathing in, I'm aware that I have a body; breathing out, I relax tension in my body.' So we practice stopping first. And then the second part of meditation

---

right effort, right mindfulness, and right meditation.

is Deep Looking. So there's a topic like looking into the four elements that make up our body or looking into the five year old child in us, looking at the five year old child in our mother, our father. So these are guided meditations that we have.

"Our practices are actually very modern. They're based on the teachings of the Buddha – like I said about stopping and contemplation – but we make it very modern. Like when you hear the telephone bell, you stop and breathe. At the time when the Buddha talked about mindfulness of breathing there was no bell. No phone. But now we use that. This is Applied Buddhism. We breathe with the bell. We breathe with the phone. And so it's very pragmatic. Because people nowadays are developing anxiety disorder, depression, and many other mental illnesses because of the stress. Stress can cause many of our illnesses. Stress is a very big factor of our lifestyle. So when people practice and they breathe with the phone they feel more relaxed, and, if they do that many times a day, they find it's very effective.

"So people don't have to sit eight hours to be in meditation. Who can afford! People cannot even afford twenty minutes a day to do sitting meditation. But our practices, when you walk, it can be walking meditation; when you eat, it can be eating meditation. When the phone rings, it can be the phone meditation. When you drive, it can be driving meditation. So it's very pragmatic."

## Wayne Coger

The Springwater Center is four hours west of Blue Cliff. It's an agricultural region, and I miss the side road to the Center on my first pass, come to a dead end, turn around, and watch more closely on the way back. Even when I pull onto the gravel road indicated, I'm not entirely sure I'm in the right place until I see a bench set up by a stream in the forested area I'm driving through.

The full name of the Center is the Springwater Center for Meditative Inquiry. Toni Packer established it in 1981 after leaving the Rochester Zen Center. Philip Kapleau had identified her as his successor at the Center, but, after a period of overseeing it during one of his absences, she decided she could no longer practice as a Buddhist. The question she found herself facing was whether or not the type of work that took place within the Zen tradition could be done without the trappings – without identifying it as Buddhist or even calling it meditation.

When I wrote to ask permission to come here, I said that I was aware the center was not directly affiliated with Zen. The Center Administrator, Wayne Coger, wrote back to me and said: "While we are not a Buddhist Center we are incorporated as a Zen Center. The late Roshi Kapleau once wrote that the 'spirit of Zen is all pervading.' So legally, and perhaps in spirit, we are in the Zen tradition."

Although there is no iconography, there are elements one recognizes from more traditional zendos. Zafus and zabutons are available, but people may also spend the scheduled sitting periods in lounge chairs by windows that overlook the grounds. Wayne believes the freedom the center provides for people "not to have to subscribe to any particular doctrine or creed to be very refreshing and very freeing." The traditional structures, Wayne suggests, aren't necessary. "That's not to be critical of someone who finds them necessary. What we are doing here has been an on-going experiment. Can this be done? Can it unfold without the trappings of a religious organization?"

It was an intriguing enough concept that, after that first visit, I came back to attend one of their week-long retreats. A couple of years later, I have an opportunity to speak with Wayne again, and I tell him that the impression I'd had during the retreat was that most of the participants knew one another. It had felt as if they had been together for a long time.

"That probably was the case at that time," he admits.

"Is it still the case?"

"No, it's not the same. We're seeing a lot of new faces. We're seeing kind of a new generation of people that are coming back. In other words, people very quickly come from being the person who's new to someone who's coming back fairly frequently. We now have – just for example, which I think has changed since you were here – I think we're a majority of people at least under 45. Which I consider young."

I ask him what meditation instruction they give to people on their first visit.

"Do nothing," Wayne says, simply.

I laugh. "I suspect if someone told me that it would just piss me off."

"Yeah."

"So what do you mean, 'Do nothing'?"

"To see that all the manipulations, all the efforting, all the self-deception, doesn't bring us any closer to the presence of this moment; to see that when we are busy doing things, we're not really listening, we're not really here. So, we're looking at the possibility that this doing is a kind of a trap. That it lets us *feel* that we're going somewhere; we're creating an illusion of kind of a goal, but, in reality, we're *here*. And what is calling for attention is *here*. I wouldn't say that we're free of the tendency 'to do.' But we're looking at looking; we're looking at seeing; we're looking at looking at the doing, at this incredibly agitated and nervous tendency to always want to have something on the fire, always to have a goal, to always have some way of measuring what kind of progress we're making. And part of this experiment is to see if it's possible to be without that."

"So, if you get rid of the wider practice context that more structured environments provide, then the energy has to come from where? From oneself?"

"Where else can it come from? The teacher can't see for you. The teacher can talk about what they're seeing, what's present for them. But the seeing has to be here. It's difficult. And it can be very frustrating. If one's looking for someone to take one by the hand, and say, 'Just do this, and everything will be okay'... I don't know if that's self-deception, but it involves both of us – if we're making that kind of contract – in a very precarious situation. I think there's much more danger for the person doing the leading, but it's dangerous for both people. We can really get a sense of inflated worth. A lot of mischief can come out of that if we're the one who's going to show people the truth, so to speak. That's quite a heavy responsibility. So the approach here is to see if we can work together, look together. In this kind of together-working, can there be a clarifying, a clarity that emerges?"

"Would you equate these moments of clarity with awakening?"

"Yes. People are infinitely capable of waking up. The coming to is not dependent on the tradition. It manifests in human beings when there isn't the kind of entanglement with our beliefs, with our sense of oneself or one's separation or one's fantasies about one's self, one's ideas. If there is a break in the continuity of that story, there can be an opening, a freshness, a seeing.'

"That," I tell him, "was an issue which came up at least twice during the discussion periods during the retreat I attended, participants questioning whether or not awakening was actually possible. And, as I remember the discussion, there seemed to be doubt about that. My feeling was – and I remember saying this – that I think people often have an inflated idea of what awakening is which can get in the way of actually experiencing awakening."

Wayne nods his head. "That the feeling or idea of what awakening consists of gets in the way of a spontaneous or a free opening? Yes, I would agree with that. I'll put it the way it happens here. We read about something – enlightenment stories or awakening stories – or we hear somebody talking about this awakening, and not surprisingly, with a lot of ideas flowing, a lot of images, and hopes and dreams. And I think within or without traditions, within the Zen tradition or other meditative traditions, when there is a genuine coming to, waking up, it's discovered it's not what we imagined or wanted or thought it was. It's none of that. It's not thought. It's not imagination. And maybe that's part of the discovery, that we're living our lives in the imagination, in the realm of thought, in the realm of ideas. Not that there's anything wrong with thought; we just think that our thought is reality, that it's all there is in some ways. And we also think that *because* I've thought something it's invariably true. Again, this work is beginning to look at thought in a more open, unbiased way. To see thought as thought."

As it happens, like Henry Shukman and Melissa Blacker, my first kensho occurred before I knew anything about Buddhism or Zen, and I recognize that that type of insight isn't dependent on any particular tradition or methodology. So I find the experiment at Springwater appealing. My one reservation is the matter of the continuity of teaching. One thing the structured context of Zen provides – through the care taken in bestowing transmission – is a means by which the teaching can be passed on from one generation to the next.

When I mention this to Wayne, he tells me:

"Toni used to say, whenever I brought up a question like that, that this work is vital; that it's important, and that it's worthwhile. I'm not quoting exactly. And because it's vital, because it's worthwhile, she had no worries about the continuity of the work. In that spirit, I don't know what will survive. I don't know if Springwater itself will survive as an institution, but the work is not dependent on Springwater, or me, or the group.

"What we're calling awakening is our natural state. It is not something outside of us, and this expression of dissatisfaction with how we're living, how we're living in conflict, how we're hurting each other, discovering how much suffering there is in the world, I don't think that's going away either. Maybe it's a germ within us, the desire to really see if there's a different way of living, a different way of being. I think, with confidence, that that won't go away either."

# 4
# ADAPTING ZEN TO THE WEST

## Dai Bosatsu Zendo Kongo-ji

Returning from Springwater to Blue Cliff along Route 17, one passes through the community of Livingston Manor, which promotes itself as the home of fly-fishing in America. If one turns north here, on 151, one will come to Beecher Lake and Dai Bosatsu. These are the Catskill Mountains where Rip van Winkle fell asleep and woke to find the world, as he had known it, changed.

All things – the Buddha noted – are relative. I had thought that Mitra Bishop's Mountain Gate in New Mexico was isolated, but to get to Dai Bosatsu, one travels along a rugged secondary road and then up a gravel road – partially eroded by recent rains at the time of my visit. I had been impressed by how large Zen Mountain Monastery – with 230 acres – had been, but the front gate for Dai Bosatsu is two miles from the main monastery building. The grounds cover 1400 acres.

The property had been the hunting preserve of Harriet Beecher Stowe's brother, and the lodge is pretty much what one would expect a wealthy 19th century family to have built for a mountain retreat, although one marvels at the challenge it must have been to construct it in an era when materials had to be harvested locally or brought in by horse-drawn wagons. Across the lake, a large bronze Buddha sits on a boulder. It tilts backwards slightly, as if the base had shifted since it was first erected. Then one comes upon the monastery itself.

The idea for building Dai Bosatsu had been Eido Shimano's, one of several controversial Zen teachers from Japan who settled in America. Shimano was an ambitious man, and he envisioned something much grander than the refurbished hot springs resort which the San Francisco Zen Center had transformed into the Tassajara Zen Mountain Center. He hired a local architect, Davis Hamerstrom, who traveled to Japan to study Kyoto architecture. In the spring of 1973, work began on what remains, arguably, the most significant Zen construction project to be undertaken in America. A Japanese-style temple of classic design was built. Its full formal name is Dai Bosatsu Zendo Kongo Ji, and it was officially inaugurated on America's bi-centennial anniversary, July 4, 1976.

The temple is every bit as impressive and improbable as I had been led to believe. Shimano and Hamerstrom modeled it after Tofukuji, the largest Rinzai temple in Japan, using imported craftsmen when necessary to ensure accuracy of detail. There are polished oak floors and tatami mats, sliding shoji screens, splendid calligraphy scrolls, and antique Asian treasures throughout. Western monks with Japanese Dharma names, wearing Japanese robes, respond with a sharp "Hai!" when addressed. Meals are eaten *jihatsu*,[51] with three nested bowls, chop sticks, and chants in Japanese. The contrast with Springwater could hardly be more stark.

Shinge Chayat and her then husband, Lou Nordstrum, had been involved with Dai Bosatsu from its beginning.

"We lived with five other people in the original building down the road," she tells me. "It was extremely cold. We had no heat, and it was a really hard winter. We would have to go out in a little pickup truck and throw down shovelfuls of salt and sand so the construction vehicles could keep coming up. And – as you know – the road is not an easy one to come up even when it's in fairly good shape. It was not a good road then.

"It was an exciting time. We were real pioneers. No one knew what this would be like. Eido Roshi had a vision. He was thinking of it as a real break from Japan, a real American Zen that would take root here. We started with great idealism, and, in a way, everything was kind of up for grabs. How we were going to form this community, and how much it would find its shape in the Rinzai container of Japan and China. How much it would find its own shape. It grew organically."

I remark that the Japanese cultural flavor is very apparent.

"At this point, yes. At this point, for sure. You really don't even know you're in America when you walk into this building. And that's because Eido Roshi wanted to bring the whole richness of Rinzai Zen to America. But he was always very open with me and others about, 'Now it will be up to you to create an American Rinzai Zen.' He was certainly very cautious about us making a lot of changes right away. I, myself, feel there are changes that I've brought about here, definitely, but I will always uphold the strength and beauty of the Rinzai

---

51. A ritualized way of eating in Zen monastic communities.

Zen practice and Japanese aesthetic that we've received. So, it's always a work in progress."

Zen as practiced in the west can often seem very foreign. The decorations and even the terminology used remain predominantly Japanese. Those who formally declare themselves Buddhists are given foreign Dharma names; the Japanese didn't take on Chinese names but Americans routinely take on Japanese – or Korean or Vietnamese – names. Practitioners generally sit either on cushions or in *seiza* (kneeling on the floor and sitting on one's heels); one bows before entering the meditation hall and before taking one's seat; meals can be eaten with chop sticks; the chants used aren't always in English. The transition to a more Western form of practice has been slow.

## Shugen Arnold

On the other side of the mountain – less than fifty miles away – at Zen Mountain Monastery, I ask Shugen Arnold how important the Japanese envelope is for contemporary North American Zen.

"Well, our lineage comes through Japan, and so the Japanese Zen aspects to our practice have been an important part of our history and training. I have reverence for that reason and a sense of respect and gratitude. Daido Roshi was very thoughtful about wanting to honor and maintain those aspects of Japanese Zen that he felt had power and meaning for western students, but he was also able to make changes or let things go as he felt was appropriate. Because in the early years there were people who came looking for a Japanese experience – and he was an American teaching in an American monastery – he thought that an important part of planting it in this country was to emphasize that, as he often said, 'Zen has always been here.' The forms came to us from Japan, but the essence has always been right here.

"I have wanted to maintain connections with teachers and monasteries in Japan, and last March, I performed some ceremonies which, within our lineage, recognize myself and the monastery within the larger school of Soto Buddhism. So I don't want to close the door. How meaningful that will be over the years to come, I don't know. How active it will be, I don't know. Daido Roshi's connection with Japan was much stronger because of Maezumi Roshi. Mine was less, because my connection was with Daido Roshi and much less so with Maezumi Roshi. My successors have almost no connection with Japan at all. I think this is a natural progression or part of our planting deep roots."

It is not only about how "Japanese" Northern American Zen needs to be, there are even questions about how Buddhist it needs to be. It was an issue Daido Loori had been concerned about. I ask Shugen if he had similar concerns.

"After all, there's just one Dharma, which has evolved into many streams, schools and lineages, which has always been – and continues to be – heavily influenced by the many different cultures and languages in which Buddhism has taken hold. But there's really just one Dharma. So Zen is the tradition that I was trained in, and that's the tradition I teach in, but I don't first and foremost see myself as a Zen Buddhist, although I have great reverence and appreciation for the Zen tradition. At heart, I am someone who's studying and practicing Buddhadharma, and I use this particular tradition as my primary vessel because it has power."

## Genjo Marinello

During a freshman English class in the '70s, Genjo Marinello was introduced to the idea that there "was a way to experience, or penetrate, reality beyond the scientific method; that you could have something called insight, inspiration, or intuition. You could tap into some fundamental truths heuristically by investigating your own internal condition." It was his effort to learn how to do that which led him to Zen.

Genjo is the abbot of Dai Bai Zen Cho Bo Zen Ji in Seattle. The structures here are not as extreme as those at Dai Bosatsu – where he trained for a while – but they are clearly based on Japanese models. I ask how important he believes these forms to be.

"I'm on the side of them being fairly important. Relative to most Zen Centers in the country, Cho Bo Ji would feel more Japanese than most. I would say we're in the 90th percentile or something like that. 'Cause we still eat at benches. We still eat with the nested bowls. We still sit seiza whenever we have tea. There's a pretty Japanese feel to it. Of course, Zen is everywhere, but in terms of passing on a practice and training that is going to bring people – without drugs – to penetrate their own ego defences sufficiently, I think you need a really strong form. Well, the Japanese have one. It could be any strong form. But the Japanese already have one. It's been handed down for centuries. A really, really strong frame and a strong form. So I'm all for America finding its own strong frame and strong form, but I think it has to be done very slowly in order for the form not to collapse. Because the form is important. I think to have a deep retreat you need that strong form. It's like a pressure cooker, and you don't want people popping out one way or another. You really want to hold the participants in the sesshin in a form that can contain the power that's coming up – both crazy power and awakened power. Since the Japanese already have a strong form, let's borrow it until it slowly morphs into an American form that is as strong."

"Looking at the centers I've visited," I remark, "the development of an American style Zen seems to be heading in several different directions. The spectrum is pretty broad. Is that something that will eventually need to be addressed?"

"I think it will sort itself out in sort of an evolutionary way. What works will stay, and what doesn't work will fall away. So I'm not too worried about it. In general, my opinion is that Zen form in America has become so relaxed that it can't bring people to the depths that I believe Zen practice can bring people to. My sense is that at more than half of the Zen Centers out there the form isn't strong enough. And I'm not talking about Japanese or American but just the form period. So I think that's eventually going to fall away. It'll just fall off because it doesn't bring people to the depth that a strong form can. And I expect there will be the light – the Zen-lite – school and the Zen 'More Hard Knocks' school, and there may be two different branches. Of course, there is the danger of it being too stuck culturally in the Japanese mode or being too culturally marginal or macho. And, no, it doesn't need to be that. We can let that fall away. That's part of the leftover Japanese samurai culture that blended with Zen that can definitely be let go of. But I still think it needs a very strong form in order to bring people past ego-defences which are *very* strong."

## Koun Franz

Koun Franz – who has a shaved head and, like Rinzan Pechovnik, wears Japanese samugi when not in full robes – tells me that, of course, the Japanese cultural forms aren't critical for Western practitioners. "What is critical is that we don't design it ourselves. Right? A spiritual practice of our own making is designed to make us comfortable. There's no way around that. This is a spiritual practice that makes us uncomfortable. That's good. It could easily be any one of a million different permutations of that, except that in order for me to do that, I have to make it, and then I'm making it so that I can be comfortable even if I'm making it so that my students can be uncomfortable. So to me, it's just a matter of here's a practice that I think, in its bones, has a lot of integrity. And I think that it bothers people in the right ways. For me, the way that I dress, for example, has a lot to do with my sense of responsibility to my teachers and also my ongoing exploration of what it means to be a priest. I have no patience with the idea that you can be a priest on the weekend or that you can be a priest only when you go to the zendo. That's crap. A *huge* number of Zen priests in North America are completely undercover. They have hair. They dress in ordinary clothes, and then they dress up when it's time. Some of them don't even do that. Now actually I'm really interested in the idea of lay teachers; I'm really interested in the idea of other ways of doing this. But if you're going to pursue this particular path, a part of it – a huge part of it – is it's a path of renunciation. And part of renunciation is that you don't get to choose what's in your closet any more, and you don't get to choose certain things about how you present in the world. That to me is important."

"I get that, but at what point does its foreignness...?"

He nods his head and responds before I finish the question. "Hugely problematic. Hugely problematic. You know, I work above a sushi restaurant; two times now, people have stopped me on the street to ask me what the hours are because they think I work there. Or people think I'm a martial artist. It's a failing, and I stick to it because I'm determined to see it through to the other side. But one of the conversations I try to bring up with my peers is that I don't think this works. I also don't think it works to do nothing. You know, if I could push the big red button – and I'm so glad nobody's asked me to push the big red button because I would abuse it – but we need a different uniform. I think we need a uniform. First of all, I think that people should shave their heads. It doesn't mean what it used to mean, but it still means something. And I think there should be some way of wearing robes. When I see the monk who runs the Sri Lankan temple we were at yesterday, he is recognized everywhere he goes as a person who's living a spiritual life. Even if people don't recognize it as Buddhism, even if people have no idea what it is, there's no question of his vocation at its core. We could do that, but we haven't figured that out. And we also come out of a tradition where, in Japan, the robes are treated as almost magical items. Which in some ways is a really beautiful tradition. But it means there's all these circumstances where you don't wear them, because you can't ever get them dirty. You can't expose them to the elements. When I see the monk at the temple mowing the lawn in his robes, there's a power to that that I feel we have given up in the Zen world."

"But if you were building a center in Halifax, you wouldn't design it to look like a Japanese temple."

"Of course not. If you build a temple in Nova Scotia it has to be Nova Scotian. It has to be local. It doesn't work otherwise. And I think I'm fortunate in that regard, because I lived in Japan for so long that, for me, there's no magic to it. I really understand if someone has only visited Japan, if they have teachers who are important to them who are from Japan, it's easy for Japan to be...uh...."

"Mythologized?" I suggest.

"Mythologized and exciting."

"Exotic."

"Yes! Exotic! And it's easy to assign a certain kind of wisdom to things that are just ordinary things. You know, one of the things that I deal with often – as the guy who was interpreting for everyone – is that people learn, for example, how to go in and out of the bath in the monastery, and then they take that back to Europe or wherever and they teach it as a Zen practice. It's just how Japanese people get in and out of the bath. Right? But now we've spiritualized it. We've made it a central part of Buddhist practice. That happens all the time. And I find that really painful, and I think we need to get over that.

"But, to me, the way you get over it has to do with not compartmentalizing it. If all the Zen priests in North America would walk around wearing robes, we would figure out what robes should look like because we'd decide that robes were important, and we'd stop looking like we were Japanese. But because we don't do that, we retain it exactly as it came to us. So when you walk into a Zen center, you're in Japan. That's a mistake."

### Bernie Glassman

When Bernie Glassman founded the Zen Community of New York, at first he kept the forms as he had received them from Taizan Maezumi. He shaved his head and donned the formal robes of a transmitted teacher, complete with attendants to position those robes correctly when he took his seat. A little later, he doffed the robes for overalls and drove a delivery truck distributing goods from the bakery he had established as a social enterprise. When I meet him at his home in Montague, he's casually dressed in a blue patterned shirt and loose white slacks with suspenders that he occasionally adjusts as we speak. He's bearded and wears his long grey hair tied back in a pony tail. Toward the end of the interview, he takes a clown's nose from his pocket and puts it on.

"In 1997, I decided I was not going to be involved in teaching any more, formally. But what I wanted to do was go around to my Dharma successors that had places and make sure that they weren't being too arrogant or thinking they knew too much. And that the best way to do that would be to pop-up unexpectedly as a clown and disrupt what was going on." So he took formal clown training.

Robert Kennedy told me about an occasion when Bernie had said, "'Some people like Zen clubs, where they can sit together with like-minded people, where they can be quiet together.' But what he did was he brought us out on the street, where we lived with the poor." It was not the type of practice in which one finds Zen monks in Japan engaged.

During my meeting with Bernie, I ask, "Given that Zen was brought to America by a small group of Japanese teachers – coming from a very different cultural background than we have here – is it still a viable spiritual path for North Americans?"

"I think so." Then he sighs. "I think so. But it's not a... To make it viable, it will not be just a single way. For me, it's equivalent to saying, 'Is Christianity viable?' I say, 'Sure. But is it just one way in Christianity? No. You can be a Protestant, a Catholic, a Baptist.' So, the same with Zen. And maybe that's part of my training, because my teacher – you have to remember – he was born in the Japanese Soto sect. His father was Japanese Soto, but he was very liberal, his father, in terms of various paths. So Maezumi Roshi also finished his studies with Yasutani Roshi and with Koryu Roshi.[52] The three different ways of study within Zen. Now, I studied with all those three, and for me it's pretty broad when we say 'Zen' what the ways can be. And I was also encouraged by my teacher to create my own ways. One thing he said which is sort of interesting, he said, 'When it comes to a new country, first what people do is they translate the sayings of the masters. Then they translate the commentaries on the sayings of the masters. And third, they make their own commentaries.' That's when you have what he called 'living *Shobogenzo*.'[53] First two is just part of that transition. You gotta get to the living."

"Can Zen exist outside Buddhism?"

"Well, Bob Kennedy's a beautiful example. You interviewed him. If you take Zen as being a school of Buddhism, then Buddhism defines as the School of Awakening. Awakening to what? Awakening to the interconnectedness of life. Now all the schools in Buddhism are different ways of helping you awaken. Zen uses meditation but not just meditation. Then where's the limit? It's not a religion in the sense of Catholicism or Judaism. It's ways of awakening to the interconnectedness of life. So I don't know who can't be called a Zen teacher if they learn upayas[54] to help awaken to the oneness of life. Now, is Kennedy a Soto Zen? No. I've never trained him in Soto liturgy. Now you're moving into a club that has liturgy and forms."

"Which at one time were important enough to you that you chose to go through a rigorous training to learn them."

"For sure. And still is important. But I don't want to limit it to that."

---

52. Koryu Roshi was a Rinzai teacher.

53. The *Shobogenzo* or *Treasury of the True Dharma Eye* is a collection of essays written by Dogen in the 13th century. They form the basis of much of Soto academic teaching.

54. Skillful means.

## Robert Kennedy

"Zen can be practiced – as it almost always is – within a Buddhist framework," Bob Kennedy tells me. "There are monasteries that are Buddhist but dedicated to Zen practice as opposed to other forms of Buddhism. So in that way Zen can be seen as part of Buddhism, but it can also be seen as a practice that is open to anyone. Yamada Roshi made that very clear, that he was not trying to make me a Buddhist but to empty me, as he said, in imitation of my Lord, Jesus Christ, who emptied himself. He was quite clear. And many Catholic priests and nuns and Catholic lay people went to Yamada Roshi because he was open to us. He did not demand that we become Buddhist in that sense.

"What Christians believe about God, Yamada Roshi said, is he transcends human experience, and Zen has nothing to say about that. Zen should not say 'yes' or 'no' with regard to the existence of God, because Jews, Christians, Muslims believe God transcends human experience. It is a different order of being entirely about which we should not say anything. Glassman Roshi said that as well, that when he first encountered Zen he felt he was a Jewish atheist, and then gradually he realized, 'I can't say "yes" or "no" to this question. There's nothing in my Zen teaching or training that would have me say "yes" or "no" to the existence of God as Jews and Christians understand God, someone who transcends human experience.' Zen Buddhism is about human experience. They might question the legitimacy of faith in general, but if someone holds it, they should have nothing to say about it.

"Maezumi Roshi made it very clear that we should make Zen American. We should not imitate the Japanese. And it is not necessary to do so. I think the Japanese can't really be imitated anyway. They're a completely unique civilization. A wonderful civilization. But it's not our job to imitate them. Our job is to find a Zen that is open to American culture, American life. It is not necessary to wear Japanese robes in order to see your own nature. And it's not helpful finally. You're just creating something artificial in a practice that imitates the Japanese. Now some Zen people will disagree with this. But I would just say that Maezumi was clear that we were to do what he could not do, which was to make Zen American. And as soon as Maezumi died, Glassman, for example, said he became himself, not only Maezumi's student but his own man as an American interested in social issues in a way that, perhaps, Maezumi was not."

When I start to ask about possible conflicts between Buddhist and Christian cultural perspectives and the challenges that could arise when Buddhists and non-Buddhists practice together, Kennedy waves the issue aside.

"Don't start thinking about other people's ideas and other people's enlightenment. Develop your own. Put those thoughts aside. That's essential.

We should not be arguing with one another. That's the great thing about Zen. It cuts off argument and argumentation and dispute, trying to prove your point or disprove someone else's point. I think Zen brings peace finally and an end to that type of religious confrontation that leads nowhere. Nobody's ever converted by argument."

"We are all the products of cultural conditioning," I point out. "But, if I'm understanding you correctly, you're suggesting that by suspending – as much as possible – discursive thought, that regardless of our cultural, historic, or faith backgrounds there is some fundamental experience or awareness that we all have the capacity to access? Something like that?"

"More or less. Like any other talent, some people who are tone deaf aren't going to be musicians, or if they're color blind they aren't going to be painters. People have different capacities. But people who have this orientation and capacity can well sit together, profit from each other's experience, as I profited from Yamada and Maezumi. They were Buddhists. I'm Catholic. But they reached out and they helped me, and I try to do that with Buddhists and non-Buddhists. I sit with them and try to – as they say – appreciate the Great Function."

"So, just to be clear, a pre-discursive reality we all have the capacity to access regardless of our religious heritage?"

"Well, I think I'd say there is no *thing* that we share together. There is no thing. It is an appreciation of where you are and – this phrase they use sometimes – the Great Function. The unity of it. Once we start talking about *things*, then it divides us. You know, dogma will divide us. We're just saying, for this time when we sit, put that aside. And that's what we share together, that common openness. We will not name the object of our devotion. We will not give a name to ourselves. We let life enter into us as things are. Things as they really are. That's a good phrase from the Dharma – you know – 'things as they are.' Not as we imagine or wish them to be."

## Henry Shukman

"I don't really believe that Zen can be divorced from Buddhism," Henry Shukman muses. He is casually dressed in a t-shirt that's a little worn and stretched in the neck. Like most of the Sanbo Zen teachers I meet, he doesn't affect any special garb outside of the zendo or very much in it. "I think there was a time in the early 20th century – with the influence of D.T. Suzuki particularly – where you could kind of talk about Zen without having to consider it Buddhist. That Zen was some kind of an aesthetic, spiritual principle that popped up all over the place. Like R.H. Blyth writing about Zen and English literature."

"There are members of your lineage – like Elaine MacInnes – who practice Zen, in her case, as a Catholic."

"Yeah, but when she's teaching Zen, she's teaching Zen. I don't think she's trying to hybridize Christianity with Zen. I know a number of Christians who practice Zen, and I'm pretty sure that she just taught Zen. You know? But she happened to be a Roman Catholic and found no conflict."

"What about your students? Do you introduce them to Buddhist teachings here? As opposed to just introducing them to the physical and mental practice of meditation?"

"Yeah, that's an interesting question." He pauses and reflects a moment. "Zen, of course – generally speaking – doesn't go into, say, the *Abhidharma*[55] or many of the traditional Buddhist teachings. It does here and there. And you can tell in the koans that a lot of Buddhist teaching was in the background at the time. And I suspect that different masters relied on Buddhist doctrine to greater and lesser extents back in China in the Tang and Sung Eras. I certainly mention the Four Noble Truths,[56] the Five Desires,[57] the Three Characteristics of Existence.[58] The Eightfold Path. I use elementary Buddhist teachings quite a bit. I guess I only know elementary Buddhist teachings. I've been right through Zen training without being exposed to much more, except to the extent that I wanted to be. I've done a certain amount of study in other traditions too."

"So could a student here practice not necessarily Zen *Buddhism* but rather what I suspect Sister Elaine would simply call Zen?"

"Yes. I mean, I wear a rakusu, which officially means I'm a Buddhist, and a number of people here do. But most people don't. And there's no need to be formally a Buddhist here. But maybe the definition isn't only a formal one, if you see what I mean. I mean, maybe you can kind of consider yourself Buddhist in the sense you... you... uh... What's the word? Ascribe? Is that the word? No, subscribe to it – you subscribe to Buddhist values – kind of... take on Buddhist views..."

"You can acknowledge the value of the teachings?" a person sitting in on the conversation suggests, "in a kind of moral, spiritual realm without necessarily ascribing to the deism of Buddha?"

"Yeah," Henry agrees.

---

55. An analysis of the sutras by early Buddhist scholars.

56. See fnt. 50, p. 93 above.

57. Also called the Five Hindrances: Sensual desire, ill will, sloth, restlessness/worry, and doubt.

58. Cf. p. 21 above.

## Joan Sutherland

My first conversation with Joan Sutherland took place while she was still living in Santa Fe, the day after I visited Henry at the Mountain Cloud Zen Center. The area had once been agricultural, and her house is a remodeled barn. Because of the building's previous use, the ceiling is higher than expected and there is still what had been a hayloft window in its peak. There is an altar to Guanyin – the Chinese incarnation of Kannon – in one corner of the room, with an unlit stick of incense in a bowl. A large calligraphy of the word "Buddha" graces a wall. There are several other Buddhist touches but also a large votive painting of the archangel Santo Miguel. "We live here," she explains. "We have to pay attention to the local deities."

"Do you consider yourself Buddhist?" I ask.

"No. Um... and I... I answer that really quickly. That's interesting to me, that I said that so quickly. I think Buddhism is a gigantic tent, and I think it includes so much. It's such a vast array of different kinds of practices and beliefs and philosophies and all of that. So I may amend what I said. If the tent is large enough to include what I'm doing, then I'm a Buddhist. But I think that Chan and Zen have a somewhat ambivalent relationship with Buddhism, which I think is part of their creative strength. There's a creative tension between Chan and Zen and the rest of Buddhism."

"Last night when I met with Henry Shukman, he expressed some doubt that one could separate Zen from Buddhism. Would you disagree with that?"

"What are we speaking of when we say 'Buddhism'?"

"The large tent."

"The large tent? You cannot separate it. It's the way the Dharma flowered originally in China, but, when it came to China, it met a very old, very established, very beautiful tradition already in place. And so what happened in China was extremely different than what happened in India. It seems to me early Buddhism was focused a lot on getting off the Wheel of Samsara.[59] Of kind of getting out. And when the tradition or the Dharma came to China, that was a problem the Chinese didn't know they had. They weren't looking to get out. And I think that shift from something that was trying to get out of life to something that was trying to get deeper into life and have a more intimate relationship with life is a really, really big change. And if you can see Buddhism as encompassing all of that, then great."

"Let me put the question another way. Is what you're doing really Zen?"

"That's a really good question, and one I ask myself all the time. It depends

---

59. The wheel of rebirth.

upon what you mean by Zen. We were just talking a moment ago about a kind of spectrum from very traditional to – what should we say? – innovative, and I would put myself at the innovative end with a big caveat, which is that the innovation is based on my understanding of the deepest layers of the tradition. I studied Chinese and Japanese. I have a Master's in East Asian Languages. I read the texts in the original. I'm immersed in them. And it is out of my understanding of those very, very old roots that something new is developing. So I don't feel at all like I'm a break with the tradition. I feel like we here in our community are trying to find how that spirit is best expressed in 21$^{st}$ Century Santa Fe, New Mexico. So, to that extent, I want to claim – I would say Chan, rather than Zen, because that distinction means something to me – I want to claim a deep connection to that tradition. The thing that makes that difficult is that the way that we've inherited Zen in particular from Japan, I am not a part of. I've trained in it. I know it. And I choose – quite deliberately – not to be part of that mainstream. So does that mean I'm Zen or not Zen? I don't know."

"The ambiance in this room, of course, is very Buddhist – St. Michael excepted. So how do you decide which elements to retain and which to allow to… to blossom in other ways?"

"Do they serve the awakening of the participant? If they do, yeah If they don't, don't need 'em. Except for those that are simply beautiful, and that's a value. They get to stay on the basis of beauty."

"For the aesthetics?"

"Sometimes. You know, they're something people love that they're used to, and it's beautiful. It has no particular meaning, but they care about it, so we do it. But also then we watch. And there have been some things that dropped away that came back. And after the initial paring down, there were other things that left. I mean, we're always watching it."

## Rinsen Weik

I ask Rinsen Weik if the members of the Buddhist Temple of Toledo consider Buddhism a religion.

"Well, let's define our terms. As I understand it, it's critical – it's absolutely critical – but how I understand it is probably worth parsing a little bit. For me, my experience of the Dharma is religious. So what I mean by that, it's communal. It involves other people with a shared experience, with a shared language and ritual, with a shared sense of tradition and history and lineage. So for me that's the religious aspect of Zen. And the spiritual element of it is the individual's experience of it in their daily life kind of stuff. Okay? So that's how I parse the terms. Spiritual means my own individual realization and experience. Religion means doing that in some kind of community that's organized and structured. So, defined that way, I think that it's absolutely critical for kensho to make any difference in a person's life long-term it has to be encountered and integrated within a context of a community that has authentic connection to the lineage and practice over time. It takes time to take an individual insight in kensho experience – or even a deep samadhi experience – and integrate that into a life so life becomes more workable, not less, and one becomes more joyful and humble and not less. That's the religious part.

"So for me, what's important – before I start working on deep wisdom stuff and kensho and all this kind of stuff – is a person needs to know how to interact in harmony with other people. Big fuckin' deal to me. I am absolutely unwilling to go into the deep end of the pool with somebody who does not know how to not be an asshole. I won't go there. So our sangha covenant is actually about treating each other with worth and dignity and respect and all that kind of stuff. So we take refuge. We make a covenant as members to treat each other well, and we have that shared vow to do no harm, practice the Dharma, actualize good for others. And I wanna see that shit come off the stove and be edible before we're gonna go into the deep end because there's lots of evidence to say that a person can have a kensho experience and so what? – you know? – still be a complete jerk.

"So for me, why Buddhism is important is what it means to me as a person, as a long-term member of a lineage of accountability and transparency wherein we have a safe pressure-cooker so that these insights into emptiness and self-and-other and absolute-and-relative and all of that stuff can actually be helpfully integrated. And the other side to it is that religion has built into it ritual empowerments, initiations, rites of passage, and acknowledgement, and I think that people are deeply thirsting for that. I think that when people don't have that – depending how they're wired – there's a kind of a sickness that comes up because just to have your own so solitary, 'private Idaho' kind of deep experience for most people leaves the itch unscratched in some fundamental way. There's this deep need to be blessed and acknowledged and seen, and so, for me, religion – which means community practice over time – provides that.

"So, for example, we just had our Rohatsu[60] sesshin two days ago. We have a midnight ceremony on the last day of Rohatsu wherein new shoken[61] students are acknowledged. And it's a very beautiful ceremony. These folks have

---

60. The anniversary of the Buddha's enlightenment in December. The sesshin associated with this anniversary is considered the most daunting of the year.

61. Students who vow to work with a particular teacher exclusively.

done a year's initiation study, discernment, and formation before they're accepted as shoken students, and they've got a pre-req before they can do that. They have to have had the Precepts[62] for at least some years and demonstrably lived into them. And then – you know – they wear a grey robe. Suddenly they have a physical manifestation of this difference that shows up in community, that's actually really nourishing; it's as nourishing as taking the Precepts, like more in some ways. And then the next day we have a public acknowledgement of that. So the Sunday Sutra Service, the kids, the families, everybody's there – the much larger community – and we have a very formal acknowledgment of that recognition of a shoken student as an actual Zen student and practitioner. And so what ends up happening is that you've got a year's formation, then initiation; you've got an intense, rigorous sesshin which is only open to shoken students or shoken initiates, that's a very, very powerful sesshin – you know – long week, whatever it was, and then it culminates in this midnight ceremony which harkens to the transmission ceremonies.

"I consciously designed it that way because few people will get to experience that, so I take a few pages from the formal Dharma transmission playbook as I've inherited it and apply it to shoken initiation and empowerment. And then, significantly, there is the public acknowledgement. And then they all offer a poem; they're acknowledged; they receive their oryoki bowls and shoken covenant, which is different from the sangha covenant, and then – significantly – the sangha blesses that. And those that have done shoken – instead of me giving a talk that day – they each stand up and give encouragement and blessings to the new initiates. So all of this ends up with a lot of sleep deprivation, a lot of heartfelt laughing and crying and really doing the work. But by the end of it, someone actually has a ritually-empowered transformative experience which is palpable, and there's no question about what happened, *and* it's happened in a community of practice – the Sangha."

"And how would that be different from the ritual experience they might get from accepting Jesus Christ as their lord and savior?"

"I don't know, 'cause I've never done that," he says, laughing. "I can't say, you know? I can speculate – you know – I can speculate, someone has a sentimental experience. They're usually crashed; they're bottomed-out. They go to a service. There's the band; there's the music; it's in the right key; everybody gets emotional; they get up and have a moment. 'Anyone who wants to witness, stand forth.' A few people shakingly do, and I don't doubt that that's an important moment for them. But I don't know but I suspect that if we took a survey of how many of those people twenty years later are still deeply informed

---

62. Cf. fnt. 37, p. 68 above.

by that spontaneous and heartfelt moment, it might be less than Christians would hope it would be."

"There are people in your lineage who don't self-identify as being Buddhist," I point out.

"Oh, sure! Sure. Lots of 'em. My view on this, really, is that I have an experience, and my teacher had the confidence in me – all the way up to *inka*[63] – saying your experience is worth sharing and trustable. And so I see my job not to say what's true and what's right but to actually share publicly my practice and how I view things. And there are other ways to practice, and I bow to them – you know – like lay teachers. I'm absolutely convinced that it can be, and I would have no idea of how to do that because I've been teaching as a priest So I hold veneration for all paths that are worthy. I'm sure my approach has shadow sides and trouble spots like they all do, but if I am going to be authentic and honest and actually teach what I have, then my experience is the only guide I have."

"What distinguishes Zen from other Buddhist traditions?"

"The disciplines and rigors of sesshin, and the reality of kensho and awakening and satori as encountered and matured through the koan system. I mean, that is a completely unique thing. That's not happening – you know – in the Tibetan and the Vipassana and stuff."

"You just blew off the entire Soto school."

"Kinda. You know? But seriously, not really, no. You know, the forms we use are Soto. I like Dogen and I hold the Soto line in the lineage of Jiyu Kennett Roshi. But, again, for me, I gotta teach according to my experience. For my entire training experience, I practiced with Soto transmitted teachers who hold the Harada-Yasutani koan system either from Maezumi Roshi's successors or my transmitting teacher, James Ford Roshi, and some of his successors. So I think that if someone was a monastic for thirty years – right? – thirty years living in the same space, breathing the same air, eating the same food as the roshi... yeah... I think that shikan taza – only just sitting – coupled with a rigorous monastic life can produce a beautiful result, and I'll never know what that is because that's not been my trajectory. What I know is a full contact worldly life with a marriage, a child, a career and other interests and a mortgage mixed with kensho and sesshin and koans to refine and work with my life within a Bodhisattva's Vow base. So that's how I teach. That's what I see, and that's what I know. Same kind of thing like if someone brings up, 'What about ayahuasca? Or tripping? Isn't that the same thing as kensho?' It's like, 'Look. It's not part of my tradition. It's not part of my experience. I can't speak to it.' I can

---

63. Inka (*inka shomei*) – "Authorized seal proving attainment." Official transmission, especially in the Rinzai School. It is the recognition by a teacher that the student has completed training and is ready to teach.

say that some people who do that kind of thing end up with a far less workable life for their effort and so I really don't recommend it."

## Genro Gauntt

Genro Gauntt receives invitations from around the world to lead street retreats.

"Mostly it's Buddhist communities who have some relation with Zen Peacemakers who invite me. They've read Bernie's books, particularly *Bearing Witness* and *Instructions to the Cook*, and they've heard about other people having done them. There are other communities too, but they tend to be Buddhist. I'm trying to think… I've done them for completely non-Buddhist, non-religious groups, and you don't have to be a Buddhist to have a transformational experience. You know? The power of these really just cuts across the board. And so I'm glad that I was able to be with people who had no spiritual experience and no meditation practice and no aspiration; they just got totally blown away by the experience. There are some people I now recognize as street retreat leaders who are doing them a couple of times a year, some. I used to do like four or five a year sometimes and now I'm down to maybe two. Something like that. But they're always by invitation, because I don't go where the energy isn't. Right? And I know if it's just my idea – you know – just my idea from my little self going, 'I wanna do it here,' it's not gonna work. But I respond to the invitations. I always say 'yes.'"

"And are these street retreats something that run parallel to your Buddhist practice or do you see them as part of that practice?"

"I don't consider myself a Buddhist."

"Yeah. I realized I'd made a presumption as soon as I said it. I should have seen that coming. But you do identify yourself as a teacher in a Zen Buddhist lineage. So, do you look at this as part of your Zen practice?"

"I look at it as part of my life-practice. It's more than Zen. For me, for many years my life has been more than Zen. My spiritual life I've had – and continue to have – many teachers from many traditions who I really love and honor and strive to imitate. So my spiritual base is huge. To call myself a Buddhist would be to limit myself. So I'm a human being with huge aspiration and know that I don't know anything, and I'm still tryin' to figure out who I am and what I do. When I teach these days, I'm not just teaching Zen sutras or texts or commentaries or any of that in the old way. I can do it, but I don't. And I never prepare myself for any talk. I walk into a room, whatever it is, and just go with whatever comes. I love to speak that way. That way I'm being taught at the same time. And I'm responding to a lot of energies coming from the heart.

So lots of traditions and lots of teaching paths are coming through me.

"We were at Auschwitz once for a Bearing Witness retreat, and we were in a Christian group doing Christian services. We do services every day. They can be Buddhist services and Christian services and Jewish services and maybe Muslim services. So people can attend any religious services they like, and most people have never gone to any other tradition. So it's a great opportunity for wideness, openness. But the priest! – wonderful priest, German priest who lives at Auschwitz and has lived there for twenty years now; he says it's his vocation to be there and hold open dialogue with anybody who comes – he was going around the circle and saying, 'What's your practice? What's your tradition?' Most people say, 'I'm a Catholic,' 'I'm a Buddhist,' 'I'm a Presbyterian,' 'I'm a Jew.' And he said, 'Genro, how about you?' And I said, 'I believe everything.'"

"What about the people you work with, do they identify you as a Zen teacher?"

"Many. Sure. Of course. That's how they identify me. I mean if I'm doing sesshin, I wear a black skirt and a shirt and a rakusu and do liturgy. I love all that stuff. It was foundational for me. But I also do Indigenous things with Lakota and other American Indian tribes and Brazilian Amazon tribes. For me, the form is so wide and beautiful. I love them all. I really love them all. And I can feel them all."

## Rebecca Li

"Buddhism doesn't need to be thought of as a religion," Rebecca Li tells me. "I often like to think of it this way: Buddhism has a religious aspect to it. So like I was mentioning how in all faith traditions there is the faith aspect. So in Buddhism there are people who find it very useful to also include the faith aspect of Buddhism. For example, putting their faith in a Bodhisattva who is out there, who will help protect them, support them in their endeavors. For some people that is useful. That's comforting. And especially for many people when they're in very challenging situations, like when they need that, when they are struggling with disease and they've done everything but it still feels they're not able to cope with it on their own, so that's comforting. So that's the religious aspect of any faith tradition including Buddhism.

"But most people that I encounter don't come to these retreats looking at it as a religious activity. Some people will find a psychological aspect of teaching sort of has helped them make it accessible. I think that's why a lot of American Zen/Chan teachers use that. It's like when Buddhism went to China, it sort of incorporated a Daoist lingo to make it accessible to the Chinese. And for here nowadays – 21$^{st}$ century in the West – I think the psychological explanation, or at least the language, psychological language, it's what helps make the Dharma accessible for many people. But I don't think people are looking for a psychological exercise. They weren't thinking they were coming to get some kind of counselling. They want to learn how to engage in a practice they can do on their own."

"So they are looking at Chan as a type of life practice but not necessarily a religious or psychological practice?"

"Yes. It's a life practice like learning how to let their life be transformed by the practice. I like a phrase a retreatant a couple of weeks ago mentioned. She called it 'more intentional.' And I think it's a good way to put it, how to talk about it, how to turn it into a verb; it's like you cultivate this clear awareness of what's going on in your mind, what's pushing you around, and then you can choose every moment you live your life. So they live life more intentionally."

### Bodhin Kjolhede

Bodhin Kjolhede is Philip Kapleau's successor at the Rochester Zen Center. His hair is short but not shaved off, and he is dressed in a navy blue short-sleeve shirt with a banded color and matching slacks. The other people I see at the Center are similarly dressed. "As part of the process of adapting Zen to the west, my teacher – Roshi Kapleau – and I didn't feel inclined to maintain the Japanese samugi," he explains. "We chose something more western, but we also wanted a way to distinguish those who were ordained. So we came up with this." Unlike a samugi, it is something one could wear on the street without appearing too foreign or exotic.

I ask him if Buddhism is a religion in the same way that, for example, Catholicism is a religion.

"Well, we get into semantics. It depends upon how you define religion. If you define religion as positing a Supreme Being, an omniscient, omnipresent Supreme Being, then no. Zen isn't a religion in that sense. It's not a theistic religion. But if you understand religion as based on faith, faith in what cannot be apprehended through the senses and the intellect, a faith in what is beyond our normal faculties for knowing things, then I see Zen as a religion. It can be, but it doesn't have to be – and this gets me back to what I said earlier – that there are people who just want to do the meditation, without the religion. And that's fine with me. They can use it as a concentration practice, and that's great. But I think that's a very limited way of practicing Zen."

"Just to be clear here, are you saying that it's possible to practice Zen without being a Buddhist, formally, although perhaps as the insight deepens one becomes a Buddhist in fact without taking the Precepts or whatever? In other words, can you separate Zen as a practice from Buddhism as a tradition, whether we call that tradition a religion or not?"

"I think so. I think anyone who crosses his legs and follows his breath is practicing Zen, but they may not be a Buddhist. Is that what you mean?"

"So one could come to the Rochester Zen Center, be committed to one's practice, enter into koan training with you, might, perhaps, flourish. But would not necessarily at any point in that process declare themselves a Buddhist per se."

"I think that's quite possible. I think it's unlikely. But it is possible. No where along the line would I say, 'Well, you have to make a claim as to what your religion is.' If you're Buddhist or not. It just isn't an issue. I think a lot of people when they come here for the first time – we have these introductory workshops – when they come for the first time, most people would not consider themselves Buddhist. But they want to do the practice. They want to join with us in the zendo to do Zen meditation. And I suspect – and this was true for me, too – they find the principles of Buddhism, the doctrine, more and more believable, that the doctrine matches their experience the longer they go along. And they just sort of ease into being Buddhist, and maybe someday they're sitting at a job application, and they might say, 'Well, I guess I am a Buddhist. I'll put that down.'"

## David Loy

I ask David Loy, "Is Zen necessarily Buddhist?"

"I'm not sure that Buddhism is necessarily Buddhist. You remember the famous story about the raft? The Buddha compared his Dharma to a raft to help ferry us across the river of life and death, but when you get to the other side you can discard the raft. The whole point of the Buddhist tradition, certainly including Zen, is to go beyond itself. All the Buddha's teachings are heuristic in the sense that they are there to help us to realize something, to transform. The teachings of Buddhism are not scripture; they're not sacred; they're not revelation. They're a roadmap. They're a guidebook to help us go somewhere. And whether we identify as a Buddhist or a Zen practitioner is not the important issue. The issue is, are we following that guidebook? And the other interesting thing, of course, is that there are a lot of other guidebooks out there in different traditions, Buddhist and non-Buddhist, and there are certainly places where they seem to overlap a lot.

"You know, Sanbo Zen is a lay organization and, in truth, in Japan it is very small and has almost no influence. But perhaps largely because of *The Three Pillars of Zen* book, it became very well known in the West, and Yamada Roshi had a number of international students, most from Europe, who also lived in Kamakura. Yamada didn't have a temple or monastery, he just knocked down half his home and built a zendo there. Some of us would practice with him in the evenings as well as doing the scheduled full-day sits and sesshin. He definitely was hoping to spread Zen to the West, and, typically, he believed that Zen was dead in Japan." He considers a moment. "Well, he would obviously know a lot more about that than I do. But I don't know that the problem with Zen is any different than the problem with any other institutionalized religion. Frankly, I don't have a very high opinion of Japanese Buddhism in general. Whether it's dead or not I couldn't say, but certainly it's very institutionalized. And there's still this big question of how important Buddhist monasticism will be here in North America. I think the emphasis on meditation for lay people is a very hopeful development. As a scholar of religion, I'm constantly struck by how the institutionalization often loses or devalues the original impetus."

"Well, the first responsibility of any institution is to maintain itself."

"Exactly. And the original idea would be that the institution is necessary to preserve and promote the teachings, the work, of the founder. But, of course, what happens is at a certain point the institution and the people in charge of the institution can't distinguish between what's good for the institution and what's good for the teachings. That's the fundamental problem that recurs just about everywhere. And I think it occurred in Buddhism too."

## Shinge Chayat

Back at Dai Bosatsu, Shinge Chayat says something similar. We meet in a room with western furniture. Her dog is curled up at her feet as she sits on a couch. Before we begin, a young robed monk comes in with a tea tray. After placing it, he does a full prostration before turning to leave.

I ask her how important she considers the Japanese cultural elements here to be.

"There are people who come here because of their love of Japanese culture as well as how it is manifesting in the path of Zen. And there are many people who are returning to an appreciation of religion as opposed to vague spirituality. They may have been Catholic at some point or Jewish, but there's something about Buddhism they immediately relate to. And the devotional aspect of Buddhism has not been at the forefront of America meditation life, and I think that now the time is coming where people can feel that sense of reverence, and so that – for example – when I'm asked by students when I give a talk, 'Is Zen really a religion or is it a philosophy?' I say, 'Yes.' Because it isn't either/or. And depending on your motivation you may feel some very deep stirrings of a devotional Buddhist sort, and we're there to provide the container for that, and to guide you into a deeper oneness with the Buddhist teachings that can't be gotten when you want to stay away from anything that seems like religion. So I think there's a need for what we're offering. Whether it's going to stay that way after I'm gone, whether the Japanese aspect will still continue, will probably depend upon future leaders."

"Can one practice Zen like most people practice yoga without any connection to its Hindu roots? Can Zen be separated from its Buddhist matrix?"

"I know people who want to do that, and who start out doing that. But really when you have an experience in Zen, it's a religious experience."

"Does one necessarily identify it as a Buddhist experience?"

"What's Buddhist? What is 'Buddhism'? The '-ist' and the '-ism' have very little to do with the awakening process. That awakening is Buddha. So you become Buddha."

"So the focus or goal of Zen is awakening, however defined, rather than any adherence to a particular teaching or philosophy?"

"The 'either/or' doesn't work here. I'll tell you why. The goal – if you want to use that word, which, of course, we don't – is to awaken, but not just to have some experience. To awaken in a way that then you are following the Buddha's path. You are following a path of caring for all beings, really looking at the unbelievable number of delusions you have that make you self-absorbed so that you cannot care for others. So you are investigating the Dharma deeply; you're investigating what those teachings are from your own awakened mind. Think about the vows [64] and the fourth, which is to walk the Buddha's path. These four vows are primary whether you consider yourself a Buddhist or not."

"So just to be clear. I could do this, I could enter into this work with you, but at no point would I be expected to declare myself a Buddhist?"

"If you wanted to take the Precepts..."

"Which would be my choice," I say, interrupting her.

"Yes. It would be your choice. And we put the Precepts in the context of Buddhism, of what the teachings of Buddha are, and following them, following those Precepts, would make you a 'Buddhist.' But, again, the '-ist' is not important. The '-ism' is not important. Become a Buddha. Become fully awake. Live that awakened life. The Buddha gave good teachings about how to do that. The Eightfold Path really works. But we don't want Buddha to become an ideology.

---

64. The Four Bodhisattva vows, frequently chanted in Zen Centers of all lineages. This is the form I became familiar with at the Montreal Zen Center: "All beings without number, I vow to liberate; endless blind passions, I vow to uproot; Dharma gates beyond measure, I vow to penetrate; the great way of Buddha, I vow to attain."

We want awakened mind and compassionate action to define you. If you want to call that Buddhist, okay."

# 5
# COMPASSIONATE ACTION

One of the Japanese protocols retained in many Zen centers is the practice of honoring the zendo – the room or hall in which meditation formally takes practice – by bringing the palms of the hands together in "gassho" and bowing before entering. Likewise, before leaving the zendo, one turns back and bows once more. At the Montreal Zen Center, where I practiced for many years, Albert Low modified this tradition by having people, when leaving, stop at the door and not turn around but, instead, bow out. It was a simple way of stressing that the practice in the zendo only has value if it impacts the way in which one behaves outside the zendo. The classical descriptions of Zen emphasize that it cultivates prajna (wisdom) and karuna (compassion) equally.

### Diane Fitzgerald

Diane Fitzgerald is the founder and resident teacher of Zen DownEast in Pembroke, Maine. She tells me that, in her opinion, compassion naturally follows from the attainment of wisdom.

"For me, the expression of practice is engagement. And while some people may find it sufficient to sit on the cushion and go to retreats and live a quiet contemplative life – and it's not my position to criticize them – but for me as a teacher and the students I work with, the natural outcome of realizing nonduality is also realizing the truth of compassion. And we really need to manifest it; that's the activity of emptiness, to be in the world and do what we can."

## Yoshin Radin

As with Mitra Bishop's Mountain Gate in New Mexico, there is no signage identifying the Zen Center located on the Lieb Road in Spencer, New York, south of Ithaca. One has to know that mailbox 56 marks the drive. Still, people find their way here.

Yoshin Radin, the resident teacher, grew up in New York, where he attended Jewish Parochial School. "It kept me out of bars and brothels." After graduating high school, he went on a trip around the world and, in places like Hawaii and India, discovered hashish and LSD. As with many others in the '60s and '70s, it led to an interest in spirituality. He did a sesshin at the San Francisco Zen Center, but the experience was "unfruitful. A lot of pain and no intelligence." Then a friend in Canada suggested he try a retreat at Mount Baldy with Joshu Sasaki. There he found his path.

"I think one of the problems with Zen teaching in America – at least the circles that I've bumped into – is that there's not enough heart in it. There's not enough love in the teaching. The teaching is do this form; do this; count your breathing; and this and that. But I think it's so much more to teach people that they can escape from the misery that their mind is creating and that by realizing certain things it's possible to take care of your mind by practicing kindness. By forgiving people. By not thinking you can undo your pain by hurting people who hurt you. Really fundamental kindness ideas that I think are absent in certain dry Zen places. I still have hippie blood."

I have no doubt about Yoshin's sincerity, but I am also aware that the teacher he admires unwaveringly – Joshu Sasaki – is one of those controversial teachers who were responsible for a great number of people falling away from Zen practice in the 1980s and '90s when stories about the inappropriate sexual behaviour, sumptuous lifestyles, and fiery tempers of teachers were rife and tainted Zen's image in the west.

## David Loy

It could be argued that compassion isn't always exhibited through kindness, but it is more difficult to dismiss the sexual predation which occurred at far too many centers during the early years of Zen practice in the west. Mitra Bishop had told me that this form of behavior was evidence that those guilty of it hadn't completed their training. The wisdom that comes from "kensho isn't anywhere near complete," she said, "until we have integrated that into our daily life so that everything we do or say or think accords with what we've realized. Kensho has to manifest in our daily life to be of any value whatsoever."⁶⁵

David Loy makes a similar point. "Something that Yamada Roshi emphasized very much is that every genuine kensho is spontaneously accompanied by the arising of compassion. And I've noticed that in the students that I've passed on Mu."

I ask how he accounts for those teachers for whom that did not seem to have been the case.

"That's an important question. What is it that gets in the way of compassionate action? I think it's very simple. Ego. Which is to say I think that there are some people running around teaching Zen whose experience is not very deep, or at least not integrated thoroughly enough into how they actually live. It's one thing to have an experience. It's something else to transform our very deep-rooted, mostly self-preoccupied, self-centered, habitual ways of thinking, feeling, and reacting to other people. To be frank, I've been in this racket long enough to see plenty of cases where the experiences that people have had haven't really changed them very much in the sense of reducing ego. Enlightenment becomes more food for the ego, one more thing to be proud of. I wonder if that points to a fundamental problem in the tradition, that we emphasize so much the moments of enlightenment, while there's relatively little emphasis upon, 'Okay, how does that actually transform how we live in the world?'

"In my own tradition there was a lot of talk about the importance of integration, that kensho/enlightenment was not enough in and of itself. But I don't remember that there was actually much done about that. I think the idea was that if you continue to practice then that will eventually take care of itself. But it doesn't always happen. I think one of the important developments in the last generation of Zen and Buddhism generally is the realization that zazen, meditation practice by itself, might not be enough. Back in the early 1970s, when I started, we had the idea that if you just sat long enough and hard enough all that psychological stuff would clean up naturally. And we can see now that that's not always true. John Welwood⁶⁶ made an important contribution with his concept of 'spiritual bypassing,' how our emphasis on enlightenment and so forth can actually reinforce some of our problematical psychological tendencies. There's been the realization that other types of practices, including Buddhist-informed psychotherapy, can play important roles in our spiritual maturation.

"I love the Zen tradition. In fact, I deeply appreciate all the Buddhist traditions. But it's not enough just to import Asian Buddhist traditions into the

---

65. Cf. p. 55 above.

66. An American clinical psychologist and practitioner of Tibetan-style Buddhism.

West or into global modernity. We need to be creative in terms of how we integrate Buddhist teachings and practices."

## Rebecca Li

Rebecca Li is a Professor of Sociology at the College of New Jersey and Director of the Alan Dawley Center for the Study of Social Justice.

"I remember Master Sheng Yen told me how the teachers at that time vowed to bring Buddhism to the US, and they believed that it would actually make it better. And so I think that's exactly what happened. Buddhism before the first part of the 20$^{th}$ century largely had been taught in these very homogeneous cultures. And so they developed in this mode and largely they did do well in accommodating a particular set of characteristics in certain cultures. But that means that if you live in those cultures and you don't have those characteristics, you won't find the Dharma very accessible – the way it was institutionalized in those times – but when the Dharma came to the United States, the marvelous thing about here, especially the development in the last couple of decades, is the utter cultural diversity here meant that teachers had to teach in a way that's not speaking to one culture. And I also think the recent years' discussion of identity explicitly – it's always been around – and the effort to push Dharma centers to pay more attention to that is really healthy for the development of Buddhadharma. Again, because think about it: a lot of the teaching activity – practice activities – are designed for certain kinds of characteristics, able-bodied or the gender segregation of a lot of practice center settings designed for this very traditional culture."

"Right off the top of my mind I can't think of any practice centers which are segregated by gender. Is that still common?"

"In a lot of Asian countries they are."

"But in North American centers?"

"At the Dharma Drum centers, the dorms are separate by gender. The dining hall in Chan settings are separate by gender. And so that's what's brought over from Taiwan. So in my retreat, I can actually arrange the setting, then the participants they sit together. Of course, participants don't say anything; they just don't come back when they don't feel comfortable. But I'm very lucky that I have a participant who's transgender who told me afterwards that the retreat was very good, but they would not recommend it to their friends because of the challenges in navigating that space. And so I created a gender-neutral bathroom in the Chan hall, but there is still quite a lot of emphasis on gender. So I think it's healthy for the institutions in Buddhism to pay attention to these issues."

## Ruben Habito

Ruben Habito's community in Dallas is called the Maria-Kannon Zen Center.

"Maria-Kannon is a figure in Japanese history when the Christians were persecuted, and they could no longer profess their faith openly, so they had to destroy or hide all their images of Jesus or the Holy Family or of the Virgin Mother that were of Western origin. So they found this feminine image of compassion in the Buddhist figure of Kannon, and they put it up on their altar and then they would recite the rosary before it. For them, it was Mary, the Mother of Jesus, but it was Kannon in public understanding.

"It is really Mary who stood at the cross of Jesus. The *Stabat Mater* is the image of Mary's compassion, bearing the wounds of her son who bears the wounds of the world, and so that compassion, of bearing the wounds of the world, is what is seen as the place of intersection with Kannon in the Buddhist tradition. And so there is the hope that we have, that those who sit in Zen are able to activate that seed of compassion in them symbolized by Mary and by Kannon."

Ruben admits that while his teacher, Yamada Koun, had demonstrated a balance between prajna and karuna in his life and in his teaching, still "the sociological face of Japanese Zen is quite another thing. It's entrenched in certain traditional formalities and hierarchical structures that may present certain obstacles to a ready way of addressing the problems of the world."

"What do you mean by that?"

"Well, in a sense, the received tradition that gets emphasized is open your eyes first. In short, experience enlightenment first by putting yourself wholeheartedly into your Zen practice, and then when you get enlightened you can go on to change the world. But before you do that, you have to really take care of yourself first. So that effort in 'making the breakthrough' takes most of the time in a life of Zen practice, and very little emphasis is given to the outflow, the expected and natural outflow, namely a life of compassion.

"Well," he continues, "the teachers want to give the practitioners what they consider the best of what Zen has to offer, namely that inner transformative experience that brings inner joy and inner peace. And so that becomes a focus and very little time and energy is left for the kind of Zen that also engages itself in the world. But if you recall, Robert Aitken, who is one of our elder Dharma Brothers in the Sanbo Zen lineage, is one of the founders of the Buddhist Peace Fellowship. So he was one of those who really brought his Zen practice to bear in a way of life that seeks to also connect with healing the wounds of the world. So, in that regard, it does come from the practice, and there are people who have been able to embody it in a more prominent way than others."

## Joan Sutherland

The Zen boom in North America coincided with a period of vigorous political activism. Young people challenged contemporary mores and questioned traditional American institutions. Many aggressively fought for an end to military induction, racial disparity, and the disenfranchisement of women. In Hawaii, Robert Aitken supported environmentalism, established the Buddhist Peace Fellowship, and encouraged his female students to examine the role of women in what remained a male-dominated practice both in Asia and North America. But Aitken was an exception. Elsewhere, Zen students were discouraged from taking part in activism.

"We inherited most of our Zen from Japan," Joan Sutherland explains, "and Japanese Zen had just been through a terrible trauma where they had aligned themselves with the imperial project in World War Two and pretty much destroyed Zen in Japan. So what we inherited was kind of a corpse. So I think there was a cultural reticence to get involved in politics because of what had happened in Japan. That's part of it. I think another part of it was that those teachers were dealing in the spheres they felt comfortable in and declining to deal with the spheres that they felt less comfortable in. And they made the mistake – either in themselves or in the way they taught – of conflating what they were comfortable with with Zen. But they are not the same thing. Zen exists mostly in the spaces we're not comfortable. But the way it came here in that first generation, it was people dealing within their comfort zones."

There is also, she points out, "the very American thing that people want transformation without having to change.

"It begins, I think, with a real thing, which is human suffering and a desire to not suffer, and that's real. I don't want to minimize it or say it's wrong. And people often want a short-cut when they want something, a bolt from the blue to come and change everything and make it okay without having to do the really hard work of integrating the bolts from the blue we get into our daily lives and changing as people. And the changes are hard. They're painful. They take a long time. They show us all the places where we have fissures in our geology and our faults and our weaknesses. And a lot of people don't want to go there. So I think that's part of it, not wanting to do what I call the 'endarkenment' work, the work of really coming to understand your soul. And also there's a fear of the 'enlightenment' part – we'll call it – where there is a fear of loss of self. People complain about the tyranny of the self and they're so unhappy in their selves and they're trying to change it, but if you say, 'Okay, let's take your self away,' they're like, 'Wait a minute! Hold on! I'm not sure I signed up for that.' And that I think is almost a biological fear of the organism, of not existing anymore.

So there's a fear that if they have these kinds of experiences they won't exist, they'll go mad, they won't be able to function in their daily lives, and all that. And that's where you see so many people hanging from the cliff edge by their fingernails not wanting to let go because they're afraid of the fall. So that's what I meant about wanting the transformation without having to do the really hard work. So then that feeds into what we were saying about some of the koan traditions. There wasn't an emphasis on realizing it in the sense of making it real in your life. There was an emphasis on realizing in the sense of having the big experience but then not doing the work of integrating it. And that, to me, is what koan work is really about. There's sort of that initial fireworks stuff at the beginning, and then there's this long process of integration. And where those two worlds aren't held separately, they inform each other. That, too, is hard and long and arduous, but wonderful."

Now that Zen has become more common in the west, teachers put more emphasis on the social implications of the practice. Joan tells me she is interested in what long-time practitioners can bring to the table for the benefit of others. "Not in terms of a list of things we should be doing but in terms of how do we do them."

"Do you think Zen practitioners address social issues differently than other people do?"

"So, for example, 'Not-knowing mind.' If you come into a situation with 'not-knowing mind' versus a sense that you already know the answers and we just have to get there, that's really going to make a big difference. And it's *possible* that we would have skills or tendencies or just practice doing things that tend to defuse situations, have a bigger view, be more interested in what the other has to say about it. Not so divisive. I don't know, but that's what I've seen in my own life with my own students.

"The philosopher, Richard Rorty, made a wonderful distinction between fundamentalism and non-fundamentalism. He said that fundamentalisms are religions or belief systems which base everything 'according to.' According to the book, according to the guide, according to the teachings. And non-fundamentalisms base everything on 'searching for.' So in an 'according to' system, you already know what's true, and you're trying to make the world conform to that. In the 'searching for' system you're endlessly alive to what's possible and how things change and how you can flow with that. Things are always changing. So we approach things not with the understanding that we're certain about them going in, but we come with a question: 'What is this?' The basic koan question: 'What is this?' And if we are really alive to the answers that come when we ask, 'What is this?' you end up with a completely different relationship to the situation. First of all, you're acknowledging that you're a participant and that you are willing to have your mind changed, willing to learn things. Even the things you hold most preciously you hold provisionally, and you're open to new information coming in. Which is, of course, fundamental Mahayana and acknowledgement of the other. And in the koan tradition, it is a desire, a delight in the other, what the other might say, how the other might surprise you. So that's a different kind of orientation.

"We used to talk about it in my community in Santa Fe as having an attitude of warmth and curiosity. Curiosity towards things. Doing a lot of listening. Not trying to arrive at a predetermined outcome, but looking for what outcome arises out of the situation when you let it. After all, you can never know what the right thing is. In the dominant culture in America, there's such an emphasis on certainty and getting it right and figuring out what the steps are. But you can never get anything 'right,' because you don't know what 'right' means. We don't know the karmic consequences of everything that happens. So it seems like a foolish pursuit to look for what's 'right.' Instead, I encourage people to look for, 'What is the most beautiful mistake you can make in this situation?' If everything you're going to do is going to be a mistake in some way – which it will, because we can't possibly gain out all the consequences – what is the most beautiful mistake you can make? What's the mistake you care most about and would like to try? And this changes your whole orientation from trying to bend reality to your belief system to really trying to see which way the Dao is going, see what's possible in this situation. Every situation is unprecedented, so what is this situation calling for?"

"Are there no limitations to – as you put it – holding the things one most cares about provisionally?"

"No limitations."

"So then are you suggesting that one shouldn't necessarily assume, for example, that sexism is a bad thing?"

"Okay, so then you get into the territory of your best guess. So my best guess is that sexism is bad, and it feels like a pretty important guess and so I'm gonna act on that. But I also hold it provisionally. I also know that I can't know for sure, that I can't be certain, but that doesn't change how my heart feels about it."

"There's a book I read recently, Yuval Harari's *Sapiens*," I tell her. "And one of the propositions he puts forth is that human society developed in part out of our ability to create fictions, what lawyers call 'legal fictions.' So, for example, money is a fiction; it isn't anything concrete or real – like, say, beaver pelts or eggs or bamboo stalks – but it's the belief in these fictions that allows people to act collectively. If we all agree that money exists, we can exchange goods and services which otherwise we'd have to barter for. He also argues that human rights are a fiction, in the sense that they don't exist in nature. There's a line in the *Dao De Jing* that I've always been struck by: 'The Dao is not human-hearted.' Human rights are a fiction that we, as a species, have created and that a large number of people have come to accept. But there is nothing in the biology of the animal that supports the concept of the equal rights of individuals. There isn't even – from a cosmological point of view – any need to assume that human beings as a species are any more important than nematodes."

"Yes. All of that is a construct or an agreement, and – boy! – in the contemporary world, that agreement's falling apart. We don't necessarily have that agreement so much anymore about human rights. That doesn't mean that you don't care about it or work to extend it in the world if your best guess is that this is a good thing, that this will enhance the sum total of human happiness. So I want to be really clear that I'm not talking about either nihilism – that nothing matters – or a passivity like, you know, there's nothing to do. The much more difficult thing is to say, 'I may not be right. I'm holding this provisionally, and I'm gonna go ahead and do this anyway because it's how I'm made.' And that's where awakening comes in, because awakening, I think, changes how you're made, and there's some things that become just… impossible. You know? You're just not going to go buy a blood diamond because you're not made that way anymore."

"So does awakening inevitably lead to a particular political/social perspective?"

"I don't see it as political. It may line up with certain things that are political, but I don't think of it as political. I think of it as a kind of natural expression of bodhicitta – really – and if that happens to line up with a particular platform, that feels coincidental to me."

I had read a magazine article in which Joan had been quoted to say that the results of practice might lead to political engagement because, over time, there tends to be a deepening sense of gratitude for the fact of existence and for what she called "interpermeation" – a term she chose over "interconnectedness" because she felt it conveyed a fuller sense of the way in which our actions impact one another. Gratitude, in this sense, is less an emotion than it is a way of living which expresses itself through generosity. I ask her if that is still her belief. She says that it may have been stated in an idealized fashion but it remains something she holds onto "as an aspiration."

"So how does gratitude arise from practice?" I ask.

"There's a little bit of a mystery to that for me. When I was teaching and working with people, and people would have opening experiences, what became obvious to me over time was that one of the diagnostics about whether they were having a true opening experience… Or… Can I say that a different way? One of the diagnostics about where they were in the opening experience was the presence or absence of gratitude. It just seems to always come up once an opening reaches a certain depth. And if a person wasn't experiencing that gratitude, that – to me – was a sign that we had more to do. There was further to go. They were in a threshold place where there were other factors at play. So this is empirical but not scientific. I came to see that at a certain point in peoples' awakening gratitude appeared naturally, that it was the emotional response to awakening."

## Patrick Gallagher

Patrick Gallagher is a Dharma heir of Sister Elaine MacInnes in the Sanbo Zen tradition.

"When people have some kind of awakening experience," he tells me, "it's just the beginning. That's the beginning of the work; not the end of the work. So you have to really nourish that and feed it and work on it. You're not transformed instantly into St. Francis. You're still the same miserable cuss you were before. You need to work on your practice.

"Sometimes it will come up in the dokusan room, people will ask, 'What does this have to do with my life off the cushion?' It doesn't come up that often, but it does come up. And it's a live question, because – as I tell people often – if it doesn't have an impact in our lives, if it doesn't make a difference to how we live our lives, it's just an eccentric hobby. And most people want more than an eccentric hobby. They want to be at the very least better wives or husbands or better neighbors. Sometimes they want to do more or they're called to do more. They want to participate in the larger social body in a way that comes out of their practice. And so it becomes a live issue for people. Not at first usually but later."

## Rinsen Weik

In the course of one of my conversations with Rinsen Weik I ask him to define his role as a Zen teacher. "What's your job description? What do you do?"

"I practice the Buddhadharma. That's what I do. And I allow students to practice with me. And I make my practice public in a certain way. And I make the content of my practice more or less available for others to interface with depending on our student-teacher relationship."

"'Practice' is one of those words we use a lot, but I'm not sure it means exactly the same thing to everybody. What do you mean by it?" He doesn't immediately reply. "What are you practicing?" I prompt. "You're a jazz guitarist;

if you tell me you're practicing in that context, I know what you're doing. You're running scales up and down the fret board or something. What is it you're practicing – and allowing others to interface with – as a Zen teacher?"

"That's a hard question actually. I mean, practicing the Dharma is one thing. Practicing as a teacher is something a little different. So, huh, let's play with that for a little bit. What is it to practice the Dharma to start with? We'll start with that one. So I think the word points to the fact that this is something that's experiential. It's not something that's just intellectual. It's not something that's just a cognitive grasping. It's something that you actually have to embody. You have to manifest it experientially. So to me, the word 'practice' implies..." He searches for the term he wants. "'Performance' wouldn't be the right word, but it's close to performing. It's actually manifesting the Dharma. Actualizing the Dharma. Making it happen. So practicing the Dharma means making it part of how we actually move through the world, how we live through the day. It has to show up in the context of the day. Now what is the 'it' that's showing up or not? Right? Well, I guess one way to talk about it would be equanimity, compassion, wisdom, creativity. I could point to the paramitas.[67] This kind of thing. There are a lot of convenient lists that I could rely on."

"What you didn't include in that description of practice is plunking down on a cushion twice a day for twenty-five minutes or so. So whatever practice is, it's not just that."

"Oh God no! No-no-no-no. So there's a difference between practice and training. So that's a formal way of practicing, like home practice. Right? So I have my zafus hanging out here, and I'll sit in the morning, every morning except the mornings I don't. So that's a formal practice. When I sit on the cushion, it's referring to all the years I've spent on retreat and all the hours engaged and all that. But in the beginning stages of Zen practice that's like tuning the guitar. That's like getting everything together and getting ready. The tune starts when I leave and go into the day. And in my case, I'm a professor and – you know – stuff happens. So it's important to have formal practice and a way for a person to touch into and integrate training as a stepping stone between training and just living daily life. So the thing is, you train in formal settings with the teacher under austere or rigorous circumstances. Okay? Sesshin. Then you go home and practice. Or even if you come to temple here and you come to a Sunday Sutra Service, that's practicing. Then, daily home sitting, that's formal practicing. But then there's practicing with the way you deal with the barista making your coffee and the sudden and difficult conversation at the office or whatever it is. And that's where the rubber actually hits the road. In the later

---

67. Cf. fnt. 49., p. 92 above.

stages of Zen training however, there's no gap between the cushion and daily life at all. So, it depends where one is in the stages of Zen training."

## Koun Franz

"You told me that what you were interested in was maturity, and that Zen provides a vehicle by which people can grow up in a profound way," I remind Koun Franz. "What's the value of that type of maturity?"

He takes a deep breath that is almost a sigh. "I think – and this connects with what I was saying about the model of the Bodhisattva – the shape of this practice is that in some way or another, you're offering each action and accumulatively you're offering your life – right? – you're living the opposite of a self-centered life. Now the people who come in and want to argue with me about philosophy, we can have a great discussion about whether that has any inherent utility or whether we should just say, 'Screw it,' and eat up all the pie that we can. But to me there's such obvious benefit in stepping away from a self-focused view that I don't really need – in my mind – to write the rest of that essay."

"Okay, so give me an example of that self-evident benefit."

"I mean, if I'm raising kids and my thoughts are primarily about me and how it affects me, I'm not going to benefit my kids. We just apply that to everything."

"Being concerned about my own kids doesn't necessarily mean I'm going to be concerned about your kids. In fact it might be quite the opposite."

"But that's the same. All that is is you're identifying with your kids. So now your kids are you. It's all about finding out what your boundaries are and expanding those. So you move from a purely self-centered view to probably a family-centered view to a tribal-centered view. You keep expanding those boundaries until you get to some place interesting. And the language around the Bodhisattva path is so unapologetically universal – always – that there's no room for my group over your group or my kids over your kids. There's no space for that at all. So to me, maturity is – in many ways – a process of learning to release the grasp on the self. Both in terms of what the self wants and in terms of the narrative we hold onto so tightly about who we are. And what I talk a lot about in the community is if you just spend time with people who have lived ninety years and who have been open to the experiences that they've had, there's a real depth of maturity that you often find there that is just like what this practice is asking of us, except that maybe it took ninety years, and Zen serves as a kind of an accelerant and says, 'Confront these issues today. How mature can you be today? How responsible can you be today?' Which is the other part of the Bodhisattva path. Right? It's saying, 'I'm actually personally responsible for the world, and I accept that responsibility, and I see it not as a burden but as a vocation.'"

## Seiho Morris

Seiho Morris is an ordained Rinzai priest whom I first met during my visit to Cho Bo Ji in Seattle. When I interviewed him later, in 2018, he was working in an addictions treatment center and was preparing to lead a retreat in Cincinnati for people engaged in Twelve Step programs. Later, he took up residence at Dai Bosatsu. He is one of the very few African American Zen practitioners I met in the course of conducting these interviews.

I had assumed that the Ohio retreat was related to his work at the treatment center, but he tells me it isn't. It is part of what he calls – borrowing a term from Nyogen Senzaki – Zen Mentor Garden practice. "It's an opportunity to guide addicts in recovery, harmonizing their physical, mental, emotional and spiritual/aspirational presence."

It's work that has personal significance for Seiho who – at the age of 52 – tells me he has been in recovery since he was 20.

"Do you ever come to a point where you can say, 'I've recovered'?" I ask.

"No, it's very much like having diabetes. I'm not recovered. There's always more healing, there's always more integration to do. Addiction is not a static thing. It's a disease and unease of the mind. The mind itself is dukkha, the potter's wheel[68] that turns in such a way that it can be difficult to create beauty. That's the nature of training both the heart and mind. It's recalibration."

He calls his work with people in recovery a "natural Dharma-field. There's a real opportunity to offer outward support for what's essentially an inside job. It's just like traditional Zen practice within a sangha, as an aspect of my day-to-day Zen practice as a monk. My role is to meet people where they're at instead of where they or others might think they 'ought' to be now that they're 'clean.' So instead of being in a traditional Zen temple or monastic setting, we're practicing together in the communities where they live, in the causes and conditions of real and imagined suffering.

"When I became ordained, I had this vision of what my practice would look like. Which is you marry, you bury, hospice, that kind of thing. But as my first Zen teacher said, 'Just like we are making choices through our actions, life and the Dharma are making choices and taking action as well. Life is not a passive canvas to submissively paint our goals and intentions on. It's a relationship.' Over time, big 'R' reality changed that vision. I realized that monks priests, yogis do far more than marry and bury. Ordained people can be part of a physical, mental, emotional, spiritual system of care to help individuals who come

---

68. Although "dukkha" is usually translated as "suffering," etymologically it suggests being off-kilter, in the way that an axle – or a potter's wheel – can be off kilter.

to them or need to be gone to."

For Seiho, the Twelve Step programs are "the perfect Zen deal. Which is, we admit that we're powerless over ego, self-rejecting thoughts, and, when we bite down and follow them, our life can become incredibly unmanageable. Step two is – the way it's actually worded is – 'we came to believe that a power greater than ourselves could restore us to sanity.' I've reframed that for myself as, 'It's the power of love, which is greater than ego, which allows us to be restored to – as Trungpa Rinpoche[69] says – "basic sanity" or "basic soundness of mind."' And then step three, is making a conscious and clear decision to turn our will or life over to God – I say 'the care of our Universal Loving Presence' – as I understand it in this moment. So, for me, that is Zen."

After the election of Donald Trump in 2016, another Dharma field presented itself to Seiho. "That was Zen Buddhism and people of color. That surprised me because it hadn't registered on my mental or emotional radar. It's been incredibly challenging for me because when you get into person of color issues – caste, racism and cultural bias, social justice, equity – that's the stuff people don't want to do. It's not the pretty side of Zen or Buddhism as a whole. In fact it's extremely messy because it goes to the heart of greed, hatred and delusion.

"That said, it was really strange being confronted with this proverbial minefield, to not just pass through it but to live within and be a part of an effort to help guide others to another shore of possibility, so to speak. I hadn't really had to deal with these issues so directly before. I never thought of myself as an activist. Zen has been a kind of gated community I've lived in. You know? But what happened was there's this thing in Seattle called Festival Sundiata, which is an African American cultural festival, but anyone can attend. It doesn't matter if you're a person of color, Black, Hispanic, white, whatever. I led two days of practice just around POC issues. At first it was extremely challenging because I hadn't actively practiced with this issue in this way, especially in the context of Zen. 'Cause, honestly, I'm usually around people who are white or Asian because it's Zen. So I don't encounter a lot of African American people within that context. I know that might sound strange, but it's true. To this day, I've never met another Rinzai Zen priest that's Black. There are some in Soto and in Vipassana but not in the tradition that I'm in, which is kind of a weird spot to be in.

"At any rate, I was sitting there and attempting to gain understanding and clarity about our shared experience, directly and deeply. And one of the things I discovered that had never occurred to me is that if you're under a lot of pressure

---

69. The Tibetan founder of the Shambhala Buddhist movement.

culturally – like the way American society is set up essentially it's a white dominant caste system and culture – and when you're the non-dominant minority in that culture, there's a constant stress and pressure where your survival nervous system is always on high-alert. So I was sitting in a group at one of these events, and I listened to all these people. It wasn't just African Americans; there were Indigenous tribal people, people who were Asian. And what I heard in their stories is there's a lot of mental health issues, anxieties, stress, depression – just profoundly so – that interferes with their inward stability, their inward harmony, and so I began practicing with people based on that.

"The first noble truth – which is dukkha – tells us that life/ego is the part of the wheel that's out of balance. So we work on concentration, presence, and mindfulness – and different Buddhist practices from the Eightfold Path – to help them to find an inward stability. It's the same as when you're in a boat on the ocean, trying to figure out how to keep the boat from capsizing when the water's choppy. Zen can be extremely helpful for maintaining harmony to the best of one's ability despite what can be adverse, unpleasant, even painful circumstances, without losing conscious contact with our inherent Buddha-nature, that Universal Loving Presence that makes up our DNA. Zen practice can teach us how to turn towards difficulty with compassion, positive action, respect and empathy."

## Bernie Glassman

"As far as I'm concerned, the purpose of Zen to is help people experience the interconnectedness of life. The oneness of life. And so there have been many upayas throughout the years of how to do that. So Zen – as you know – means 'meditation.' And that's been a major upaya. But even in Zen, all kinds of techniques and tricks have been used to help people to have the experience, and my concentration of that is to bring them to these Bearing Witness retreats, which I think have a huge effect in that regard."

The Bearing Witness retreats engage participants in a recognition of the historical consequences of failing to recognize the inherent unity of human life.

"In '76, I had an experience which changed my venue of teaching from the zendo – the meditation hall or the temple or the Zen Center – to society. And I was looking at ways of doing this in all of society. I had an experience of what I call the 'Hungry Ghosts' – which is a term in Buddhism – an experience of the thirsts and the hungers of everything around. And simultaneously I experienced it as myself, as that these were all aspects of myself. And a vow came up to try to satisfy those hungers. Those were hungers for food. Hungers for power. Hungers for love. Hungers for status. Acknowledgement. All kinds of hungers.

So my work really moved into whole different spheres."

Even before he left Los Angeles for New York, his attitude to practice had begun to shift. He engaged ZCLA in social action, establishing, among other things, a medical clinic – with a Dharma sister, Chozen Bays, who was a physician – to respond to the needs of the generally lower-income people living in the neighborhood where the center was located.

"I've always felt comfortable in poor areas. And where the zendo was in LA was a poor area. So I started that clinic. And I founded a number of businesses. Already my thinking was moving that way, but still my main interest was helping people to become One. And I started with a standard kind of enlightenment experience. But my definition of 'enlightenment' kept shifting to now where for me the enlightenment experience is an awakening to the interconnectedness of life, *and* it keeps deepening.

"So at first it's awakening to the oneness of oneself. And then of the family. And then of the group. And then of the society. And then of the world. Then of the universe. Almost any Zen workshop I'm in, I'll start by defining what I mean by enlightenment – the experience of the interconnectedness of life – and I'll quote the Japanese teacher Kobo Daishi who said that you can tell the depth of a person's enlightenment by how they serve others.

"When I first got very heavily involved in socially engaged Buddhism, almost every Zen teacher was criticizing me, saying that I was 'defaming the Dharma.' Which was, for me, weird. You could talk about compassion, but if you made compassion your practice that was defaming the Dharma. That's changed over the last twenty years. Nobody would think... Well, there's probably some people who would say that. But now there are many people doing socially engaged work.

"In the Zen Peacemakers we have three tenets. First, not knowing. Then, bearing witness. Then, loving actions. And they come pretty much out of standard Zen. But putting them in English that way and talking about them from up front is a little different. So in koan study, the first koans are hoping to help you get the experience of not-knowing. Bearing witness – zazen is bearing witness. Shikan taza is bearing witness to the wholeness of life. But I use it in those terms, and having techniques to help you get to this place of not-knowing. 'Not-knowing,' in my terminology, means not having any attachments. Being totally open. And, of course, it's endless."

He makes a careful distinction between meditation – which remains the basis of Zen – and the concept of "practice." "'Cause I use 'practice' for the whole thing. And I'm constantly having to correct people, 'cause people will say, 'Well, first you practice, then you do social action.' I say, 'No! Social engagement is *a* major practice. Zazen is *a* major practice.' For me, the word 'practice' means to get rid of the dualistic subject-object relationship. So that can be done in anything. You can wash dishes as a practice. Now that's pretty common Zen too, bring water, that whole kind of work. But people would look at me and say, 'I can see where chopping firewood, that's a practice, or cutting a carrot a certain way, that's a practice. But working with homeless? How can that be a practice?' I was constantly contradicting this. To do things in your life, whatever you're doing in your life, and doing it in a way which decreases the subject-object relationship – in other words that helps you experience the interconnectedness of life – that's practice."

The Bearing Witness Retreats – which take place at places of genocide such as Auschwitz, Rwanda, and Wounded Knee – grew out of the street retreats among the homeless in New York City. I'm curious about the instruction he provides students who are used to more traditional zazen settings before they take part in their first street retreat.

"You know what I'd tell a traditional Zen student? Or anybody? Anybody. How you're filling your time? Being here now. When you're on the streets there's nothing to plan. You're not thinking about your business. I mean, you are the first half day you're there or whatever. But after a while, all you're worried about is, 'I gotta pee. Where am I gonna pee? I'm hungry. Where am I gonna get food?' I call it a 'plunge.' My Bearing Witness retreats, generally they start off with plunges. It's a way of getting you to just deal with what's coming up.

"So, like I said, the first tenet is 'not knowing.' And I created these plunges as a way of helping you experience 'not knowing,' bringing you into a situation where your rational mind can't fathom it. The experience of 'not knowing' is hopefully to not be attached to your ideas. Have lots of ideas, that's fine. Have lots of knowledge, that's fine. But to not be attached. And not thinking that this idea or this process is going to take care of the situation. Go in completely 'not knowing.' And the plunge is helping you to do that because it's bringing you to a place where your mind, your ideas don't work. And your mind doesn't know how to rationalize this. And that's sort of an instantaneous sensation.

"'Bearing witness' means – to me – to stay in that situation. So it takes time. It's not enough for me to say, 'Go into the streets and meet with a homeless person.' But live there, be in that. And if we create the environment right, then people will experience 'bearing witness.' Being in that state of nonduality. So it's getting you into a state of nonduality.

"Auschwitz, same thing. I do an annual retreat at Auschwitz. In any of the Bearing Witness retreats, there's no teaching. What I'm doing is setting an environment. So the environment at Auschwitz is I bring as many different kinds of people as possible. 'Cause the Auschwitz retreat – for me – is around diversity and the 'other.' It's an icon for a place that killed everybody that was an 'other.' But in our daily life, the main way we deal with the 'other' is to ignore them. So we don't invite them to dinner. We won't listen to them on TV. You know? We don't read those books. I mean, we all have our own club that we feel comfortable in. Anybody else, that's the 'other.'

"So Auschwitz was an extreme case where you kill everybody who's not an Aryan. It's a place where you kill the gays. You kill handicapped. You kill the Romani. You kill the Jews. You kill Catholics. You kill Polish intellectuals. You know, they all didn't fit Hitler's club model. But – you know – we did lynchings of Blacks. We do bashing of gays. So, it's a common thing. So Auschwitz, for me, is an icon. And I bring as many types of people as possible. We always have Romani. We have survivors. We have the children of survivors. We have children and grandchildren of SS people that ran the camps."

## Genro Gauntt

Genro Gauntt first participated in one of Bernie's street retreats in 1997. A year later, he was helping to lead them. "I still lead them. I've led more than fifty around the world. I've led them in many countries and in many cities in the United States and Canada. In Brazil and Europe and, yeah, many places."

To be in a street retreat or a Bearing Witness retreat, he tells me, "is to do like years of practice in a couple of days because a lot comes off. The mind, because it's not familiar with the context of the world that you suddenly find yourself in, it can't process it. It can't identify with it. And it makes us be awake and aware and mindful, because there's a lot to be mindful of when you're living on the streets. You're not in your room or on your couch. And then dealing with homeless people in soup kitchens and being regarded as a nobody. And eventually what happens is the mind's not really processing it as data and information; it's something that needs to be understood. What happens is a deep sort of freeing and happiness arises for the great majority – the great, great majority – and, you know, these are people, middle-class/upper middle-class, who have never done anything like this, never dreamed of doing anything like this, but for some reason were drawn to do it. And they're terrified coming in; there's so much to worry about. How am I gonna find a bathroom? What are we gonna eat? What if I need this or that? We beg for everything, and they've never begged before. And after maybe the second day, after the second day of a four-day retreat, they go, 'Oh, my God! I've never been happier in my life, and I really wish this retreat would last a few more days.' Because they have a freedom they've never known before. From themselves, from their own routines and in their minds about who they are, about what life is. Yeah. It's beautiful. So what's the relation to Zen? Buddha is not-knowing; it's coming from this space of openness and non-judgement and non-criticism and just wide-open experience. That's what happens."

The Bearing Witness retreats started not long after Bernie began the street retreats. "Bernie went to Auschwitz to attend a multi-faith conference on peace. It was being hosted I'm not sure by who, but it was held in a conference center adjacent to the Auschwitz-Birkenau camp. And he walked into the camp – it was part of the program – and he was just overwhelmed by the presence of what he described as souls and spiritual energy, and he said, 'This is an incredible place for people to experience.' He didn't know what would happen, but he wanted to bring people there to experience it. And he knew the souls there wanted prayers and presence. And that particular concept was confirmed later by Rabbi Zalman Schachter. He told Bernie, 'Yeah. Go! It wants you. It needs you.'

"So that was '94. The first Auschwitz retreat was '96. I don't know if it was called a Bearing Witness Retreat in that year. I was there, but we just called it Auschwitz-Birkenau Retreat I'm sure. The Bearing Witness aspect came up very soon thereafter. And it was very, very powerful. Very powerful. I was recently divorced and was in between the transition of my regular daily life and working fulltime with Bernie and crew. And I was depressed. I was in bad shape. For who knows what reasons. Right? I was about to be tested and have a major life change. There had been a lot already. So I went there with 150 others, basically. It was the first time any of us had ever been there."

He pauses for a while, struggling to find a way to continue. "I knew what Bernie was talking about when he said the spiritual atmosphere was dense. I mean, it really was. It was quite palpable. It was like, there are places on Earth where you walk and you go, 'My God! Something happened here!' And it for sure happened there. You could feel it. So days on end we're doing meditation on the tracks between the two main crematoriums and listening to testimonials from people at night, from survivors and from Polish people whose families were directly involved one way or another, and children of Nazis from Germany, and Israeli Jews who found the courage to go there somehow and were children of survivors. It was a big, huge, experience and testimony. And the third day – fourth day maybe – of five days, I was alongside Peter Mathiessen,[70] and he said, 'Genro, how you feeling?' And I said, 'I feel great!' He said, 'I do too. I was depressed before I came here.' I said, 'So was I.' Something major – some transformation – happened. It's not the way we sell it; we don't say it will happen. But this is the experience, and then something happens. Then the Auschwitz retreats continued annually even though there was no plan to do it more than once.

---

70. A writer, naturalist – and former CIA operative – who was one of Bernie's disciples. His novel *In Paradise* is about the Auschwitz retreats.

But for the next several years, it was heavily attended and over-subscribed. We had to turn people away. Street retreats continued. So those Bearing Witness Retreats continued. And ideas about other things – you know – came up. And social service in various ways was being taken on by many people who had experienced the street retreats in particular and Auschwitz as a Bearing Witness Retreat. Various inspirations came to people, and they acted on it."

During a retreat in 1998, Genro noticed that although people from many religious traditions were involved, there were no representatives from Indigenous spiritualities.

"So I said, 'Let's invite somebody.' And so we had a contact, one of our members had done a film on the Pine Ridge Reservation in the early '80s, and he had some contacts there, so I called him. And he said, 'Yeah. Call so-and-so.' So I called an elder in the community – a quite well-known elder, really, a wonderful man – named Birgil Kills Straight. And this is a man, I learned later, didn't talk much especially to white people about Indians. But he came out right away. He said, 'I would love to do that. I would really love to come. But I can't. I've got other obligations. But I'm gonna send somebody.' So he sent a Lakota from Pine Ridge named Tuffy Sierra, who came that year. Never been out of the country. Didn't have a passport. Got his passport the day before he left the country and came. So Tuffy asked Birgil Kills Straight, 'What am I supposed to do when I'm there?' Birgil Kills Straight said, 'Pray.' So that's what he did.

"So he was there for a week with us, and I got to know him. And maybe a couple of months later I said to myself, 'Oh, my God! For somebody to be with us and to do something with us, that's a huge offering that they made. I've got to do something with them.' So I called up Birgil Kills Straight, and he said, 'Great. Come do the ride.' What he meant was the Big Foot Ride, which is an annual two-week horseback ride, several hundred miles from Northern South Dakota, from the Standing Rock reservation where Sitting Bull was; it's the path travelled by Big Foot and his band who were seeking refuge with Red Cloud on the Pine Ridge reservation, and, of course, it ended up with the Wounded Knee massacre. So in 1985, Birgil – by vision and dream – went to another man who had the same vision and dream and started that ride. So I went and joined the end of it, and Tuffy Sierra, my friend from the Auschwitz retreat, came, and I spent a few days with him. Spent a few days with Birgil and his family. Met medicine people. Incredible stories. Lots and lots happened. And that was the beginning of my relationship with them, only as a friend, only as a student. I didn't go to teach anything. I didn't go to provide any social service. I was just there to learn from them and be a friend. So fifteen years later, the Black Hills Bearing Witness Retreat happened, and since then we're now in our fifth or sixth year."

# COMPASSIONATE ACTION

## Genjo Marinello

Genjo Marinello has participated in several Bearing Witness Retreats.

"I think they've done a very good job in bringing Zen out of the box and translating Zen into a kind of modern idiom that is more easy to grasp – or get your head around – than ancient Chinese or Japanese koans or poetry or even haikus. I mean, I've spent thirty years trying to understand that stuff and feel as though I get a lot out of it. But Bernie really brought it out of the box. His three tenets – not knowing, bearing witness, loving action – I know exactly where these derive from in Buddhism, but there's nothing Buddhist in those tenets *per se*. And I think that's brilliant to bring it out in that way and to put it to some practical use. I think it's been practical in the sense of helping to heal these sites where genocide has happened. Bernie's sort of a genocide-junkie, and maybe I'm one too; I don't know. But there's something about *being present* at a place where genocide has happened, and just sitting there and absorbing it, that seems to help those who are witnessing – bearing witness – but it also seems to help the culture heal. That's what it feels like. So that's pretty damn good. I mean, it's wonderful what happens in the zendo, but this is really bringing it out into the world in some practical, healing way. And then the idea of council, their way of bearing witness through council, is very old and ancient – it kind of goes back to Indigenous cultures sitting in a circle around a fire – but that way of counsel, of hearing and listening deeply and spontaneously to each other without crosstalk as a way to communicate, share, and heal, that's another great offering"

## Hozan Senauke

Zen practice, Hozan Senauke suggests, is about "knowing where your feet are. Knowing where you're standing at any given moment. Building that awareness. So it's a very grounded awareness. It's not rarified. But it's like, where am I standing? And that is literal, and it's metaphorical, and it's also psychological. Knowing when some strong afflictive emotion arises, knowing that it's arising, rather than it blowing you off your feet so you get caught up in reactivity or some kind of dysfunctional action. And I think this is energized by bodhicitta. It is energized by the Bodhisattva vow to awaken with all beings, including one's self. That's what I understand to be both the means and end of Soto Zen."

"What do you mean by 'awaken'?"

"A very good question. What I mean by 'awakened' is 'awakened activity.' I mean action that is premised on our common humanity. Thereby, some fundamental kindness. To respect that kindness doesn't always mean that everything's nice and gentle, but it means seeing the all-pervasive nature of Buddha Nature and really challenging yourself when you're not seeing it, which certainly comes up a lot in our social world. Nonetheless, even if I'm not seeing it in relation to this person or this situation, how do I want to act? That's where I come back to knowing where my feet are. How do I want to act in the face of this? And that – to me – is enlightened activity. And I tend to look at people – or evaluate, if you will – on the basis of what they do. What they say and what they do. Because I really don't have any way of evaluating what type of meditative experience they might have had. And also I don't think that those experiences are necessarily transformative."

"You're referring to awakening or kensho experiences?"

"Yeah. I mean, it's not that they're unimportant, but they have to be able to affect your behavior – you know – your relational capacities. So that's kind of the standard I use."

## Phap Vu

The practices promoted by the Order of Interbeing, Brother Phap Vu explains to me, are "based on two concepts in the Mahayana tradition. The first is dependent arising. All things are dependent on other things for their manifestation, for their being. The other comes from the *Avatamsaka Sutra*, interpenetration. That I'm in that, and that is in me. And what these two things are looking at, what these two things are describing in the human experience, is that there's a larger version of us. There's a larger interconnectedness of us, of all things. Nothing exists within itself. Everything is connected with everything else."

The goal of Zen practice, then, is to bring about a shift in perception. "Either it's realizing the interconnectedness of all things, or realizing how one could respond to the difficulties in life. And the difficulties in life can be anything from a relationship with another person, or the difficulties in life could be economic. Or it could be something like a global catastrophe. Global crisis. How do we approach this? How do we respond?"

The current "global crisis" he talks about isn't something theoretical. Thich Nhat Hanh has been blunt in telling his disciples to acknowledge the impact human activity has had on the interconnected whole and the consequences of that activity. "Civilizations have been destroyed many times and this civilization is no different," he wrote. "It can be destroyed."

I wonder how one comes to terms with a concept as bleak as that.

"What is it that you hope for for the people you work with?" I ask Phap Vu.

His answer is one of those deeply profound statements that inevitably sound naïve: "To love themselves. To have compassion for themselves."

"You sense that's something lacking in people?"

"Well, I had a lack of that capacity to see myself in another way. To see that you are much more than you think you are. You know, we live our lives, we do our work and school or whatever we do with family or whatnot. And sometimes we're stuck in this mode. And we put ourselves in boxes, give ourselves labels. And society puts labels on us and puts us in boxes. And we're not aware of that larger aspect of ourselves."

Nhat Hanh calls this larger aspect "home." "Our true home. Every spiritual tradition has this. In Christianity it would be like the Divine nature. It's the interconnectedness that we're a part of the divine basically."

## Sunyana Graef

The Vermont Zen Center is located in Shelburne, a small, artistically-inclined community outside Burlington. Perhaps because there had been one outside my office for several years, I notice the Peace Pole[71] at the foot of the Center's drive before I see the official sign set in a small flower bed.

The grounds cover some 72 acres and are lovingly tended. It happens that my visit takes place in May when the magnolia trees are in full bloom, their bases littered with large white petals. The rhododendron is in flower, along with many colorful bedding plants. The center's teacher, Sunyana Graef, informs me that when the house was purchased it was in the middle of an alfalfa field and there had only been a single tree, a pine which now towers over the property. The sangha celebrated its 25th anniversary the year I visited, 2013, and a spruce they planted when they first took over the property is now almost as high as the pine.

The center itself is a refurbished farmhouse that has had several extensions over the years and can now comfortably house sixty people during sesshin. The first room one enters is a living room with stuffed furniture and a big fireplace. "When I was looking for a place for a Zen Center," Sunyana tells me, "one of my chief requirements was not a zendo but a living room. What I was looking for was a place where people would *have* to walk through the living room to get to the zendo. The reason for that is simply that I wanted a sangha to form. And this is where sangha is formed. Not when you're sitting in silence but when you come together in a social environment. So that's why I loved this place. You come in, and you have to walk through the living room. And people would sit here and chat and get to know each other."

Throughout our conversation, Sunyana discusses some of the differences between her center and the Rochester Center where she had trained with Philip Kapleau. "I have a much stronger emphasis on the Bodhisattva of Compassion,

---

71. Peace Poles originated in Japan in 1955. The sides of the pole declare "May Peace Prevail on Earth" in four different languages.

Kannon, because her presence in my life was so important, always has been since the day I met her. And so, Kannon is everywhere in the center. Another huge difference is the fact that we don't have staff. And that affects all aspects of life here, because everyone takes responsibility. So our practice is our life. Our life is our practice. And I hope I never hear from *anyone*, 'I don't know what this has to do with my life.' And I did hear that in Rochester. 'We're doin' this, but what effect does it have on my life?' And it doesn't. It takes a while for it to affect your life, but you need to make that connection from the beginning. So that's what I hope people see. That this is everything we do. It's the way we brush our teeth; it's the way we drive our car; it's the way we talk to our loved ones and strangers; it's the way we walk outdoors and smell the flowers. There's nothing that isn't practice. Nothing. So I hope people will get that. We didn't *exactly* get that in Rochester. That wasn't the focus that I knew about then."

"What was the focus?"

"Wisdom. Enlightenment. That was it."

"And here there's a greater focus on compassion?"

"I hope so. Well, not necessarily more but more evident? My teacher actually actively discouraged us from social outreach. And that's definitely *not* the case now in Rochester. But at that time, it was. And, of course, this was the '60s, the '70s, when there was so much activism going on, and he thought we needed to focus our attention within to develop ourselves. We were so immature and so scattered and so undisciplined and so drug-hazed that I think he was probably right about that. It's just that there were repercussions to that. And one repercussion was that we thought there was nothing more important in the world than enlightenment, and the more deeply enlightened you were, the *better* you were. Somehow you were more Buddha-ish or something. So that had its effect necessarily. It was not a good one. We were conceited as all get-out.

"So I began teaching Loving Kindness to my students. At every sesshin, there would be half an hour where we would do Loving Kindness, sending it to yourself, to a friend, so on and so forth. And then I started giving classes outside sesshin, and there are people who sign up for those classes and don't do anything else, but they often come back. And it's been a very important part of our community, teaching that. Teaching that way of loving acceptance."

## Bodhin Kjolhede

Although Kapleau dissuaded his students from being politically engaged, he did seek ways of involving them in the local community. He adapted, for example, the traditional Buddhist activity of begging – *takahatsu* – by sending his students out to clean the streets around their neighborhood.

"It's a lot different from walking through the streets and asking for donations," Bodhin Kjolhede concedes, "but in keeping with his insistence that we not appear too foreign, that we adapt to something that's consistent with our own culture, he came up with this idea of going out in disciplined groups in silence, eyes mostly down, just picking up trash in the neighborhood. And we've continued that. What it has in common, I suppose, with traditional takahatsu in Japan is that we're bringing into public a demonstration of the Zen principles of concentration and 'no self.' It's just this element of service that isn't there in Japan."

It is because of his commitment to conserve the practice as he had received it from Kapleau that Bodhin is cautious about the degree to which he involves his students in social issues. "The danger of it is if you become too one-sidedly engaged – socially or politically – then you run the risk of losing the real root of Zen practice." But members of the Rochester Center have served in hospices and worked in soup kitchens in the past.

"There's a whole kind of blossoming of ways of engaging with the wider world outside the walls of the Zen Center. For example, I'm trying to give some leadership in the whole spectre of global warming. In fact, recently we had a meeting where we talked about how we might have a public demonstration of the spirit of Zen the way that we did about thirty years ago when the Minnesota Zen Center organized a three day Zazen Vigil in New York City. This was on the occasion of public protests in New York regarding the proposed deployment of Cruise Missiles in Europe. And so the idea came up of inviting Zen Centers to convene across from the United Nations in a place called the Peace Park and just sit for three days. That had quite a strong effect on me. I thought it was powerful, something I could get behind more than waving protest signs and marching. So I'm trying to get something like that going regarding climate change."

If Zen – as Bernie Glassman and others have put it – is about discovering the interconnectedness of life, then environmental issues are a natural subject of concern for practitioners.

# 6

# Ecodharma

## Taigen Henderson

It's not only personal circumstances that draw people to Zen or other spiritual practices. Social events can be powerful motivators as well.

I have only visited the Toronto Zen Center twice, the first time to conduct interviews and the second to do a book reading, but it's a sangha I think I would feel comfortable belonging to. I found the people to be warm and welcoming, and the teacher – Taigen Henderson – is one of those individuals one naturally feels at ease with. That might, in part, be due to the fact that he and I share a career history. We both worked in aluminum home improvements.

The conversation in which Taigen told me that enlightenment no longer seemed to be on the radar for many people took place in September of 2018. Less than thirty months later, the world was a very different place. Wildfires linked to climate change had destroyed some 47 million acres in Australia. In the United States, the police killings of George Floyd, Ahmaud Arbery and Breonna Taylor re-energized the Black Lives Matter movement and sparked demonstrations around the world protesting systemic racism and police violence. And, most bizarrely, after Joe Biden was elected President, supporters of Donald Trump – bolstered by white-supremacists and Q-Anon conspiracy theorists – stormed the Capital in Washington, DC, and tried to overturn the election. All of this, of course, in the midst of a pandemic that continues to rage at the time of this writing and is currently responsible for more than 3 million deaths, one fifth of those in the US.

Looking back on that 2018 interview, Taigen wonders if it hadn't taken place at "the end of an era. Which is why it seems so distant, even though it was less than three years ago! Canadians are shielded from the extremes of the

US, so there is less angst here, but I do see more now. And as a result, there is genuine searching going on. That's one of the outcomes of the tumultuous times we're now in."

## Domyo Burk

Shortly before I was scheduled to interview her in December 2019 – a month before the first COVID-19 cases were reported in the US – Domyo Burk was arrested and spent the night in jail.

"I heard through my network of climate activist groups that something was going to go on and that if people were interested in civil disobedience they should sign up, and that it was going to be run by experienced people. So I signed up, and we went down to the state capital and occupied Governor Kate Brown's office, insisting that she come out against the giant liquefied natural gas pipeline and liquefication plant that's a big project in Southern Oregon. A Canadian company wants to pipe fracked gas through the pipeline and then, in Coos Bay, liquefy it, load it onto ships, then ship it overseas to be sold in Asia. It's just wrong at so many levels. The pipeline goes through tribal lands, public lands, private land through the right of eminent domain, which should only be used when it's in the public good. So it all hinges on that ridiculous argument that it's in the public good as opposed to good for an enormous multinational corporation, besides the fact that this is just – in terms of climate change – the exact opposite of the direction we should be going. So, there was a big rally out in front of the capitol. Then everyone went inside, singing, and filled the atrium with song. And then a bunch of us went up the stairs into Governor Brown's ceremonial office and just hung out there for eight hours." She chuckles at the memory. "And after the building closed, Governor Brown even came to talk to us, but she wasn't willing to come out publicly against the pipeline, so we stayed, and twenty-one of us stayed past the point where the state troopers warned us that we would be charged with trespassing and arrested if we didn't leave."

She admits that not everyone sees the connection between environmental concern and Zen, but, as she put it in one of her podcasts, "My own Zen practice feels shallow and inauthentic unless I talk about the climate and the ecological crisis we're facing."

"You know," she tells me, "sometimes you get a message from Buddhism – sometimes more by omission than anybody stating outright – that 'You shouldn't care about the state of the world,' or it's all 'empty.' I don't know, sometimes people say stuff like that. And when I get a message like that, I experience complete resistance to it. I just think, that cannot be the case. Roshi Kennett[72] would say, 'When you encounter something in the Dharma that doesn't seem right, you're right to doubt what you think it means.' To me that means not necessarily the Dharma as Buddhism but the truth, the deeper truth that we are trying to reach through Buddhism or whatever our faith path is. When it sounds like a spiritual tradition suggests we should let the world burn, that just can't be the case, not if it's a legitimate spiritual path. You can't just leave out the Earth and all beings. My response to such a suggestion is, 'What!? That's insane. I don't even want to be part of anything that leads to that.' But sometimes it's difficult to find in Buddhism something that says you should get your ass off your cushion and go out and do something to help – you know – all beings, including animals and plants and everything. But then I was just reading Shantideva's Bodhisattva vow. Well? It really can't be much clearer than that."

Shantideva was an 8th century Indian Buddhist monk and scholar still greatly admired in Tibetan Buddhist traditions. The vow to which Domyo is referring comes from the *Bodhicharyavatara* (*Guide to the Way of Life of the Bodhisattva*) and begins:

> As earth and the other elements together with space
> Eternally provide sustenance in many ways for the countless
>     sentient beings
> So may I become sustenance in every way for sentient beings
> To the limits of space, until all have attained nirvana.

A briefer vow chanted at Zen Centers of all lineages puts it much more succinctly: "All sentient beings, I vow to liberate."[73] All sentient beings, of course, include not only those with which we are familiar but any yet to be discovered on places like Kepler-621.

## Shodo Spring

Shodo Spring is a Dharma heir of Shohaku Okumura in the Soto tradition. In 2013, she gained acclaim for her Compassionate Earth Walk, a three-month spiritual hike along the proposed Keystone XL pipeline route in the Great Plains. Following the Earth Walk, she founded the Mountains and Waters Alliance at her farm in Fairbault, Minnesota, where she leads retreats

---

72. Peggy Jiyu-Kennett was the first woman to be authorized to teach Zen in the West. She founded Mount Shasta Abbey in California where Domyo trained.
73. Cf. fnt. 64, p. 120 above.

emphasizing human interdependence with the natural world. The retreats had been suspended because of the pandemic when I spoke with her.

She tells me that she grew up in a Lutheran family in Ohio and admits she was "one of those obnoxious super-religious people until I was in my late twenties." Eventually, she left the church and her marriage and came to live in Minneapolis where, one day, she saw a notice on a bulletin board for an introductory Zen class at Dainin Katagiri's Minnesota Zen Center.

"I went to it. And they had stuff that wasn't interesting, but they gave us zazen instruction, and I had to sit for fifteen minutes, and I liked it. So I started sitting at home. I had no idea why people sat together or any of that. But I was sitting by myself at home. I made a cushion which had lots of bright colors in it and was stuffed with rags and was made out of scraps."

"You said they had stuff that was *un*-interesting?" I ask, to ensure I'd heard her correctly.

"It was not interesting. I knew everything, you see?" she says with a laugh. She was 35 at the time.

She did, however, visit the center on occasion and eventually registered to attend a sesshin. "Most of the time I did not have knee pain, and I did have energy rushes, and, on about the third day, Katagiri Roshi's talks started making some sense. I no longer remember much about what happened during it, but I remember that I came out realizing that I didn't know anything, and I was really excited about that. So then I became a regular."

"And if someone from your Lutheran past had asked you, 'What is this Zen thing all about? What does it do?' How would you have answered them?"

"What does it do for you? You know, 'what does it do for you' is really easy. Of all the religions in the world, Zen is the one that actually helps you with your daily life. Well, Buddhism is. Christians pray. I haven't noticed that helps a lot. They think somebody's gonna help them. But Zen actually gives you tools to make your life work. It helps me to be alive. It helps me to be here with the life that I have, and it helps me to be happy. For me, Christianity was always intellectual. I know it wasn't supposed to be, but my sense of religion was out in the fields and trees. The things that were supposed to be meaningful in the church, they didn't click, although I kept trying and trying.

"And let me say this: Christianity has this teaching about sin, and the definition of sin that I always liked since I discovered it in fifth grade is that sin is separation from God. Well, what my Buddhist practice helps me do is not be separate. They say that God is everywhere, God is in everything. Well, that's not just words. That's for real. You know? God is a word – to me – that describes the incredible power of the universe. And we use that word to talk about something that can't be talked about. It's something that you can't name, something you can't say. Shouldn't even speak it. That's for real! That's not just an idea, that's for real. And so practicing Buddhism, I get to actually live the life that I just heard about and read about in the church."

After our conversation, she wrote to me to clarify some points we had discussed.

> First – Zen is present in this moment, not abstract or philosophical. It offers no support for excuses, for abandoning this world in hopes of something better, or withdrawing into intellectual realms or even states of bliss.
>
> Second – There is a fundamental equality, expressed in the term "all sentient beings." This coincides well with my early history in physics, where I learned to regard matter and energy as variations on the same unnameable essence. Sentience is hard to name, and people disagree about what has it and what does not. To me, all matter is alive and sentient: animals, plants, rocks, drops of water, and molecules, electrons, empty space. So humans are neither lords of creation nor its saviors.
>
> That last point is very relevant in working with environmental implications: We are not alone. We – roughly speaking, industrial humans plus agricultural humans but not all humans – have done this damage as a result of our illusion of being in charge and being separate. That illusion is the cornerstone of the society which first mined coal and oil and built a very complex technological structure then persisted in being willing to destroy everything to keep its conveniences intact.
>
> The core point of Mountains and Waters Alliance is that we are not alone, and perhaps the other sentient beings would be willing to help if we would – well, ask. Or make space for them to help. Or stop trying to kill them.
>
> People practice something called Zen for many reasons – to calm down, to feel cool, to understand something. And those reasons do not of themselves support ethical, social, and environmental work. Zen is fundamentally not a personal practice – a key departure from classical Buddhism – it is something that happens, that is called forth by the world, enacted in our bodies, and in our sanghas, and requires the kind of ethical conduct that is as natural as eating, sleeping, and generally caring for one's own body. The whole takes care of itself by expressing itself in us as individuals and

communities.

Her Compassionate Earth Walk was an example of a physically enacted Zen practice. The idea for it came while she was taking part in an ango[74] at SFZC's Tassajara practice center.

"So I'm sitting in the zendo and I keep seeing these images of people walking – you know – walking, walking, walking. And so I finally gave in and said, 'I have to do it.' I talked to teachers. Steve Stücky[75] said, 'Yeah. I think you have to do it.' And then he said, 'I'll come.' And he did come for four days. It was a meditation. It was a ceremony actually. It was a ceremony that mostly consisted of walking and some sitting, and it actually turned out to be, 'Oh! The Earth!' It was about my relationship with the Earth."

She described the walk more fully in a call she sent out to other Zen practitioners inviting them to join her:

> This walk is zazen. In the same way that we meet ourselves on the cushion, here we meet our collective selves while putting one foot after another on the ground. As we face our own thoughts and emotions, here we face that great injury in the Earth, that expression of the break in our collective human spirit. As well as we can, we meet it without turning away.
>
> As in zazen, we walk in the middle of all beings, receiving life from them, offering life to them, allowing the whole to heal itself. We throw ourselves upon the mercy of the universe. We give up attempts to control even our fellow human beings. We attempt to give up our attempts to control.
>
> The walk is also a ceremony of gratitude to the earth, which has never abandoned us, and an expression of our love for all earth's creatures including humans. Someone said, "When you sit, you call upon Avalokiteshvara."[76] Thus the walk is also a prayer.
>
> Finally, for me this walk is in response to seeing the faces of my small grandchildren, each of whom innocently trusts

---

74. An extended – usually 90 days long – training period.

75. Steve Stücky was the Central Abbot of the San Francisco Zen Center from 2010 until shortly before his death on December 31, 2013.

76. A male figure identified in India as the Bodhisattva of Compassion. It changed name and gender when it was imported into China and later Japan. As I wrote in *Cypress Tress in the Garden*, such transformations are inevitable when a system of belief or practice travels from one region to another and is adapted to a new environment.

that the grownups will take care of the world and deliver it to them in good condition. It is eight years since I looked into my infant grandson's laughing eyes, deeply felt that trust and committed to live up to it. It is eighteen months since I accepted the vision of this walk as my appropriate response.

## David Loy

David Loy is a co-founder of the Rocky Mountain Retreat Center where he and Johann Robbins – of the Insight Meditation tradition – offer "Ecodharma Retreats." I suspect that Shodo's Compassionate Earth Walk, Bodhi's climate change vigil, and even Domyo's night in jail are examples of what he means by Ecodharma activity.

"'Ecodharma' is a particularly modern development of Buddhism that applies basic Buddhist teachings to our ecological situation today." The connection between the kensho experience of nonduality and Ecodharma, he tells me, is a deep one.

"At the core of the eco-crisis is that both individually and collectively – as a global civilization – we feel disconnected from the rest of the biosphere. It seems to me that there is a remarkable parallel between what Buddhism has to say about our individual predicament – the illusion of separation – and the fact that a comparable sense of separation seems to be at the heart of our ecological predicament. Basically, we as a species feel separate from the rest of the natural world, which means we feel we can use it and abuse it pretty much any way we like. And that also seems to be a pretty good example of karma that's now coming back to haunt us. Because we're not separate, of course, we – as part of the biosphere – are also suffering the consequences of our actions."

The Ecodharma Retreats arose, he explains, from a desire people had to do nature retreats.

"They were looking for a suitable place to do meditation in nature. And that remains an important part of what we offer. But now there's increasing concern about asking ourselves what can we do in light of the cascading crises that have started to occur. What does Buddhism have to offer that can help us understand and respond to the kind of ecological crisis we have today?

"So some of our retreats are straight nature retreats. Some of them aren't even nature retreats, people just using the lodge, which can accommodate about twenty-five people. But Johann and I also offer a ten-day Ecodharma Retreat which is mostly meditation, usually outside on our 185 acres, or nearby, but it's partly workshop as well. To some degree we model ourselves upon

Joanna Macy's *The Work That Reconnects*,[77] helping people get in touch with their gratitude but also their grief about what's going on, since many of us are closed down emotionally because we can't cope with our grief. We're afraid of it, because we don't know what we personally can do to make a difference. And our approach is we've got to get in touch with that grief, to start to face it and work it through together, in which case it can empower us to respond more directly to what's going on.

"One important issue for Johann and me is spending as much time as possible out in the natural world. Even when we can use the lodge, we're not meditating much in there. Weather permitting, we're meditating outside. We're taking people on walks. When it's time to meditate, people find their own spot. Think about the life of the Buddha. Today there's so much emphasis on meditating inside comfortable zendos and Dharma halls, with temperature control and windows with screens for keeping out insects. So we're wondering, 'Wait a minute! Is something being lost here? What about reconnecting with the natural world?'"

David doesn't consider these necessarily to be Zen retreats as such.

"There's a different kind of meditation we encourage – we don't require it – that is more sensory-based, in the sense of not going into your head and reciting Mu or working on a koan, but opening up to the natural world. That's one thing. And another is, we encourage gratitude practice – feeling gratitude – with the realization that gratitude isn't just something we feel (or don't feel), it's a practice we cultivate. As Brother Steindl-Rast[78] said, we're not grateful because we're happy; we're happy because we're grateful. Again, we're doing this outside, feeling and expressing our appreciation to the trees, the wildflowers, the burbling creek.

"Following on from that, what Johann and I do – and this is the workshoppy bit – is offer readings and discussions that help us get in touch with our feelings about what's happening ecologically. That often becomes quite emotional, as you might expect. We open up and share feelings, to the extent that people feel comfortable doing that. Then everyone goes off on a solo, with their own tent and sleeping bag. In the last retreat we did, it was a two day/two night solo. Those who are less confident might choose a spot closer to the lodge, but, in any case, people pick their own location and they're there by themselves for two days and two nights. During that time, we encourage them not to have an agenda but to continue to be open to what's happening. To notice, what does

---

77. Joanna Macy is an environmentalist and Theravada Buddhist.

78. David Steindl-Rast is a Benedictine monk and mystic whose published work focuses on the relationship between science and spirituality.

the land, what do the trees and the meadows and the large and small animals have to offer? And that can be quite powerful. There can be a kind of 'spirit quest' edge to the solo, depending on how people want to do it.

"After it's over, we come back together, we share what happened, and then during the last day or so we talk more about the Bodhisattva or Ecosattva path. Buddhist traditions in Asia developed in a very different context, so they can't offer anything very specific about *what* we should do today. But the Bodhisattva path says a great deal about *how* to do what we decide to do. How might that inspire and motivate us? It's gratifying to observe how this type of retreat changes people, empowers them and makes them want to be more engaged. They feel the urgency more and how what they do might make a difference."

"In his Bearing Witness Retreats," I note, "Bernie Glassman insisted that he wasn't the teacher. He said it was the location – the street or Auschwitz – that was the teacher."

David nods. "That's our sense too, that the beautiful, unspoiled land where we practice is the real teacher. And the whole point of our schedule and program is to enable and maximize that process. But let me make a couple of distinctions here. Bernie was wonderful in the ways he focused on social justice. And that's a huge question, all the more so today. But whereas Bernie focused on how humans relate with and often oppress other humans, our focus has been more on how humans relate to and exploit the rest of the natural world. In other words, I'm very concerned to integrate social justice issues into ecological issues, but not to the extent that we ignore the problem of what might be called *species-ism*. Trees don't vote, don't march or protest. Right? The whole point of Ecodharma, as I understand it, is realizing that we need to expand the moral sphere of responsibility beyond human beings to incorporate the rest of the natural world, not only animals but forests and lakes and ecosystems. That's a little different from what Bernie was focusing on, although I think it fits in quite well. And there's this concern now within Zen Peacemakers today, which is moving in this direction. But I should mention that, within American Buddhism in general, it's taken a while for ecological concerns to develop. We haven't been all that progressive. It's been a slow development."

I mention another parallel that strikes me. "One of the things Nhat Hanh talks about, one of the things that he advises – maybe 'encourages' is too strong a term – one of things he advises his followers to do is contemplate that the human species isn't immune to extinction. We aren't, as a species, going to last forever."

"I think a growing number of us have that sense today. There is an interesting parallel with our awareness of our individual mortality. Buddhist practice helps us get in touch with our own impermanence, our own insubstantiality.

That's an important part of it. And part of the challenge of Ecodharma, I believe, is that it raises similar questions about the fate of the human species and certainly modern civilization as we know it today."

"So then, what do you hope for for the people who participate in these retreats?"

"That's easy to answer. I would hope for them, first, to come to feel a deeper connection with the natural world. And gratitude will normally follow naturally from that. I would also hope that they are able to get in touch with their own grief about what's happening to the natural world. It's not that we work through that grief once and for all, but it's something that shouldn't be denied when it arises. Painful though it is, opening to our grief is necessary for the transformation – the kind of enlightenment – that we need today. But my most important hope would be that those who undertake this process be empowered and motivated to become ecologically and socially engaged. As Joanna Macy says, the world – the Earth – has a role to play in our liberation."

## Rinzan Pechovnik

"Since I was a kid," Rinzan Pechovnik reflects, "I've always been concerned about the environment. I don't know why. But I've always felt we have too many people on the Earth, and we're not caring for the Earth. And it would hurt me and pain me to see the way the Earth was treated. And in my teenage years and with my drinking, I withdrew from environmental engagement because it was too painful. I didn't like seeing the way the Earth was being treated so I withdrew, and found other things like alcohol. Then at Great Vow,[79] Chozen Bays was holding this retreat called the Grasses and Trees Retreat, and I said, 'I'm going to go do that,' and I knew it was going to be difficult because I had closed my heart to something I really loved and I would be sitting in the midst of it letting my heart break open. We spent almost all of the retreat outside the zendo, sitting in woods, sitting in fields – you know – being outdoors. And I was terrified because I knew it was going to really hit my heart. And I was being intimate with something that I felt was dying. That this Earth was not being cared for in the way we want, and it's painful to see a beloved one being mistreated. Dying.

"So I was sitting in a kind of reverie during the retreat, thinking about grief and loss and what-have-you, and I felt this dropping into my heart, and a great sadness and sorrow welled over me. Later I was out in the field, just sitting with this feeling, and doing exactly what I'm describing, sitting, being open, just

---

79. Great Vow Monastery is located in Clatskanie, Oregon. It was founded by Chozen and Hogan Bays – Dharma heirs of Taizan Maezumi – in 2002.

this great doubt, this great question as Hakuin points to. 'What is all this?' And a crow cawed, and it shattered my mind. It was perfect. And then every blade of grass shone forth distinctly. A cow mooed in the field" – he laughs at the memory – "and my heart deepened even more, and then I burst into tears, and everything was alive and speaking and in communion with me. It was this immediate communion and this overwhelming sense of tenderness. All over me. Just an overwhelming sense of tenderness. I think 'tenderness' is a good word because it also implies 'tending to.' But that tenderness welled over me.

"And I later went to sanzen with Chozen – who was my teacher at the time – and she saw me crying, and she said, 'What's going on?' And I just said, 'It's all so *tender*.' And she said, 'Welcome to living without skin.' So I've never forgotten that opening. It got into my pores, and it reoriented me. Over the years that tenderness has continued to gestate and grow and become cultivated through this practice.

"So it made me more and more willing and more and more capable of touching and being close to suffering and caring. I think that's an aspect of practice, that we shed our barriers. We're more and more able to be with this world of suffering. Usually, our strategy is to block ourselves from this world of suffering. But when we're open to the world of suffering, we're going to have a more natural responsiveness and a willingness to want to be with other people in their suffering."

"I had been going to ask if the practice helped cultivate skills which might be of use in addressing the social, environmental, political issues of the day, but you've pretty much answered that with a 'yes.'"

"Yeah. And I wonder if I could expand on that. I'm going to throw out a few tidbits here. Doing zazen in and of itself doesn't teach us any of those skills. Doing zazen in and of itself does not. But a life of practice – you know, we could call it Zen practice, it could be Christian contemplative practice – but a life of practice where I'm bringing that attention, that awareness, and that openness out into every aspect of my life *will* heighten my responsiveness. I hear it when I'm on the internet and they're talking about Buddhist action and what-have-you, that the only Buddhist response is a loving response. Or they'll say, 'As Buddhists we need to be able to do it like this.' In my view, the only Buddhist response is a non-attached response. And the skill that our Zen practice teaches us is how to not be attached. Now that doesn't say not to be engaged, because I think it does call for us to be engaged, but it does say, 'Don't be attached.' And so if I say, 'The only response is a loving response,' then I'm attached to a loving response. And that's going to close out the possibility that maybe a harsh or an aggressive response is called for in that moment, and I simply have to be open to that possibility. At times it may be a hug, and at others it might be a shout. In my own life, 99.9% of the time, it's a hug. But we have to be non-attached to what response is going to come out of us, so we can be truly responsive. And along the way we're going to stumble, we're going to fall, and we're going to make mistakes, but we also have to be non-attached to the sense that I know what is right and what is wrong. And again, it would be a mistake to say since I don't know – fundamentally, Zen is the religion of not-knowing – I can't lay claim to anything and I should just sit on my hands. Then I'm just denying my own interaction with the world. So, though I 'don't know,' this is what's comin' forth from me now, and I'm going to put it into the field of play to see what happens. Maybe it will be helpful. That's my hope. I'm trying to put out what's helpful. And so if the moment calls for a shout, or it calls for a protest, or it calls for something more aggressive, I'm gonna try it. Not because, darn it, I know what's right, but because this seems to be what's coming forth. And this touches what Bernie Glassman was doing with not-knowing and bearing witness and see what's next. Obviously, sometimes, if I let out a shout, the next thing to do is say, 'I'm so sorry; I shouldn't have shouted.' Maybe that's the next response, and maybe that's the healing response. But maybe another response is, 'Good! I woke you up. Can we talk now?' What comes next after that? So I'm non-attached to being right, but I must also be willing to let what comes forth come forth.

"Koan study is key in this. I think koan study offers more clues because there's a call-and-response in koan study between koan-teacher and student that says *do* something. Give me something here. Don't just talk about it. Don't give me silence. You know, the great koan, 'When meeting a person of the Dao on the way, greet them neither with words nor with silence.' How do you greet them? You have to do something. You have to let yourself out there into the world somehow. And then, finally, I think you have to be non-attached to attaining or getting any outcome. I think over and over again in this practice zazen teaches us there's nowhere to get. So if I go out to save the world and it's my own narcissism and it's my own inflatedness, if I go out to say, 'We have to save the earth!' I must recognize that that's what's rising up from me in this particular moment and so I go with it. But I also have to be open to the possibility that the Earth is in hospice right now, and that our civilization is in hospice, and that we may be saying goodbye to it. Now if all I want to do is save the Earth, I'm not going to be able to be of service to an Earth that is dying. Similarly, if I have a beloved one who is dying of cancer, and I have the idea, 'We have to save this person' or we have to make it be a certain way, then I'm going to miss the point, which is, 'We've tried everything, and now how do I show up to be with you? How can I be with you now?' It's not, 'Well, it's pointless. You're gonna die. Sorry. I'm gonna go on to try to save the next person.' At some point we say, 'Okay, my hopes are gone. So I just need to be with you right now. And I'm curious how I'm going to be with you in these closing days in a way that's intimate, tender, non-attached to how I am, non-attached to how you are.'

"So I think this is the dynamic that comes out of a life of Zen that interacts with the world that's just flux. It's complete flux. And, you know, I think some Zen practitioners get caught in, 'It's all mind, and it just comes and goes.' It's true, everything comes and goes. But how can I be so deeply engaged that I allow my heart to break, I allow myself to weep, I allow myself to touch, and I allow my *self* to be part of this dance at the same time?"

## Joan Sutherland

In the course of one of my conversations with Joan Sutherland, I am reminded of something the astrophysicist Carl Sagan – who had little respect for spiritual traditions – said: that human beings are the way in which the Universe becomes aware of itself. "One could say that we are the universe 'buddha-ing,' if you will," I suggest to Joan.

"Yeah. Yeah. I think that's true. I read a little bit in physics and I probably know just enough to get me into trouble, but there are these ideas now that down at the quantum level – the level that's sort of at the bottom of everything – consciousness may be an element down there. In the same way that quarks and muons and neutrinos and things are elements, that consciousness is kind of there from the beginning. And then it grows and becomes more refined or something as matter becomes more complicated. I like that idea I think that's kind of true. So that's the science view. And then D.T. Suzuki used to talk about how the universe made a vast vow to exist, which I always thought was so beautiful. And then he said our vow, our Bodhisattva vow to aspire to being Bodhisattva-like, was our way of answering the universe's great vow to exist."

"It has always seemed self-evident to me that although we tend to look at matter as being 'dumb' or 'mindless,'" I say, "in point of fact from the very beginning there had always been the potential for consciousness inherent in matter. We're the evidence of that."

"Yeah. It couldn't happen if it weren't there, unless you believe in some kind of divine intervention. There's no way for it to get into the system."

"It's something I've taken comfort in," I tell her. "I remember when I was in school though – in my early teens, maybe even just 11 or 12 – I read somewhere that eventually the sun will consume the Earth. It's inevitable. And I remember feeling at the time that, in that case, everything is pointless. I found the concept thoroughly enervating. Over time one learns to accommodate to it the way one learns to accommodate to so many things, essentially by ignoring them, by pretending they're not there. It's also a fact that current human activity could result in such a dramatic change to the ecosystem that our existence as a species – at least as we currently exist – is going to be jeopardized."

"Yeah. If I go back to what you were saying about realizing that the sun was going to swallow up the Earth one day, you said we deal with that the way we do most difficult things by pretending it's not there. I would suggest that there's another way to deal with it, which is to accept that that is, in fact, going to occur. Part of this present moment is the fact that in 8 billion years – or whatever it is – the Earth will be consumed by the sun. And, in that case, a direction we could go is, 'Doesn't that make this moment precious? Doesn't that make this moment tender?' And isn't it amazing how everything on the Earth persists in the face of certain annihilation? You know, it gets up every morning and grows and turns its face to the sun and then curls up in the dark. I mean, how beautiful that impulse towards life is in the face of certain death. So it can go in the direction of tenderness and preciousness and love for the world.

"Another thing I would add is that when we are confronted with something of such enormity as species extinction and the end of the human race and climate catastrophe, it's important to feel our grief as well as our outrage or our denial. And that's part of what I call 'endarkenment,'[80] allowing yourself to be heart-broken, and then asking, 'What do I do with that broken-heartedness?' And I think pure outrage is a hard place to act from over time. And so in terms of how it affects how you do things, there's a kind of desire to find a longer term way of being engaged in these helpless, hopeless problems. And, for me, part of that has to do with acknowledging sorrow. Because I think all the energy we spend not dealing with that sorrow weakens us and takes up a lot of our time and energy. So how does this sorrow keep us open and alive to what's going on rather than turning away from it?"

## John Negru

John Negru (Karma Yönten Gyatso) is the founder of the Sumeru Press, the publishing company which has released most of my books. He has an interesting background story which includes a fifty-year Dharma practice with a variety of teachers in different traditions, extensive community service, pilgrimages, and even three days in 1980 at Bodhgaya with the Dalai Lama. But he doubts that there is much value in retelling it.

"People ask me, 'What's your story?' And I tell them that my story is irrelevant. Nobody else is going to be able to replicate the lived experience that I had,

---

80. Cf. p. 128 above.

the meetings with teachers that I had when I had them in the cultural milieu that I found myself. So if I'm telling you that story, Rick, I'm just telling you an interesting bedtime story."

The point is that it is interesting, and one significant element is the way in which, as a young adult, he become involved with and later disaffiliated from two Buddhist communities he now describes as "flawed." One was the Montreal Zen Meditation Centre established by Tyndale Martin who claimed, falsely, to have been authorized to teach by Philip Kapleau. The other was in the Tibetan tradition.

There were several such groups during the Buddhist boom of the 1960s, '70s, and early '80, and many participants – several of whom had dedicated years to their practice – fell away in discouragement. John, however, points out that there had been positive aspects as well. "We had the marvelous opportunity to meet many authentic, accomplished Buddhist teachers who allowed us to glimpse real practice and a real life devoted to the Dharma. And so in that sense I'm very grateful, but there's a lot of sadness and dukkha associated with that time."

He no longer identifies with any particular school of Buddhism but has come to feel that "there is value in every lineage. So I'm happy to support every lineage but not commit to any one lineage." One of the ways in which he provided support was by becoming a publisher.

"My goal is to support the Dharma in any way that I can. I'm not going to be a highly enlightened teacher. I'm not going to run a profoundly transformative Dharma center. But I can help the people who do those things, and I'm happy to serve in that way. In order to make it a realistic thing, I've chosen to make Sumeru a company." Over the course of Sumeru's history, proceeds from book sales have provided financial assistance to various Buddhist enterprises. "I think that's kind of like a trifecta. You get the Dharma out there, you validate the work of all these different traditions and help them financially, and you give an opportunity to people such as yourself to engage in a deeper form of practice themselves."

His current focus is on the way Buddhist practice often leads to social action and environmental concern.

"Buddhism is about recognizing reality and acting skillfully within it. It's about recognizing interdependence, karma, non-self. All of these different concepts and the practices of training that enhance those concepts, that state of mind, are based on understanding reality as opposed to our delusions about what reality is, which is driven by our desires and our hatreds and our preferences and so on. Like it says in the *Hsin Hsin Ming*,[81] 'The Great Way is not difficult for those who have no preferences. But make the smallest distinction, and Heaven and Earth are set instantly apart.' So here we are – 2021 – in the middle of a pandemic, in the middle of a global climate crisis, mass extinctions. You look at the nine planetary boundaries that we have crossed or that we are on the threshold of, and the only one that we have been able to pull back from has been the ozone hole. So this is our reality. So any looking away from our reality – focusing on our personal psychological development – really isn't showing awareness.

"Ron Purser is an ordained Korean Buddhist monk who is also a Systems Management professor at San Francisco State University. He wrote a book called *McMindfulness*, and I heard him on the radio the other day saying that the original version – the Buddhist version – of mindfulness also contained a discernment component which has been jettisoned along the way. So when you have discernment, when you look at the current situation in the world, you say, 'Well, okay, this is what's happening.' As the Dalai Lama says, 'I am a servant of seven billion people.' So if you're going to take that position of being a Bodhisattva, and you look at this situation with discernment, how could you *not* act? How can you say, 'Well, I am going to rarefy my *samatha*[82] practice' or 'I'm going to dig deeper into the four *jhanas*'[83] without being in the world that we live in? Right? It just doesn't make sense to me that you could separate those things. That's where I'm coming from."

Which brings us back to his work as a publisher.

"I've been involved in environmental activities since the early 1970s. It isn't just a vague, 'Hey, let's get on the climate crisis wagon.' Publishing books from an Engaged Buddhist perspective and doing environmental community development projects with different sanghas is something much more evolved and specific that I can do.

"We need to reconceptualize the performative aspects of what it means to be a Buddhist community leader within the larger context of the modern world. The Buddhism of the Future cannot stay bound to old ways of practice if it's going to remain relevant to our children and the generations to follow."

## Diane Fitzgerald

Fifty years ago, Diane Fitzgerald marched in the "very first Earth Day parade in New York City. It was kind of a random occurrence that I happened

---

81. Composed by the Third Chan Patriarch of China, Jianzhi Sengcan.

82. Tranquility of mind. One of the fruits of meditation practice.

83. Stages of meditation practice.

to be there and joined in as a fourteen-year-old. That was the start."

Diane is the founder and resident teacher of Zen DownEast in Pembroke, Maine. Google maps informed me that it is less than two hours from where I live in Island View, New Brunswick, and I made plans to visit her which were disrupted when the border between Canada and the US was closed because of the pandemic. We meet by Skype instead, and I ask her about the EcoSattva program associated with her community.

"The term is the combination of the words 'ecology' and 'bodhisattva,' and it refers to a person who takes compassionate care of the Earth. Part of the practice is an acknowledgement of the importance of environmental ethics. Just like the Buddhist Precepts guide our lives because we're not perfectly realized human beings, so we also have a set of environmental ethics to guide our lives in this particular practice."

Our conversation naturally turns to the significance of Buddhist teaching during the pandemic. It was a topic she had recently discussed with her community.

"The standard teachings in Ecodharma is first that our practice is to meet reality as it is arising, not turn away. Another is studying the self so that we can learn what our engrained habit patterns are – our blind spots – and seeing the ways we construct the self, which helps us identify the many cognitive biases that we have and the psychological defences we develop individually and communally when we're faced with a crisis of this magnitude. Another is the teaching of interdependence and non-separation. So at this time we're very much aware of our bodies and how this tiny virus can invade and rearrange us to produce more of itself. And then there's the truth of impermanence. So our whole world seems upside down. We have this great sense of groundlessness, and we keep grasping and trying to find something of the old routines and the old normality. But this also provides an opportunity to recognize that the true reality of our existence is groundless. After all, at some point we will die. We often lead our lives without needing to confront that, but this situation brings it front and center. So how can we find some freedom in that groundlessness that allows us to be more compassionate, more open, less afraid of uncertainty, less afraid of paradox?

"Something else I think particular to Ecodharma is the practice of what Joanna Macy calls 'Active Hope,' where we don't need to be optimists, but we do envision a goal or values that we adhere to. And our work is to commit ourselves to what we believe to be right and not be attached to what the outcomes may be. So it is in practicing what we believe to be right and true that we find our commitment flowering. In times like this, when everything is so unknown and unpredictable, how can we continue to practice Active Hope which is not

Pollyannaish? It doesn't require optimism, it just requires a commitment to these values that we hold dear because of our practice. And it does reference the refuge that we take in sangha or community. That is one of our vows,[84] right? And how community, even though we're practicing social distancing – as some people have said, it doesn't have to be social-isolation – how we really do need each other, and we do need to be aware of the most vulnerable members of our community and the world. How does that 'taking refuge in sangha' allow us to bring forward our natural compassion and empathy for the community that's ours, the whole of Earth as our community?

"So we meet the reality of what is arising. We see how the conditions of the environment can contribute to viruses, to respiratory problems, to the transfer of disease from animals to human beings. How forestry is creating all kinds of ecological complications for us as our world continually expands. So we see the reality of that as well as seeing the reality – without turning away – of what we, as humans, are doing in response."

Diane organized a workshop on "Eco-Anxiety" to help individuals acquire the skills needed to function in the current circumstances.

"And the first part of it is, in Zen we turn toward instead of away from. Right? So we turn *toward* the source of our suffering, we turn toward our anxiety, we turn toward our depression. We recognize it as actually a sane response to what is happening in the world. And in responding to the crisis, I think we can work with our own mind to understand our defenses – this is Dogen's study of the self – to understand our blind spots and all of the psychological defenses we have. Because responding to this crisis is ultimately our generation's suffering. So that is something that we can offer as students of the way.

"And another thing people have talked about is that if we want to actually respond, we have to change the metaphor. Which is it's not about fixing the problem. Ultimately, it's about realizing nonduality. Right? Realizing that we and the earth and all the beings are not separate and that the earth is alive and breathing and sentient and not separate from us. And to see the interconnection of all of life, sentient and insentient. And so when we're able to change our perspective, that allows us to act from a place that's very different from a place where, 'Here's a problem and I'm going to stay in the human realm and figure out how to fix it.'

"And one of the things we work on within the EcoSattva group is how we can include and work with others in the community who are not Zen Buddhists. So we're quite cognizant of not employing terminology that would

---

84. The Three Refuges is a formula developed in early Buddhism. Individuals seeking to join the order vowed to take refuge in the Buddha (the enlightened one), the Dharma (his teaching), and the Sangha (the community of his followers).

be off-putting. So I couldn't talk to somebody off the street about nonduality, but I could talk to people about their appreciation of Native American traditions which value the Earth and Being and see them as alive and to be respected as much as humans. Right? Equals. So finding ways to express nonduality in a way that people can relate to and understand. I think that's the challenge for us. But ultimately what we really are doing is teaching the Dharma; we're just trying to use the most skillful means we can in teaching it. And the way that we, as Buddhists, take on impermanence – right? – understand and actually appreciate it."

"The way Buddhists understand and appreciate impermanence?"

"Right. Appreciate it. Groundlessness in uncertainty. For the average person, uncertainty is very anxiety-provoking. So how do you make friends with uncertainty? How do you learn to live into it in a way that feels enlivening instead of fearful, fear producing. Right? So, again, using our Buddhist teachings and translating them into a way that people can understand. Because the more we fear uncertainty, the less we are able to act or even take it all in.

"I've done, like, a ton of reading on all of this, and one of the psychological defences is that the people who are *most* anxious and concerned about climate change are the ones who will immediately turn off any sort of discussion or conversation about it because it is so anxiety-provoking to even talk about it. So how can we reach people who you might think are climate-change deniers, but, in fact, they're just denying the reality of their internal state."

I point out that there are, of course, many people in North America who apparently do doubt the reality of climate change.

"Yes. So, again, how do you talk to resistant communities? Whether they're individuals or communities. And I know in Maine there are a large number of people who feel that way, who think that environmentalism is sort of an alternative religion, and that it is somehow contrary to their religious beliefs, and there's just this deep identification they have with being anti-climate-change. So how do you talk to those people? I think the only way you talk to them is on the level of what is happening in their lives that matters. For example, in Machias, where we're working, there's a real risk of flooding from the Machias River. Very low-lying areas. Can we have conversations with people about their anxieties with the flooding or what can be done about the flooding? Can we meet them in some place where they feel that they can have a conversation with us without having any illusion that we are going to change people into being activists in the way that we are? I think there is some possibility – and I have seen it – of dialogue with communities who would otherwise be wary.

"I also think our motivation is not to change climate deniers into climate activists. It's to find some points of intersection where we can work with them.

And for us, we're not looking for markers of success in what we're doing. This is another Zen teaching – right? – that we are not attached to outcomes. We give our hearts openly to this without knowing what the end result will be, without attachments to rewards. And we even do it if everyone in the community is resistant.

"My group has been doing a large campaign on ocean plastics for the last three years, and we have brought it to the community in different places like the libraries and community centers, things like that. The university. And it's surprising, lobstermen will show up who would be climate deniers basically, but they all show up and talk about the movement of the lobsters northward and the increasing temperatures in the Gulf of Maine. So I think that, too, is part of our practice of not-knowing. That there is not some solid truth that is available to us, and how can we practice open-heartedly and convey the practice by *how* we are, not what we say. I think that's what it's about."

She applies the concept of "not-knowing" to the possibility of human extinction as well. "We have no way of knowing this. And like so many things, we don't attach ourselves to some theory. Like, in Zen, we don't even talk about reincarnation. It's more, 'I don't know. Maybe. Maybe not. It doesn't really matter with where I'm practicing now.' So it's open. So maybe it's true; the human species will die out, and – you know what? – we're alive now; we're all present now. And we are being called to give ourselves to a really exciting adventure. And just like all the great movements in the past – the civil rights movement, the women's suffrage movement, the movement for marriage equality – the people involved in those movements didn't have any sort of expectation of a positive outcome. They didn't know what was going to happen. But they gave themselves to it fully because that's what they valued. That is what I think needs to happen. We can't just be taking solace that some bacteria are gonna survive. I mean, maybe they will. I don't know. But that's not what's happening right now."

## Koun Franz

There may be – as Joan Sutherland implied – skills Zen practice cultivates which allow practitioners to tackle social and environment issues in ways that others might not, but not all Zen students are engaged in such activity, and the majority of the people who are involved in addressing these concerns have no Zen training at all.

"I think we've talked about trying to make a distinction between Buddhism and the Dharma," Koun Franz reflects during one of our conversations. "You know? Buddhism is a fabrication of the mind. The Dharma is something that we can kind of work with. But anyone can. And people work with the Dharma all the time without ever calling it that or thinking of it as that. And I would say that anyone who is making real strides to undoing the systems that are causing climate change and that are perpetuating racism and that are perpetuating misogyny are working with the Dharma. They're just not calling it that. That's fine."

As Koun and several other teachers have told me, almost everyone comes to Zen – in a certain sense – for the wrong reasons. They come because they are dealing with matters of personal need, with difficulties in their lives and the hope is that, by taking up Zen practice, things will get better. And, Koun tells me, what they find when they seek him out in Halifax, "is a guy who's saying, 'We offer nothing. There is nothing here for you, and you will be disappointed for the rest of your life. Would you like to sit with that?' Right? And some people resonate with that and some people don't."[85]

Not everyone, of course, can face toward their own suffering as Zen calls for them to do, much less face issues like climate change. We all begin where we are – there is no other place we can start from – and we deal with what we need to deal with. There is nothing else we can do.

In Koun's view, Zen is about maturation, what Mitra Bishop – citing Torei Enji – called the Long Maturation. Maturation is not a process that ever comes to an end, nor can we know where it will lead. And that "not-knowing" is part of the Zen tradition as well – not knowing where the path is leading but persisting nonetheless.

---

85. Cf., p. 53 above.

# Epilogue in Island View

There is a story Elaine MacInnes is fond of telling about a Little Salt Doll who went on a journey to explore the world. She had many new experiences and saw many interesting places. "Then one day she came to the edge of the sea and was quite astounded by the restless surging mass of water. 'What are you?' she cried. 'Touch me and you will find out,' answered the sea. So the little salt doll stuck her toe in, and had a truly lovely sensation. But when she withdrew her foot, the toe had disappeared. 'What have you done to me?' she cried. 'You have given something of yourself in order to understand,' the sea replied.

"The little salt doll decided that if she really wanted to know the sea, she would have to give more of herself. So next she stuck in her whole foot, and everything up to her ankle disappeared. Surprisingly, in an inexplicable way, she felt very good about it. So she continued going further and further into the sea, losing more and more of her self, all the while understanding the sea more deeply. As a wave broke over the last bit of her, the salt doll was able to cry out, 'Now I know what the sea is. It is I.'"[86]

•••

There is a room attached to my garage which a previous owner had used as an art studio. The property is located on a high, steep bank overlooking the river that the First Nations community – to which my great-granddaughter belongs by virtue of her father's family – call the Wolastoq, or Beautiful River. The people refer to themselves as Wolastoqiyik, People of the River.

I use the room as a private zendo. It is also used for winter storage and for several months of the year includes lawn furniture and bikes as well as my meditation cushion and mat. There is a wood stove, which I seldom have to use

---

86. Elaine MacInnes, *Zen Contemplation: A Bridge of Living Water* (Ottawa: Novalis, 2001).

because the sunlight coming through the large windows warms the room even in winter. The tree tops I see through the north window as I sit are actually rooted fifteen to twenty feet further down the bank. Eagles frequently glide by on the air currents over the river, as many as a dozen at a time. Wildlife biologists suggest they are always on the lookout for food, but it's hard to escape the notion that they are just frolicking for pleasure.

Every morning – except for, as Rinsen Weik put it, the ones I don't – I come out here. On some winter mornings, it is dark enough that I need to light a candle. There is a Buddha figure placed not so much on an altar as on a shelf beneath that north window. There is also an abstract Haitian statue of the Virgin at the foot of the Cross, a Stabat Mater which I acquired when I was doing fair-trade importing. I light a stick of incense without any ceremony, then sit on the cushion, fold my legs, and sit in zazen until the incense stick expires. Outside, there is a set of wind chimes which frequently accompanies my sit along with the occasional sound of critters scurrying about in the rafters. And most mornings – except for those I don't – I look forward to this time.

In the flower bed outside, below the south window, there is a large garden Buddha now partially covered by moss. Like most of the Buddha and related figures I have, it was a gift from someone. I know only a handful of people in central New Brunswick who formally practice any form of Buddhism, but most of the people I know are aware that I seem to. They tend to be tolerant and treat it – if I may use Patrick Gallagher's term – as an eccentric habit. It's too difficult to try to explain that I don't consider myself a Buddhist but rather a Zen practitioner. It isn't a distinction that even always makes sense to those few professed Buddhists I know.

I have mobility problems, so I have not attended sesshin since Albert Low's death. I do, however, still host the small sitting group which he asked me to organize in Fredericton. It has a core membership of about eight. The local Shambhala community has – for almost twenty years now – graciously allowed us to use their center one night a week. When Koun Franz's Thousand Harbours Zen holds extended sits in Halifax, I try to attend. Both of these were, of course, suspended during the pandemic, so for over one full year my practice has been solitary except for bi-weekly Zoom conferences with Dosho Port with whom I am inching my way through the koan curriculum. I'm not in a hurry, and at my current pace it will another decade before I complete it. Given that I have passed the biblically allotted three-score-and-ten-year lifespan, it's possible I never will.

On rare occasions I will be asked about my practice. The question is usually posed something like, "What do you get out of it?" And the honest answer is, "I don't know." This is something I have been engaged in now for fifty years.

I have no idea how my behavior, my way of viewing things, my attitudes and values would have been different if I'd followed another path.

No one's experience in Zen is the same as anyone else's, although there tend to be – as these interviews have demonstrated – some commonalities.

When I was in my 20s, before I knew anything about Zen or Buddhism, I had a spontaneous experience. I had carelessly endangered another person through an act of gratuitous cruelty. I regretted my actions immediately and spent the rest of that evening, with some others, working to rectify the situation. It was nearly dawn before things were resolved, and I was able to return home. I was living in a small cottage, called Birkenbrae, on the outskirts of Fredericton. It was on a two-acre plot filled with wild flowers, fruit trees, and abandoned goat sheds. There was a wrought-iron bench in front of the house, and when I returned I was too exhausted to go to the door and unlock it, so I sat down on the bench. I was thoroughly ashamed of what I had done and felt disgusted with the type of person I had become. And then it was as if I was just too tired to maintain the effort of being "Rick" any longer. I simply let go of that effort, and, immediately, it was like finding a clear signal on the radio dial. You move closer to the source of the signal as you drive or you nudge the dial just a bit and the static drops away and a signal comes through with absolute clarity – a signal which had always been there, but which you couldn't pick up until the conditions were right.

It was an overwhelming feeling of connection with the entirety of Being and a sense that everything that exists is united in some way by love in the on-going process of creation which science calls evolution. That was how I expressed it to myself at the time. It was also absolutely clear to me that this was what people – although they weren't aware of it – meant when they used the word "God." It would be more than a year before I encountered the concept of Dao and recognized that, if a designation was needed, it was a more appropriate one.

I didn't doubt the validity of this perception, but I did question what I had done to deserve it. In some ways, it was consistent with – although more intense than – experiences I'd had on psychedelics, which, perhaps, made me more open to accept it. I was also pretty sure that I couldn't be unique; other people must have had similar experiences. The event redirected the academic work I was engaged in at the time and eventually led me to books on Asian spirituality in which I recognized a similar perspective. For a long time, I had an inflated sense of my own – wholly unearned – spiritual accomplishment. Many of the faux spiritual leaders of the period – like those whom John Negru encountered about this same time – had similar conceptions of their self-importance. Some even gathered disciples.

I, instead, was fortunate in discovering Zen practice. My Birkenbrae experience was acknowledged to have been an awakening, but it was also made clear to me that by itself it was of negligible significance, was little more than what Koun Franz referred to as a "burp of the mind." It was only the first step in Torei Enji's Long Maturation. That maturation remains an ongoing process, through which I have cultivated several qualities I treasure.

There is a sense of wonder that anything at all exists, a continual amazement at the reality of the universe and the fact that consciousness is inherent in it.

There is a sense of awe at the interdependence of Being in all its beauty and horror.

There is a – at times overwhelming – feeling of gratitude.

And there is sense of reverence, perhaps similar to what Rinzan Pechovnik referred to as tenderness with its connotation of "tending to."

I may well have acquired these ways of understanding the world and my place in it without Zen; my initial insight, after all, came about before I had any awareness of Asian spiritualities. Nor am I proselytizing. But it remains the case that I have a sense of being understood when I speak of these matters – as I seldom do – with people engaged in Zen practice.

It is also possible that we are just journeying in tandem.

Above the river, two eagles are in synchronized flight, almost wingtip to wingtip, flying in giant loops over the water. Perhaps they are looking for food, but it seems as if they are just having fun.

A monk asked Fuketsu, "Without speaking, without silence, how can you express the truth?"

Fuketsu observed, "I always remember springtime in southern China. The birds sing among innumerable kinds of fragrant flowers."[87]

---

87. *Mumonkan*, Case 24 – Senzaki/Reps rendition.

# THE INTERVIEWS
## [Index]

Arnold, Geoffrey Shugen – August 14, 2018. Pp. 71; 101-02.
Atkinson, Chimyo – Sept 5, 2018. Pp. 69-70.
Bishop, Mitra – June 3, 2013; Oct 8, 2013; Oct 1, 2019; Nov 5, 2019. Pp. 54-55; 124-25.
Blacker, Melissa Myozen – May 3, 2013. Pp. 38-39.
Burk, Domyo – Dec 10, 2019; Feb 18, 2020. Pp. 54; 88-89; 150-51.
Chayat, Shinge – June 12, 2013; June 22, 2018. Pp. 39-40; 100-01; 119-21.
Coger, Wayne – June 19, 2013; July 26, 2018. Pp. 95-98.
Fieleke, Mike – Aug 23, 2018. Pp. 58-60.
Fitzgerald, Diane – Jan 21, 2020; March 31, 2020. Pp. 123; 164-68.
Franz, Koun – July 22, 2018; Feb 12, 2020. Pp. 44-45; 52-54; 87-88; 103-05; 134; 168-69.
Gallagher, Patrick – June 15, 2013; Jan 20, 2014; May 25, 2016; Sept 23, 2019; Nov 26, 2019. P. 132.
Gauntt, Genru – March 10, 2020. Pp. 29-31; 115-16; 140-42.
Glassman, Bernie – July 15, 2013. Pp. 28-29; 105-06; 137-40.
Graef, Sunyana – May 2, 2013. Pp. 145-46.
Habito, Ruben – July 9, 2015; July 23, 2015. Pp. 83-84; 127.
Henderson, Taigen – June 17, 2013; Sept 12, 2018. Pp. 57; 149-50.
Kennedy, Robert – July 24, 2013. Pp. 12; 31-33; 107-08.
Kjolhede, Bodhin – June 20, 2013; Jan 22, 2016. Pp. 117-18; 146-47.
Li, Rebecca – March 3, 2020; May 8, 2020. Pp. 55-57; 116-17; 126.
Low, Albert – April 28, 2013. Pp. 49; 70; 87; 123.
Loy, David – Aug 13, 2020; Aug 25, 2020. Pp. 34-36; 50-51; 118-19; 124-26; 155-58.
MacInnes, Elaine – June 15, 2013. P. 73.
Marinello, Genjo – Oct 18, 2013; Feb 19, 2014; April 28, 2014. Pp. 102-03; 143.

McLean, Myokyo – April 29, 2013. Pp. 48; 74-75.
Morris, Seiho – Aug 28, 2018; Oct 10, 2018. Pp. 135-37.
Negru, John – Dec 29, 2020; Jan 10, 2021. Pp. 162-64.
Nghiem, Dang – May 23, 2014. Pp. 92-95.
Pechovnik, Rinzan – Feb 21, 2019; Oct 23. 2019. Pp. 63-64; 77-80; 158-61.
Phap Vu – May 23, 2014; Nov 19, 2019. Pp. 67-69; 144-45.
Port, Dosho – July 14, 2013; Sept 7, 2014. Pp. 71; 90-91.
Radin, Yoshin – Jan 15, 2014; May 25, 2014. P. 124.
Rhodes, Bobbie – July 8, 2013. Pp. 36-38; 91-92.
Rynick, David Dae An – May 3, 2013; Oct 7, 2019. Pp. 75-79.
Senauke, Hozan Alan – Oct 29, 2019; Jan 2, 2020. Pp. 23-28; 73-74; 143-44.
Shukman, Henry – Oct 3, 2013; May 18, 2018. Pp. 40-41; 60-63; 85-86; 108-09.
Spring, Shodo – March 7, 2020. Pp. 151-55.
Sutherland, Joan – Oct 4, 2013; Sept 24, 2019; Oct 8, 2019. Pp. 41-42; 49-50; 84-85; 110-11; 128-32; 161-62.
Tarrant, John – March 24, 2013. Pp. 86-87.
Waldinger, Robert – Aug 16, 2018. Pp. 9; 21; 43-44; 58; 87.
Weik, Rinsen – Aug 2, 2018; Oct 15, 2019; Dec 17, 2019. Pp. 51-52; 80-83; 111-15; 132-34.
Zen Mountain Monastery – June 7 & 8, 2013. Pp. 66-67; 70-73.
Zummach, Tetsugan – Sept 7, 2014; Aug 7, 2018. Pp. 64-65.

# Glossary

**Abhidharma** – A collection of sutra commentaries, probably dating back to the 3rd Century BCE. Part of the Tripitaka (Three Baskets) which make up the canonical scriptures of Buddhism.

**Advaya** – Sanskrit term for Nonduality, see below.

**Ango** – Ninety day intensive training period.

**Angya** – Pilgrimage.

**Avalokiteshvara** – Bodhisattva of Compassion in Indian Buddhism. Later became identified with Guanyin/Kannon.

**Awakening** – One of several terms referring to achieving insight into the basic interconnectedness of Being.

*Blue Cliff Record* – See *Hekiganroku*.

**Bodh Gaya** – Village in the Indian state of Bihar considered to be the site of the Buddha's enlightenment.

**Bodhicitta** – The intention to achieve awakening for the benefit of others.

**Bodhidharma** – Legendary Indian figure who brought Zen to China. Bodhidharma is considered the 28th patriarch of India Buddhism and the first patriarch of Chinese Zen.

**Bodhisattva** – An enlightened (Bodhi) being (sattva). Certain historic or legendary Bodhisattvas function much the same as saints in the Christian tradition.

**Buddha** – Literally, "The Awakened One." When used with a capital B, usually referring to the historic Buddha, Siddhartha Gautama. With a lower-case b, it refers to any enlightened being.

**Buddha Hall** – In temples, the hall where devotional activities such as chanting are carried out. The hall normally contains an image of the Buddha.

**Buddhahood** – The state of being fully awakened.

**Buddha Nature** – The inherent ability of all sentient (and in some views non-sentient) beings to realize their True Nature.

**Caodong** – The Chinese name for the Soto school.
**Chan** – Chinese term which the Japanese pronounced as "Zen," meaning meditation.
**Chi** – Energy or source of energy.
**Dai-** – A prefix meaning "great," as in Dai-kensho.
**Daigo tettei** – Complete and unsurpassed awakening.
**Dao** – Formerly "Tao." The "way." The term originates in Daoism (Taoism) and refers to the fundamental nature of reality.
***Daodejing*** – Formerly *Tao Te Ching*. The basic text of Daoism. It is a collection of eighty-one chapters written in verse attributed to Laozi.
**Dharma** – A term with multiple meanings, but generally referring to the teachings of Buddhism.
**Dharma Heir** – The heir of a Zen teacher whose understanding of the Dharma qualifies them to be a teacher as well.
**Dharma Transmission** – see Transmission
**Dhyana** – Sanskrit word for meditation, from which both "chan" and "zen" are derived etymologically.
**-do** – A suffix referring to a room or space dedicated to a specific activity or purpose. A zendo, for example, is a space in which Zen (meditation) is practiced.
**Dogen Kigen** – 13th century Japanese Buddhist credited with bringing Soto Zen to Japan.
**Dokusan** – Private interview between student and teacher. Cf. Sanzen.
**Dukkha** – Unsatisfactoriness. Sometimes translated as "suffering."
**Eightfold Path** – see Four Noble Truths.
**Emptiness** – A basic and easily misunderstood Buddhist concept regarding the nature of Reality. Essentially, emptiness refers to an intuition (rather than an intellectual understanding) of the fact that all things are empty of self-nature, i.e., are composed of a variety of elements which are in a constant state of flux and are interdependent with all other elements. The term may also refer to the formless – and yet creative – Void from which all things arise and to which they return.
**Engaged Buddhism** – A term coined by Thich Nhat Hanh for Buddhist practice which addresses social, political, environmental, and economic issues.
**Enlightenment** – Recognition of one's True Nature; insight into the basic interconnectedness of Being.
**Five Hindrances** – Sensual desire, ill will, sloth, restlessness/worry, and doubt.
**Four Noble Truths** – 1) All of existence is characterized by suffering

(dukkha); 2) Suffering is caused by craving; 3) Suffering can be ameliorated by overcoming craving; 4) Craving can be overcome by following the Noble Eightfold path, which consists of right view, right intention, right speech, right action, right livelihood, right effort, right mindfulness, and right meditation.

**Four Vows** – 1) To save (liberate) all beings; 2) to eliminate endless blind passions; 3) to pass innumerable Dharma Gates; 4) to achieve the great way of Buddha.

**Gassho** – To bring the palms of the hands together, often accompanied by a bow. It is a sign of respect and reverence.

*Gateless Gateway* – see *Mumonkan*.

**Gautama** – The Buddha's given name. See Siddhartha Gautama.

**Guanyin** – See Kannon

**Hakuin Ekaku** – 18th century Japanese Zen monk and reformer of the koan tradition.

**Hara** – The abdomen understood as a person's center.

*Hekiganroku* – A classic koan collection, also known as the *Blue Cliff Record*.

**Huineng** – Dajian Huineng (638-713). The Sixth Patriarch of Chan Buddhism. All current forms of Chan and Zen derive from his school.

**Hungry Ghosts** – "Pretas." Hungry Ghosts are images of the unquenchable appetites to which all beings are subject.

**Inka** (*inka shomei*) – "Authorized seal proving attainment." Official transmission, especially in the Rinzai School. It is the recognition by a teacher that the student has completed training and is ready to teach independently.

**-ji** – A suffix meaning "temple."

**Jihatsu** – A set of nested bowls used for meals. Cf. Oryoki.

**Joshu Jushin** – See Zhaozhou Congshen.

**Kannon** – "Quanyin" in Chinese. The female Bodhisattva of Compassion.

**Karma** – Literally, "action." The concept in Asian thought that actions have consequences. Popularly viewed as one's past actions, in this or previous lives, resulting in one's current situation.

**Karuna** – Compassion.

**Kensho** – Seeing into one's True Nature. Enlightenment.

**Koan** – (The plural of "koan" is "koan.") Usually an anecdote from the lives of the Zen masters of the past – primarily those in China – often expressed in the form of a question. The question or situation described becomes the focus of a Zen student's meditative practice and helps the student attain insight. While koan cannot be resolved through reasoning, an understanding of them can be achieved through intuition. Individual koan are referred to as "Cases," in the sense of legal precedence in jurisprudence.

**Kwan Um** – The Korean School of Zen established by Seung Sahn.

**Kyosaku** – "The Encouragement Stick." A long stick tapered at one end, used by monitors during zazen to encourage (or wake up) meditators.

**Linji** – The Chinese name of Rinzai.

**Mahayana** – "The Greater Vehicle." The Buddhist tradition which evolved from the earlier Theravada tradition. Zen is a form of Mahayana Buddhism.

**Manjushri** – Bodhisattva of prajna/wisdom.

**Mantra** – A word, phrase, or short prayer which is repeated as a focus of meditation.

**Metta** – Loving-kindness.

**Mu** – "Wu" in Chinese. Meaning, "No, not, nothing." Usually refers to the opening koan in the *Mumonkan*: A student of the way asked Joshu, "Does a dog have Buddha Nature?" Joshu replied, "Mu!"

***Mumonkan*** – A classic koan collection, also known as *The Gateless Gate*.

**Nonduality** – "Not two." The recognition that elements which seem to be distinct are, in fact, not separate but are aspects of a single wholeness.

**Oryoki** – A formal way of eating using three nested bowls. Cf. Jihatsu.

**Osho** – Priest.

**Ox-Herding Pictures** – A series of ten illustrations portraying the stages of growth in Zen practice. The illustrations show a young man seeking, finding, and taming an ox.

**Paramitas** – The Six Perfections: generosity, ethical behavior, tolerance, diligence, concentration, and insight.

**Six Patriarchs** – The successive teachers credited with establishing Chan Buddhism: Bodhidharma, Huike, Jianzhi Sengcan, Dayi Doaxin, Daman Hongren, and Dajian Huineng.

**Prajna** – Wisdom.

**Precepts** – Ethical teachings which Buddhists commit to abide by.

**Rakusu** – A bib-like garment representing the robe of the Buddha.

**Realization** – Realization of one's True Nature, and therefore realization of the True Nature of all of Being. Awakening.

**Rinzai** – The School of Zen practice derived from Linji Yixuan.

**Rinzai-ji** – "Rinzai Temple," Joshu Sasaki's primary temple located in Los Angeles.

**Rohatsu** – The anniversary of the Buddha's enlightenment in December. The sesshin associated with this anniversary is considered the most daunting of the year.

**Roshi** – Literally, "Old Teacher." In North American Zen, it has come to mean a fully qualified Zen teacher.
**Samadhi** – The state of concentration or absorption.
**Samsara** – The repeated cycle of birth, life, and death.
**Samugi** – Work clothes.
**Sanbo Zen** – Formerly, Sanbo Kyodan. A school of Zen prominent in the West which combines Soto and Rinzai practices. Also known as the Harada/Yasutani Lineage.
**Sangha** – The community.
**Sanzen** – Private interview between student and teacher. Cf. Dokusan.
**Satori** – Awakening, enlightenment.
**Seiza** – Traditional manner of sitting on one's heels in Japan.
**Sensei** – Teacher. In American Zen, usually implying less authority than a Roshi would have.
**Sesshin** – (The plural of "sesshin" is "sesshin.") A Zen retreat, traditionally seven days long.
**Shikan Taza** – Simple awareness as a meditation practice. In shikan taza, the meditator does not have a particular focus, such as the breath or a koan.
**Shinjin Datsurakuh** – Casting off body and mind.
***Shobogenzo*** or ***Treasury of the True Dharma Eye*** – A collection of essays by Dogen.
**Shoken** – Taking individual vows with a single teacher.
**Siddhartha Gautama** – The Buddha's given name.
**Soen** – Korean term for Zen.
**Soen Sa Nim** – In Korean Zen, a term meaning "Zen Master." In Kwan Um Zen, it generally refers to Seung Sahn.
**Sokoji** – Ethnic Buddhist temple in San Francisco to which Shunryu Suzuki was assigned.
**Soto** – The School of Zen descending from Sozan Honjaku and Tozan Ryokai.
**Sotoshu** – The administrative headquarters of the Soto establishment in Japan.
**Sutra** – In Buddhism, scriptural writings usually, but not always, attributed to the Buddha.
**Takuhatsu** – Ritual begging.
**Tao** – see Dao.
***Tao Te Ching*** – see *Daodejing*.
**Teisho** – A formal talk given by a Zen teacher.
**Thien** – Vietnamese term for Zen.
**Theravada** – "The Teachings of the Elders." Generally considered an earlier

form of Buddhism from which the Mahayana was derived. The form of Buddhism now common in Sri Lanka, Myanmar and Thailand.

**Three Characteristics of Existence** – *Annica* (impermanence), *dukkha* (suffering), *anatta* (no permanent self).

**Three Gems** – see Three Refuges

**Three Poisons** – Greed, ignorance, and hatred.

**Three Refuges** – Buddhists take "refuge" in the Buddha, the Dharma, and the Sangha.

**Three Treasures** – see Three Refuges.

**Transmission** – Formal recognition that an individual has completed their training and may teach independently.

**True Nature** – True nature is characterized by nonduality and interdependence with the whole of Being.

**Upaya** – Skillful means. The variety of techniques used by a teacher to assist a student to come to awakening.

**Vedanta** – Hindu philosophy.

**Vipassana** – Meditation techniques associated with Theravada Buddhism

**Wu** – See Mu.

**Zabuton** – The mat on which a meditation cushion (zafu) is placed.

**Zafu** – "Budda" (fu) "seat" (za). A meditation cushion.

**Zazen** – Seated (za) meditation (zen).

**Zen** – Literally, "meditation." Zen Buddhism is the meditation school of Buddhism.

**Zendo** – Room or hall in which Zen is practiced.

**Zenji** – A teacher of the Dharma.

**Zhaozhou Congshen** – Ninth century Chan master. His "mu" (cf.) is one of the most commonly assigned initial koans.

# Author's note

In a few cases, passages in this book have been used in earlier works I've released. At times, there are differences in the manner in which those passages are expressed. This is due to changes requested by those to whom they have been attributed.

www.ingramcontent.com/pod-product-compliance
Lightning Source LLC
Chambersburg PA
CBHW032026230426

**43671CB00005B/213**